THE ADVENTURES OF AN IT LEADER

THE ADVENTURES OF AN IT LEADER

ROBERT D. AUSTIN
RICHARD L. NOLAN
SHANNON O'DONNELL

HARVARD BUSINESS PRESS
BOSTON, MASSACHUSETTS

"A hero ventures forth from the world of common day into a region
of supernatural wonder: fabulous forces are there encountered and a decisive
victory is won: the hero comes back from this mysterious adventure
with the power to bestow boons on his fellow man."

—Joseph Campbell, *The Hero with a Thousand Faces*

Library of Congress Cataloging-in-Publication Data
Austin, Robert D. (Robert Daniel), 1962-
  The adventures of an IT leader / by Robert D. Austin, Richard L. Nolan, Shannon
O'Donnell.
    p. cm.
  ISBN 978-1-4221-4660-6 (hardcover : alk. paper) 1. Information technology—
Management. 2. Strategic planning—Data processing. 3. Management information
systems. 4. Information resources management. I. Nolan, Richard L. II. O'Donnell,
Shannon. III. Title.
  HD30.2.A936 2009
  004.068'4—dc22

                                                                2008041014

The paper used in this publication meets the requirements of the American National
Standard for Permanence of Paper for Publications and Documents in Libraries and
Archives Z39.48-1992.

CONTENTS

Contents

PART FOUR: THE HERO BREAKS THROUGH

PART FIVE: MASTER OF TWO WORLDS

INTRODUCTION

The Adventures of an IT Leader invites readers to "walk in the shoes" of a new CIO, Jim Barton, as he spends a difficult year learning IT leadership at the IVK Corporation, sidestepping the pitfalls that make the CIO job the most volatile, high-turnover job in business.

Although this book is based on the authors' years of firsthand experience with diverse companies and managers, the IVK Corporation and its staff are fictional. As the story begins, the midsize growth company is attempting a turnaround following a period of slowing business performance. The stock price has fallen substantially as investors have adjusted their expectations of the firm's growth. An aggressive new CEO, Carl Williams, takes over and assigns a new management team. In the process, CIO Bill Davies is fired and Jim Barton, former head of Loan Operations and a talented general manager, is appointed CIO. Barton has no background in IT—none at all. The story follows Barton as he figures out what effective IT management is all about and deals with issues and challenges of the job. The financial and other information about IVK in chapter 1 provides a cogent snapshot of the company's situation as the story begins.

The Main Characters

In order of appearance . . .

Jim Barton: The new CIO of IVK. A talented and ambitious general manager, Barton knows little about IT. He sets out to learn quickly and to lead the IT department toward renewed growth, stability, and strategic partnership within the company—but not without facing serious challenges.

1

Introduction

Carl Williams: This bold turnaround CEO is high on ambition and short on patience.

Maggie Landis: A savvy management consultant and Barton's girlfriend, she often provides Barton with valuable insight, references, and perspectives.

The kid: Wise beyond his years, this twenty-something tech nerd, whom Barton mysteriously meets only at Vinnie's Bar, proves a useful sounding board and source of surprisingly good advice.

Bill Davies: Former CIO at IVK, Davies was fired in part because he struggled with management-level communication. He tells Barton that he "won't last one year" in the job of CIO.

Bernie Ruben: As the director of the Technical Services Group and longtime IVK employee, nearing retirement and thus mostly immune to concerns about risk to his career, Ruben frequently provides Barton with the candid advice, knowledge, and context he needs to make key decisions.

Raj Juvvani: As director of Customer Support and Collection Systems, Juvvani is part of Barton's core IT team.

Tyra Gordon: As director of Loan Operations and New Application Development Systems, Tyra worked closely with Barton when he was head of Loan Operations and takes the lead on several new IT projects under his management.

Paul Fenton: As director of Infrastructure and Operations, Fenton manages a large and important domain, including IT security, and is part of Barton's core IT team.

Gary Geisler: As director of Planning and Control, Geisler works closely with Barton on IT financials.

John Cho: IVK's outspoken resident security genius, Cho has a distinct fashion sense and provocative musical talent.

Jenny: Barton's ever-dependable executive assistant.

Several additional characters populate the story, but are described in context.

PART ONE

THE HERO CALLED TO ACTION

CHAPTER ONE

THE NEW CIO

Jim Barton sat motionless in a blue leather chair, one of several positioned around an elegant glass table at one end of the CEO's expansive corner office. At the other end, Carl Williams stood looking out a window. The silence grew long. Finally, Williams turned to look at Barton.

"Speechless" was not a word most people could imagine applying to Jim Barton. His energy and outspokenness as head of the Loan Operations department made him one of IVK's most dynamic executives, a key player and a likely CEO someday—of a different company, if not this one.

But the news Williams had conveyed moments before had left Barton silent, dumbfounded.

A few minutes earlier Barton had rushed to William's office, summoned for *his* turn with the new chief. All morning, leadership team members had marched down that hallway one at a time, each after receiving a phone call, each on a journey to discover his or her fate. As the executive assistant greeted him courteously and waved him in, Barton allowed himself some optimism.

Most likely, he thought, he was about to receive a promotion. He'd done a good job, been a big contributor as the company had grown to its present size. Something like "Chief Operating Officer" would fit him quite nicely.

5

On the other hand, to hear that he was being asked to leave would not have enormously surprised him. He hadn't done anything to warrant such treatment. But unexpected things happen when companies are in crisis. The logic behind executive appointments, retirements, resignations, and firings was rarely transparent. Sometimes, Barton thought there was little logic to it at all.

The timing of his meeting gave Barton reason for hope. According to word going around, firings, resignations, and forced retirements had been handled in the first meetings of the day. Since midmorning, he'd heard mostly about reassignments. Executives involved in early-morning meetings had departed as soon as they'd finished, but for a while now people emerging from meetings with the CEO had been staying. It was late enough in the day that he might just be in line for that plum job.

But his mood darkened when Williams, standing by the window, not looking at Barton, began to speak. The CEO's words struck Barton with near-physical force.

"Jim, I don't think you're going to like this very much."

Barton's mind raced. *Why would he wait this late in the day to fire me? What have I missed or misunderstood?* He pulled himself together well enough to answer: "Just tell me, Carl. We're all grownups here."

Williams chuckled. "It's not what you think. We're not asking you to leave or anything like that. But when you hear what I have to offer, your first inclination may be to think along those lines yourself. Though I sincerely hope not."

To Barton, William's gestures, standing across the room, staring out the window—the entire scene—appeared overly dramatic. Although the view from the thirty-fourth floor was enticing, Williams wasn't simply lost in admiration, he was avoiding eye contact. Barton glanced around the room, seeking additional clues to what might be going on. The office, he noticed, had been completely transformed, all signs of the previous occupant vanquished. That was too bad. Barton had gotten along well with Kyle Crawford, the former CEO. There had been rocky moments, but suddenly, looking back, those didn't seem too awful.

"As you know," Williams continued, "the board is determined to get things on track. They want us back on our earlier, steeper growth trajectory. They believe, and I agree, that the controversy that has dogged us for the last eight months has been a damaging distraction. When they brought me in from outside, they asked me to take a look at the company and to formulate a recovery plan.

"As you probably suspected, the board asked me to reconstruct the leadership team, to clear away the 'rot' that might remain from the way some things were done in the past. To recommend the composition of a team that could rise to the challenges we are facing in the coming months. I'd like you to be on that team."

Relief. It didn't sound like a demotion. Williams continued.

"It has been a difficult process. I haven't told anyone else this, but the first time I went to the board with my proposed team, they balked. They asked for additional changes. I had originally proposed a very different role for you than the one you've ended up in."

An unusual assignment. I can live with that. Spirits lifting, Barton made a constructive noise: "I'm willing to do whatever will help," he offered. "You know me, Carl. I'm a team player."

"I'm delighted that you are taking that attitude," said Williams, who smiled but maintained his place at the window.

"You see, after a considerable amount of shuffling and reshuffling, and having discussed this with the board extensively, we've . . ." Here Williams drew in a deep breath, "Well, we've decided that you should be our new chief information officer."

This was the news that had knocked the air out of Jim Barton, reducing him to his unfamiliar wordless state. After allowing Barton a moment for thought, Williams finally turned away from the window. Barton felt the boss's gaze burn into him. Finally, Barton managed to babble: "CIO? You want me to be the CIO?"

"Davies has been overwhelmed in that role. You've been one of his most outspoken critics."

"I know, but . . . I've got no background in information technology."

"By all accounts, you have a lot of thoughts on how IT should be run. A lot of people think you have pretty good thoughts about this. I think you've said a few things along those lines to me, even in my short time here. Unlike Davies, you'll report directly to me."

Not yet able to unpack a tangle of additional objections all crammed together in a ball at the top of his mind, Barton simply repeated himself: "But I've got no background in IT."

"And Davies has a lot. That clearly doesn't work, so we've decided to try something else." Williams moved to the table and sat down. The CEO learned forward, now locking eyes with his subordinate. "You're a good manager, one of our best. You may not know much about IT, but we think you'll figure it out."

"I'll figure it out?"

"Yes." He nodded and leaned back in his chair. "It's very important, you know."

"I know it's important. I've been saying that myself."

"A lot of people have heard you, loud and clear. The members of the board of directors agree. We're not a small firm anymore. Haven't been for a while. Increasingly, we're more of a financial services factory. But we don't come close to running the company that way yet. That's got to change. And a huge part of the change will be IT."

Barton was helpless to disagree. Williams was paraphrasing arguments that Barton himself had made many times. When he'd made these arguments, though, he'd never imagined that it might become *his* job to act on them. The sobering thought that he might need to figure out how to implement his own recommendations helped him recover.

"What's going on with Davies?" asked Barton.

"Gone," said Williams. "This morning."

So there would not even be a transition period. Just as well. Barton had never gotten along with Davies. Davies didn't like Barton, and who could blame him? Barton had been very critical of IT. He wasn't proud of it, but he'd even occasionally stooped to making fun of Davies's weird taste in neckties.

"Carl," said Barton, "I just don't think I'm the right choice. It's not the place I can add the most value. Can I ask you to reconsider?"

Williams stood, strode to his desk, ready to move to his next meeting. "It's done," he said. "I know it's a shock, but I think this is a fundamentally sound choice. Think about it. If you can manage a modicum of objectivity, I think you'll see that it's a good idea. As unexpected as this may seem, it's not a punishment. IT is a problem area. You are a highly regarded fixer. It's going to be hard, but if you succeed, it will be very good for this business."

"I just can't see it at the moment," said Barton.

"Give it time," said Williams, impatience creeping into his voice, "but not too much time. I sincerely hope you won't do anything stupid, like walking out. Let me know what you decide."

The meeting was over. Williams still had many others to talk to before his day was finished.

Barton stood and shuffled toward the door, but turned back as he approached it.

"Thanks, Carl," he said, automatically.

Williams looked up, trying to determine whether Barton intended sarcasm, deciding that he did not. "You are most welcome," he said. Then he looked down at a sheaf of papers on his desk, to remind himself who was next on the day's meeting schedule.

Friday, March 23, 2:41 p.m. . . .

A small crowd was forming outside Barton's office. All day, eager IVK employees had been working on a big whiteboard in the back of a storage room to create a chart showing the new management team for the company, as well as they could discern it. It was detective work, following clues to possible scenarios and likely conclusions. All of it would be announced soon enough, of course—probably as soon as Monday—but curious souls could not wait that long. Besides, it was fun, in a fatalistic sort of way, this sleuthing for facts that might have implications for all, their jobs and careers. Certainly more fun than fretting or doing their desk jobs.

Much was known. Some executives had told people of their new assignments. Others' roles had been determined by mysterious, undisclosed means. Still others had been escorted from the building and were presumed gone for good.

Jim Barton remained the biggest puzzle. He was still present, but had said nothing to anyone about what Williams had offered him, and he was an obvious fit in *none* of the remaining slots. When inquisitiveness overwhelmed them, people gravitated to the corridor outside Barton's office. The bold ones squinted through glass and half-closed blinds to try to see what he was doing.

Barton was oblivious to their attention, lost in a thick fog, oscillating between anger and excitement, as unsure as he had ever been about anything. One minute he'd decided to resign, the next he was jotting notes for improvements to IT processes. He'd skipped lunch, a bad idea he realized now. At 1:35 p.m., he'd swiveled his chair around to the computer screen and had begun searching the Web. Now his eyes were locked at a focal distance of about sixteen inches, on the surface of the computer monitor. From within his sphere of intense concentration he could not have seen people peering in at him even if he'd looked right at them.

The first thing he had typed was "IT Management." Google informed him that it had located 1,240 *million* Web pages on that subject. He clicked on the first of these; what looked like a table of contents for a magazine appeared. He scanned it. "Outsourcing to India." That seemed like a legitimate management issue. The next few items, reviews of new devices, not so much. Then came stories about companies that had succeeded with things that had techie-sounding names: "Virtualization." "Managed services." Acronyms lay strewn about the page: SaaS. SOA. PLM. ITIL. SSL. VPN. Most of it didn't look like "management" at all. This was one of Barton's pet peeves. He used to say it to Davies, all the time: "IT management has to be about *management*. Talk to me about *management*. Profit. Risk. Return. Process. People. Not Trojan this or blade server that."

He stood up, moved to his whiteboard, and erased everything on it. Then, at the top, in big, green letters he wrote, "IT management is about management." He underlined the second occurrence of the word "management" and looked around unsuccessfully for a pen of a different color that he could use to emphasize the word even more.

> ### IT management is about <u>management</u>

For a while, he just stared at what he had written. Then he rolled his eyes and slapped the green pen back onto the whiteboard tray. "That helped a lot," he said sarcastically.

He moved back to his chair and started surfing from link to link, not pausing to read most pages. In the blur of passing pages, a sentence caught his eye, prompting him to stop: "More than any other group within a company, IT is positioned to understand the business end-to-end, across departmental boundaries; no other department interacts with as many different parts of the business as IT." *What a bunch of crap,* he thought. As he'd seen again and again, IT people did *not* understand the business. That was one of his big problems with them. But as he read the sentence again, as he thought about it carefully, he realized it didn't say "IT understands the business better than any other group." It said IT is *positioned* to see better into more corners of the company. IT people have an advantage in gaining a deep understanding of the business. Doesn't mean they do a good job in seizing that advantage. The potential, though, interested Barton. He had never before thought of it that way.

He surfed. Pages and more pages filled with gibberish. He stopped on a page with a pair of diagrams. The first claimed to portray the usual state of affairs in IT management situations. It showed business knowledge ("smarts" in the diagram) and technical knowledge having no overlap, but needing to be pushed together:

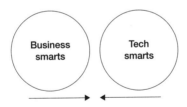

The text that accompanied this diagram suggested that one of the top responsibilities of the IT manager, one of the most useful things that he or she could do, would be to take actions that pushed the two circles closer together. If this effort was successful, that would then result in a changed diagram:

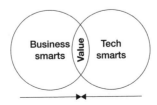

Hmm, thought Barton. *Overly simplistic, maybe, but consistent with my understanding of the situation and the problem.* He wasn't sure what actions might push the two circles together—he'd think more about that. Education, training, came to mind, but there had to be more to it than just that. This way of thinking about the problem suggested, at least implicitly, that communication issues were a big deal. That, too, fit with Barton's IT-related experiences. If business people and technology people shared more knowledge—more understanding—the end result of that would be an improved ability to communicate with each other, which should result in getting work done more smoothly. The discussion that accompanied the diagram also suggested—helpfully, he thought—that people able to operate in that area of overlap where "Value" was created were a resource to be hired, retained, and cherished. You could keep track of how many people you had who were like that, whether they were business-savvy types in the IT department or tech-savvy people from business units. And you could try to increase their numbers.

Again, Barton surfed. Not far from the circle diagrams, he found a picture that he liked even more:[1]

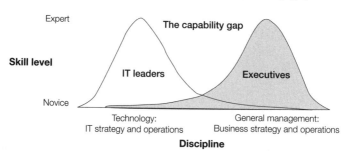

The IT leader/general manager capability gap

Something about this diagram better captured the anxiety he felt as he considered accepting the CIO job. He believed he resided at the top of the "Executives" hill in the picture, near the peak of understanding the company's general management, business strategy, and operations issues. Moving across to acquire understanding of IT strategy and operations would, according to this depiction, involve crossing a threatening chasm. If he accepted the position, he'd need to come up with a way of building a bridge between the two hills, or crossing from the top of one hill to the top of the other. He had no interest in spending a lot of time down in the valley between the two disciplines. But that wasn't the only source of his anxiety. The idea of tiptoeing across a rickety bridge between the two summits held little appeal. It would be all too easy to fall through a crack in the bridge and plummet to his (career's) demise. Even *thinking* of hanging out there in the middle of such a bridge called forth in Barton an acrophobic surge of adrenalin. The words to an old Elton John song, "Rocket Man," floated through his mind: it would be lonely for Barton out in that space.

The text that accompanied this diagram argued that the valley could be spanned from either direction. A career technical employee could acquire enough understanding of the business to be an effective IT leader. Or a career business employee could acquire enough understanding of technology. It suggested, even, that it might be a bit easier and more viable for the career business leader to work the problem from that side. The rationale: technical knowledge, as much as you needed to know as an IT manager, was relatively explicit and learnable, whereas a lot of the understanding that made managers effective was tacit—mastery of relationships, understanding of political factors, and so on. This argument also rang true. It was in those softer, tacit areas that Davies had repeatedly had problems. Half the time, the guy couldn't even dress himself to be taken seriously in a business group. No one would've even thought of taking him to a meeting with customers, although he had suggested exactly that on numerous occasions.

Barton returned to Google and typed "CIO." This time only (only!) 134 million entries resulted. He began clicking through them. *CIO* magazine and *CIO Insight* were the biggest hitters among the first ten entries. After working his way through a few more pages of entries, glancing quickly at some, he came across a PowerPoint presentation called "A Short History of the CIO Position" and clicked on it. It looked like a presentation prepared by a professor from a school Barton had never heard of. Some of the content was cryptic, but the gist of it was clear.

The presentation described the last decade of the CIO job as a "roller coaster ride." In the late '90s, the Internet explosion made tech start-up companies glamorous. This created difficulties for CIOs as some of their best employees left for possible IPO riches. But these events also raised the prestige of the average CIO. Established firms looked to their own IT managers to acquire some of that start-up magic. Technologists, keepers of the magic, became *cool*. In annual reports, blue suits and white shirts gave way to khakis, neat haircuts to ponytails, b-school types to nerds.

IT managers rode enthusiasm for the Internet to new heights. Higher status meant bigger budgets. IT practitioners throughout corporate hierarchies became vital consultants to business-area partners. Companies reorganized, extracted IT departments from beneath finance, where they often resided (for historical reasons—"data processing" started with payroll and accounting), granting them equal stature with organizational areas such as finance, marketing, and operations. According to the statistics in the presentation, by 2002 barely 10 percent of companies continued to house the IT department within finance.[2] With reorganization came a seat for the CIO at the senior management table. In a few companies, CIOs ascended to CEO, seemingly altering the historical career path for IT managers.

But the story ended badly.

The NASDAQ peaked in March 2000, then plummeted. Within a year, former high-flying companies crashed. IT workers, accustomed to setting their own salaries, suddenly couldn't find jobs. People took notice of how few Internet companies seemed capable of generating profits. Established firms whose strategies had evolved vigorously under threat from the IT "revolution" tossed out the new strategies and reverted to old ones.

Revenge of the nerds gave way to revenge of the cost accountants, dot-com to "dot vertigo."[3] With consummate bad timing, large IT projects, such as ERP and CRM implementations, stumbled.[4] Costs overran budgets; benefits undershot expectations. IT project failure was nothing new, but as technology lost its luster such failures earned renewed scrutiny. Projects were cancelled, budgets slashed.

By 2003, IT managers were living in what one consultant phrased a "hunt-kill-eat" climate. Grand visions and strategies that had seemed so important a few years earlier now elicited disapproval. Executives who had been eager to discuss IT-enabled futures were no longer in the mood. These harsh realities descended on IT managers and put them into basic survival mode: *hunt, kill, eat.*

Cost savings became the project mantra du jour. Subject to tightening budgetary control, the typical IT organization became reactive, with few new applications being developed. Press accounts in 2003 traced the CIO's fall from grace. Old organizational arrangements, such as having the CIO report to the CFO, reappeared.[5] The need to comply with new legislation such as the Sarbanes-Oxley Act of 2002 once again made the CIO job seem closely aligned with finance. The number of CIOs reporting to CFOs doubled, and the average CIO salary dropped.[6] *CIO* magazine ran a cover story called "The Incredible Shrinking CIO" ("Their budgets have been cut, their work's been outsourced, their staff's been downsized, and they've been pushed off the executive team").[7] The roller coaster that once carried IT managers so high now hurled them earthward.

By 2006, the presentation concluded, many CIOs had lost seats at executive tables. Their organizations were increasingly being shipped off to vendors, both domestic and overseas. On the other hand, the emphasis on IT as purely a cost-cutting tool was easing a bit. Improved economies had CEOs looking for ways to increase revenues again, turning their attention from bottom to top lines. In some companies, IT was enjoying a mild renaissance as a possible enabler of new growth. A few companies drew senior IT executives closer into corporate governance by establishing IT oversight committees on their boards of directors.[8]

Barton thought back through the history of IVK. During the dotcom craze, IVK had been very small, one of a breed of corporate creatures that was rare in those days, a non-tech startup company. When the bottom had fallen out of the tech market, it was a very good thing that IVK had never quite gotten on board the Internet express. Throughout much of the crash-and-burn period for Internet startups, IVK had managed to grow.

The part about IT being a potential source of growth for a firm excited Barton. He wasn't quite sure what it meant, but he wasn't ready to discount it either. He remembered Davies arguing that superior technical features that could be effectively demonstrated to clients could be a factor in closing deals. That's why he'd wanted in on meetings with customers. The idea of Davies and his weird neckties sitting down with customers had obscured serious consideration of this argument.

Surfing just a bit more, thinking about wrapping things up and taking his decision home for the weekend, Barton stumbled across a sentiment that he appreciated. It proposed that IT managers try a thought experiment:

> *Imagine your day-to-day work. How much would be left to do in a day if a moratorium were declared on discussions about specific technologies? In how you think about IT management, how much would there be—principles, philosophies, practices—that could be said to be independent of the underlying technologies?*

Because the world was still reeling from the aftershocks of the Internet crash, this article said, it was essential that IT managers understand and demonstrate to others that the need for shrewd IT management does not vanish when over-hyped technologies do. If the field of IT management was to mature, to take its rightful place in the pantheon of management ideas, it must have substance beyond the specific objects of its actions. The article finished with a flourish:

> *The core of IT management—the management content—is not transitory. Just as the fundamentals of, say, finance or marketing, remain relatively stable at their core, so are the fundamentals of IT management.*

If this was true, Barton thought, then there was hope for him in the CIO job.

He shut down his browser and stood up, reaching for the coat on the rack behind his chair. Finally, looking toward the door, he noticed the sizeable group of people gathered outside his office.

"What is it?" he asked them, as he emerged with coat on and briefcase in hand. No one said anything. He looked from one to another of their sheepish expressions. Then he singled out someone who worked for him—or who *had* worked for him—in Loan Operations.

"Jackie, what's going on?"

Jackie gathered her courage and told him: "We've been trying to figure out where you fit in the new management team. We've figured out pretty much everyone else, but you're a puzzle. And," she quickly added, "of course those of us who work for you hope you'll continue to be our boss."

Barton laughed. "I'm afraid you're out of luck."

Perplexed faces told him that no one had the slightest idea what he meant by that. He looked around, gathered his own nerve, and tried on a phrase that had never before passed his lips: "I'm the new CIO."

Several people in the room gasped. Barton did not wait for further reactions. He headed for the elevator, leaving stunned silence in his wake.

REFLECTION

Why would Carl Williams ask a non-technical manager to assume the CIO position?

If you were Jim Barton, would you take the job?

What do the IVK Corporation exhibits (1-1 through 1-6) tell you about the current state of the company? Given this information, what does IVK need from a new management team under CEO Carl Williams?

IVK Corporation Organization Chart

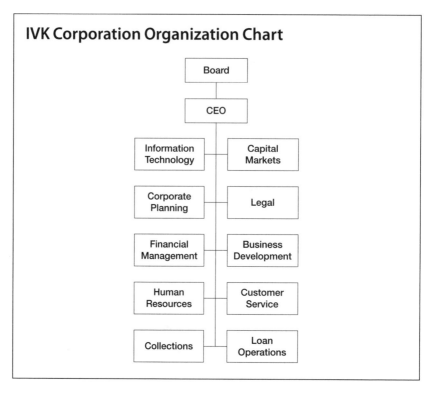

Market Share of IVK Corporation Versus the Two Leading Competitors

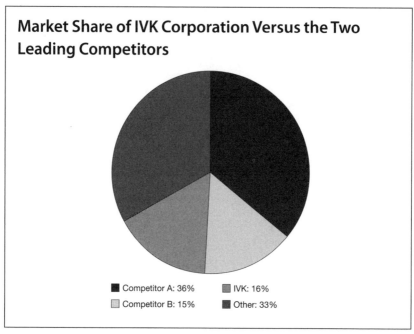

Competitor A: 36%   IVK: 16%
Competitor B: 15%   Other: 33%

IVK Corporation Statistics for the Fiscal Year

- 2.2+ million customer inquiries
- 530,000+ applications processed
- 180,000 loans funded

Financial Statements—Consolidated Balance Sheet

	June 30	
	Year X	Year X–1
Assets		
Cash and other short-term investments	$152,551,539	$17,175,191
Total cash and cash equivalents	$152,551,539	$17,175,191
Service receivables:		
Advisory fees	34,835,164	10,785,983
Residuals	107,795,378	43,617,465
Processing fees	6,352,356	2,539,735
	148,982,898	56,943,183
Other receivables	438,934	155,833
Property and equipment	15,336,144	6,255,447
Less accumulated depreciation and amortization	−4,227,745	−1,877,339
Property and equipment, net	11,108,399	4,378,108
Goodwill (People's VK acquisition)	3,229,497	3,347,697
Prepaid and other current assets	23,031,274	478,634
Other assets	1,800,990	0
Total assets	$341,143,531	$82,478,646

continued

Financial Statements *(continued)*

	June 30	
	Year X	Year X–1
Liabilities and stockholders' equity		
Liabilities:		
Accounts payable and accrued expenses	$26,343,374	$13,333,047
Net deferred tax liability	41,143,125	14,365,987
Notes payable and capital lease obligations	9,723,003	283,864
Notes payable	6,233,853	6,374,320
Total liabilities	$83,443,355	$34,357,218
Commitments and contingencies		
Stockholders' equity:		
Preferred stock, par value $0.01 per share; 20,000,000		
Shares authorized at June 30, Year X; no shares authorized		
At June 30, Year X–1; no shares issued or outstanding		
At June 30, Year X or June 30, Year X–1	0	0
Common stock, par value $0.01 per share; 100,000,000		
Shares authorized; 63,543,662 and 56,731,054 shares issued and outstanding at June 30,		
Year X and Year X–1, respectively	639,780	531,954
Additional paid-in capital	183,572,199	13,269,353
Retained earnings	73,488,197	34,320,121
Total stockholders' equity	257,700,176	48,121,428
Total liabilities and stockholders' equity	341,143,531	82,478,646

Financial Statements—Consolidated Income Statement

	Years ended June 30		
	Year X	**Year X–1**	**Year X–2**
Service revenue:			
Advisory fees	$89,194,767	$69,346,698	$14,761,226
Residuals	74,894,813	61,027,105	11,834,993
Administrative and other fees	4,113,746	2,814,617	474,888
Processing fees	65,456,570	39,566,486	14,191,953
Total service revenue	$233,659,896	$172,754,906	$41,263,060
Operating expenses:			
Compensation and benefits	54,879,252	26,805,902	11,488,553,
General and administrative expenses	65,695,724	31,062,928	10,651,614
Total operating expenses	120,574,976	57,868,830	22,140,167
Income from operations	113,084,920	114,886,076	19,122,893
Other expense:			
Interest expense	717,392	1,563,305	1,824,493
Interest income	–814,894	–116,983	–91,220
Other income	–2,412	–2,200	–130,447
Total other expense, net	–99,914	1,444,122	1,602,826
Income before income tax expense	113,184,834	113,441,954	17,520,067
Income tax expense	43,539,727	42,214,388	5,106,933
Net income	69,645,107	71,227,566	12,413,134
Net income per share, basic	$1.18	$1.33	$0.24
Net income per share, diluted	$1.10	$1.26	$0.23
Weighted-average shares outstanding, basic	59,047,914	53,699,115	52,632,000
Weighted-average shares outstanding, diluted	63,543,662	56,731,054	54,574,266
Stock price (at year-end)	$30.74	$60.22	$25.10
Market value (stock price × shares, in millions)	$1,953	$3,416	$1,370

Stock Price for IVK Corporation

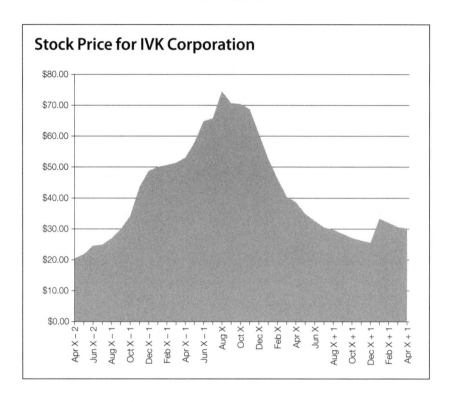

CHAPTER TWO

CIO CHALLENGES

Friday, March 23, 9:48 p.m....

By late in the evening, a sense of foreboding had settled over Barton. He wandered from one room to another through his upscale condo, stopping to flip TV channels, sound muted, without perceiving the images that flashed on screen. Several times he tried to telephone Maggie, the woman he'd been dating for the past several months. Barton was frustrated that, on top of the day's events, he was stuck home alone on a Friday night because Maggie, a management consultant, was on temporary assignment in another city. She was probably with clients, but it was odd that she was not answering her mobile phone. Given his overall state of mind, Barton was inclined to assume the worst.

He thought about going for a run, but he preferred mornings for that. Logging on to his computer, he discovered that his nephew, a technology, music, and video game buff, had "gifted" him some music. Jack often sent Barton things via e-mail, like videos or links to interesting Web pages. Barton and his nephew had a special relationship, although they didn't see each other very often (Jack lived in the suburbs, which might as well have been in another country as often as Barton made it out there).

Delighted with the distraction, he downloaded music by a band called Black Box Recorder. Barton hoped for something that would lift his spirits, but he could see immediately from the song titles that he was out of luck: "Girl Singing in the Wreckage" and "It's Only the End of the World" didn't sound upbeat. Barton cued up the new tunes and tapped on the remote to channel the music to his high-end sound system, cranking up the volume. About halfway through the album, the lead singer offered some breathy advice that struck Barton as useful: *Life is unfair*, the singer whispered, against a stark backdrop of percussion and bass, *Kill yourself or get over it*. It made Barton laugh. Seizing the energy in this burst of levity, he decided to get out of the condo for a while, take a walk, find something else to lift his spirits. Grabbing a coat, he left without turning off the music.

Forty or so minutes later, hitched up to a bar, he found himself in a serious conversation with a kid who, Barton assumed from his looks and the way he talked, did some kind of computer work for a local business or university. The guy was in his late twenties, Barton guessed, just a decade or so younger than Barton himself, but total kid and total nerd in the way he interacted. In the time it took to drain a martini, Barton had unloaded his story, told his sad tale of career misfortune. The kid had advice. He kept repeating a phrase that Barton couldn't quite follow:

"You've got to know what you don't know."

"Huh?" responded Barton.

"What you don't know. You've got to know it."

"How can I know it if I don't know it?"

"No, I don't mean you should know the things that you don't know. I mean that you should know the things you know, and know what you don't know."

Barton shook his head, perplexed.

"How are those things different?"

"The things you know and the things you don't know? Because you know one and you don't know the other."

"Yeah, but you think I should know them both. I see how to know the ones I know but it's that know-things-you-don't-know bit I'm tripping over."

"Let me start over," the kid said. "In taking on a new assignment, such as the one you've been given, you have to . . . you have to *realize* that there are some categories of things that you know, and some things that you don't. And you have to know what is in which category."

"Oh, I see. I think. I don't have to actually *know* things I don't know, I just have to know what they are and realize that they're in the don't-know category."

The kid drained the last of a mug of Coke and slammed it down hard on the bar. "That's it!"

Despite himself, Barton felt proud. He took a sip of his own drink, a second martini not nearly as good as the ones he sometimes made for himself.

"So, what about it?" the kid asked.

"Huh?" said Barton.

"What about it? Do you think you . . . you *realize* what categories of things you know and what categories of things you don't know?"

Barton thought about this. "Yes," he said. "I definitely don't know the techie stuff. I definitely do know the management stuff."

"Hmmm," the kid said.

"What?" asked Barton.

"You sure about that?"

"About what? I'm sure I don't know the techie stuff."

The kid raised his eyebrows, a gesture that suggested wisdom Barton thought he could not possibly possess. "So what about the 'management stuff,' as you put it?"

Barton was indignant. "Of course I know that stuff. I'm the best manager they've got. That's why they've chosen me for this job."

"Okay," said the kid. He motioned to the bartender, ordering another Coke. The bartender shouted down to Barton, "You want another too?" Barton shook his head. He was still fixated on the kid and what he was saying.

"You don't seem convinced."

"Are you?"

"Yes."

"Hey, fine. Whatever."

"But you don't believe me. Even though you don't know me and have never seen me manage anything," observed Barton.

"It's not that," said the kid, receiving a new, frosty mug from the bartender and taking a sip. "It's nothing to do with you personally."

"What is it then?"

The kid shrugged. "I'm a technical guy, what do I know?"

"I'm not asking you what you know; I'm asking you what you think."

"It's just," he said, now turning to Barton with a slightly vindictive tone, "that I've worked for a lot of people who think they're good managers, and what they don't know is that they don't know a rainforest from a desert. So nothing personal. I just think most people who think they 'know the management stuff' probably don't really. You might be an exception." He shrugged again.

Barton thought about this. It sounded like the kind of thing one should keep in mind when taking on a new job. The boundary between technical and management stuff might not be clear-cut. "Fair enough," he said to the kid.

The kid seemed surprised. "You might be an okay manager after all," he said.

"So if you were me," Barton asked, "what would you do on Monday? What would you do on your very first day?"

"Easy," the kid responded. "Start trying to figure out who on your team is really good. You don't know the 'techie stuff,' as you put it, so it won't be easy for you to tell who in the department is really good and who isn't all that good. Lots of managers never really know that. And, to pick up on our earlier conversation, they don't know that they don't know it. Which makes them do stupid things, like reward dolts and underappreciate genius. Put people on the wrong projects. Insist on objectives that make no sense. Everyone realizes it when a manager doesn't know what he or she doesn't know. It's a state of blissful management ignorance. There's definitely a talent in it, don't get me wrong. Some people get paid quite a lot of money not to know a rainforest from a desert. They succeed mostly by managing the appearance of success rather than actual success."

Just then, Barton's phone rang. It was Maggie.

"Hi Jim, looks like I missed several calls," she said. "Everything okay?"

"Not really," he answered, "but nothing dire or life threatening. If you've got some time, I'll tell you about it."

"I've got time now," she said. "We had a team meeting that went late or I'd have called you back sooner. Where are you?" She'd heard background noise.

"I'm at Vinnie's."

"Uh-huh. And how many drinks have you had?"

There was no use feigning innocence; she could tell that he hadn't been drinking coffee. "A couple," he admitted.

"How about," she said, "if we talk while you walk home?"

This was fine with Barton. He was eager to tell her about the day's events. He and Maggie chit-chatted while he paid the bar tab, then he turned to go, nodding to the kid. A few steps toward the door, he suddenly stopped and turned around.

"Hold on a minute," he said into the phone. Then, out loud, to the kid: "Hey, kid. Want a job?"

The kid laughed. "Not right now. But ask me again in a few weeks. Maybe then. And you can tell me how it's going."

"Fair enough." Barton exited the bar, returning to his phone call and pouring out his sad tale to Maggie while she made satisfyingly sympathetic noises at the other end.

Sunday, March 25, 8:15 a.m. . . .

Barton sat on cold pavement, legs outstretched, reaching for his toes, prepping for a long run around the park. He needed it. His late-night activities Friday had caused him to skip running on Saturday. Having missed the daily ritual, he'd felt unsettled all afternoon, as he hit the dry cleaner and drug store, stopped in a grocery to grab some ready-to-cook dinner. He'd spent Saturday night watching TV and listening to the music that Jack had sent him, and then he'd gone to bed early.

The relatively mindless Saturday pursuits had left him with plenty of capacity to think about his first day as CIO on Monday. The obvious first thing to do would be a meeting of his direct reports. He'd have sent out notice of the meeting on the weekend, but he realized that he wasn't even sure who the direct reports to the CIO were. Sending the notice on Monday wouldn't be too much of a problem; they would all be expecting it.

At the meeting, Barton intended to propose a day or two of off-site meetings sometime in the next two or three weeks; he would ask his managers to present the current status of the activities within their areas, the challenges that needed to be met in the coming months, and opportunities to create value for the company. Using the current situation as a basis, he then wanted them to work together to construct a future vision for the role of IT in the business. Before too long, they'd need to hold an all-hands department meeting, the first for Barton as their new leader; they could begin to plan that also.

That would be the morning. In the afternoon, he wanted to spend some time with the Planning and Control guy. Gary Geisler was keeper of the financial information that pertained to IT budgets and expenditures. Barton expected to field questions from the CEO's office about how much IVK spent on IT. Right now, he didn't even know the right categories for analyzing IT spending (but he knew he didn't know, right?).

As Barton began to jog down a path, he suddenly had a disturbing thought. Sometimes, he recalled, Bill Davies jogged around here. Barton had occasionally encountered him on this very route. Davies surely knew by now who his chosen successor was, but Barton was unsure how Davies might react to the news. There was more than a little irony in the fact that his most vocal critic had been stuck with his job. Davies might relish that. But it couldn't feel very good to get fired; Barton had never experienced that, didn't care to.

A few minutes later, two paths converged and—to Barton's horror—he found himself running almost side-by-side with Davies, who didn't seem to notice at first. If Barton stopped suddenly, he would just have drawn attention to himself. Worse than that, it might have conveyed to Davies a message that Barton was intimidated or embarrassed, and he was deeply averse to communicating either sentiment. Instead, he felt inclined to reach out to Davies. Not to apologize exactly, although that might have been appropriate, especially for some of the wisecracks he'd made about Davies's "benevolent dictator" leadership style and rather quirky wardrobe. But maybe to say "no hard feelings," to convey some respect for the work the other man had done. And maybe—just maybe, Barton realized—to create the option of consulting Davies about things in the future. This was not something he would be inclined to do at first, but there might come a time when it would be useful. Barton did not believe in burning bridges.

So when Davies slowed down and stopped to rest and stretch, Barton did also.

"Hi, Bill," said Barton.

"Hello, Jim," responded Davies.

"Nice day."

"A bit cold for March."

A pause grew uncomfortable. Barton broke it: "I guess you heard . . ."

"I did." Said too quickly, to cut off whatever else Barton was about to say.

Barton waited to give Davies time to say more, but he didn't. Barton opted for brevity to fill the new silence: "Ironic, huh?"

"I laughed for about half an hour when I heard."

Davies said this in a monotone. Barton looked closely, trying to discern whether the remark was a friendly joke or a hostile gesture. The guy's social skills had never been great, so Barton figured this might just be awkwardness. He might not mean anything at all by it. Maybe it was just poorly calibrated candor.

Barton made a peace offering: "Hey, I just want you to know—we had some disagreements."

"We sure did."

Again, Barton could not read the sentiment behind the words. He continued: "I was out of line at times, and I feel bad about that." Davies shrugged. Barton pressed ahead: "I guess I just want to say 'No hard feelings,' not on my part."

Confusingly, Davies began to laugh. Soft at first, the laughter gained volume and power until Barton began to wonder if the guy might be coming unhinged. Barton looked around to see if anyone else was nearby, embarrassed for Davies, a little worried what he might do. Just when Barton thought the laughing could grow no louder, it stopped. Davies turned to Barton, looked him in the eye and said: "What you don't realize, Jim, is that you'll be gone soon too. That company is a madhouse. Nobody could succeed running IT in that place. You won't last a year."

Barton started to answer, but Davies wasn't finished: "Don't feel bad for me," he added. "I start a new job on Monday. I even got a raise. And you're going to need all that feeling-bad capacity for yourself when *you* get tossed out on *your* butt."

Without waiting for a response from Barton, Davies sprinted away, making it clear that he didn't want to be followed.

Barton couldn't have followed anyway.

The offer of the CIO job had provoked many strong reactions in Barton. He'd felt put-upon. He'd patted himself on the back for being a good guy, willing to "take one" for the team. He'd supposed himself the most flexible member of the senior management team, imagined how grateful his CEO and management peers must be, seeing him act in such a selfless manner. He knew that the job would be hard and had considered that he might even fail at it. But until this moment—until Davies had said what he'd said—Jim Barton had not once considered the possibility that the company might unceremoniously boot him if they didn't like what he did with the IT department. But how could they? It would be like spitting in the face of a hero.

But as Barton contemplated Davies's words, he knew they contained truth. In business, memories were short. Nine months from now, no one would remember what a great guy he'd been to take the job. They'd just know it was *his* job, and if they thought he was doing it badly, they'd feel no more loyalty toward Barton than he had felt toward Davies. A lot could—and would—change in a short time.

So if he was going to take this job—if Jim Barton was going to become the CIO of IVK—he would need to expect to be judged on his performance, regardless of the deficit of experience in the area that was his starting point. It was obvious, really—the kind of point he might have made to Davies in a past discussion. He'd been deluded to think otherwise, and the sudden "shoe on the other foot" reversal shook him to his core.

Sighing deeply, he set off down the path in the direction Davies had not taken.

Sunday, March 25, 3:15 p.m. . . .

By early afternoon, Barton had gotten over Davies's challenging assertion and reverted to a more helpful mode of thinking about concrete first steps in his new job. One obvious idea would be to meet with CIOs of other companies who might be willing to confide in Barton how they thought about their jobs. But he wasn't sure how to go about this. He'd never been a CIO and did not have a network of CIO associates. Maggie was his ace in the hole, however. She worked closely with many IT managers and knew many CIOs. It would be a matter of telling her the CIOs, or the companies, he'd like to approach.

He wasn't sure what to tell her when she asked about this, however. Competitors wouldn't do. They couldn't be counted on to be forth-coming, and there might even be legal issues. On the other hand, he'd have to be careful about whether the way very different kinds of companies used IT would be relevant to IVK. To some extent, of course, which companies he met with would be determined by the willingness and availability of the people he approached.

After a few minutes of thinking about this, Barton phoned Maggie.

"Hey there," she said. "I was just about to call you. How are you feeling today about the fast-moving events in your life?"

Barton laughed. "A little whiplashed, but okay, I guess. How about you—you spend a lot of time with CIOs already—sure you want to be *involved* with one?

"You mean, will I still love you if you turn into an IT nerd? I'm not sure. But I think I can handle it."

"Gee, I sure hope so," said Barton trying on a nerd voice, realizing he was no good at it, then reverting to normal tones: "Seriously though, I am getting more practical about it, thinking about how to do it. If I do it."

"That sounds like a good thing."

"I think so. I was wondering if it might make sense for me to meet with some other CIOs, others who might know a lot about how to do this job. But I don't actually know anybody helpful—"

"Ah, but you're thinking maybe I do?"

"Yep."

"Yet again, you want me for my knowledge."

"Among other things."

"Well," she sighed playfully, "okay. But it'll cost you. Want me to set up some lunches?"

"That sounds about right."

"It's a terrific idea. But what you get out of it, Jim, I'll tell you right now, is going to be highly variable."

"Okay, Maggs. Why's that?"

"Because to get to the level of discussion that will be really helpful, you're going to have to get to know these people. Surface-level stuff will help some, but to get into the next level of discussion, you'll have to have a relationship. So I think you should meet with some of them not just once, but periodically. The most valuable guidance will come in time, not right away."

"Makes sense. How about if we set up some first meetings, then we can figure out who seems promising for repeat engagements?"

"Yeah. I'm thinking local metro area, but you'd probably be willing to fly an hour or two for the right lunch date, right?"

"Absolutely."

"Any thoughts," she asked, "on which companies, which CIOs?"

"I don't really know any CIOs," Barton answered. "And I'm not sure how to think about which companies."

"How soon would you like to start?"

"Not sure about that either. I'm tempted to say 'as soon as possible,' but maybe you think there's some level of expertise I should acquire before I start this process?"

"No, I don't think that's the issue, unless that would make you more comfortable. Tell you what, why don't you think about it some more and send me an e-mail? Tell me how you want to choose companies or CIOs, when you want to start, how often you want to meet, any other details important to you. I'll probably vary from your guidance where I think it's a good idea, but this would give me a basis to start."

"Thanks, Maggs. I'll do that as soon as I can, next couple of days. I'd do it today, but I'd like to get a bit of a read from some of my new management team."

"Doesn't sound like you're thinking about this assignment hypothetically anymore. Decided to take the job?"

"Let's just say that I haven't decided to leave, so I guess maybe that's the same thing as deciding to accept."

"You okay with me setting up some meetings with other industry folks, not necessarily CIOs?"

"I think so. Who do you have in mind?"

"Some industry analysts, the ones who have a clue, and maybe some key people who work for IT vendors or service firms, people who I know are smart. Maybe some industry movers and shakers, people who are involved as investors, or who have other reasons to want to keep track of where they think things are headed in the IT industry."

"Wow. That'd be great. I might find it particularly helpful to talk to people who have a business view into IT."

"Have you thought about whether there are other strategic lunch engagements you should seek out? How about meeting with customers?"

"I know all our customers pretty well. I was head of Loan Ops until about forty-eight hours ago, you know."

"But you don't know them as the IVK CIO. You might be surprised by what you don't know that they might tell you if you present yourself as the new CIO and ask questions about how well IVK is meeting their business needs with IT."

"I see. That's a good idea," said Barton, though privately he was less than fully convinced. If his customers had been having trouble with IT, he'd have known about it.

"By the way, Jim, I saw a presentation the other day about how the CIO's position is changing. I took some notes to send to a couple of my staff. I can send them to you, if you like."*

"I'll look forward to seeing them. Thanks, Maggs," said Barton.

"Anyone else you want to meet with?"

"With all these ideas you're coming up with, I'm going to have to prioritize a bit. Can't meet with them all right away."

"You give it some thought, I'll give it some thought. We'll formulate a plan."

"Right. Let's figure out what to do."

"Then do it."

"Right." Barton shifted gears, "So, how are things there? That handsome banking client behaving himself?"

"Jim, Jim, Jim," Maggie said, feigning disappointment, an exasperated headshake conveyed in the rhythm of her words: "Is that your way of saying that you miss me?"

*See "Maggie's notes on 'The New CIO Role'" at the end of this chapter.

REFLECTION

How do you interpret the kid's advice, "You've got to know what you don't know"?

Why do you think Davies got fired? How likely is it that Barton will be fired within the year?

What kinds of questions should Barton be asking of CIOs, analysts, investors, customers, and other IT movers and shakers? How should he prioritize and organize these meetings?

Maggie's Notes on "The New CIO Role"

Gap in CIO's "Strategic Aspirations"

- According to an IBM survey of 176 CIOs worldwide, the number-one barrier that impedes the CIO in becoming a business leader:

  - Misperceptions of the CIO role: 31%

  - Lack of business skills and competencies: 26%

  - Failure to understand importance of IT: 12%

  - Lack of time to spend on strategic issues: 12%

  - Poor collaboration with lines of business: 8%

  - Lack of support from CEO/Board: 7%

  - Insufficient authority or responsibility: 4%

- 86% of CIOs said they wanted a more strategic role, a greater role in making or shaping strategy.[a]

Global Trends Affecting the CIO Role

- Majority of companies have become more focused on increasing market share, moving past emphasis on cost cutting

- Increasing options for outsourcing IT services: financial benefits, increasingly sophisticated offerings from service providers

- CEOs expect IT managers to manage people, finances, and materials, not just technology

- CEOs expect IT to contribute to a firm's strategy flexibility; they must be able to absorb change

- In many firms, CIOs fall short of going beyond operational focus; in many firms with progressive IT capabilities, enlightened CFO, COO, or CEO is the real driver, not the CIO

- CIOs called on to take a broader role in corporate leadership

Some Key Factors in Future CIO Success

- Enhancing and maintaining relationships with other business leaders

- Ability to develop an organization of talented technologists who understand the business

- Ability to educate CEO and peer executives on new possibilities enabled by IT and on key business trade-offs implicit in technology choices

Some Possible "Next Steps"

- Work systematically to develop (or rebuild) the business credibility of the IT organization

- Position IT as a strategic and competitive necessity; make sure IT plans, actions, and capabilities are clearly linked to company objectives and goals

Imperatives

- Speak the language of business, inside IT and especially with business partners

- Keep a strong connection with the CEO and business peers

- Don't lose sight of efficiency; be a relentless cost reducer

- Understand impacts of IT on the revenue and cost sides of the income statement

- Invest in agility of systems and IT architecture

- Establish a robust governance framework; manage the project portfolio to maximize return

CIO Challenges

- Manage sourcing and partners

- Manage talent; build a smart organization

- Enable innovation; enable change; be competitively relevant

- Safeguard the information assets of the organization; maintain robust infrastructure and assure business continuity

Source: This exhibit is loosely and partially based on S. Sadagopan, "Meet the New CIO," *Opinion,* November 19, 2007, http://www.sandhill.com/opinion/editorial.php?id=161.

a. "The CIO Profession: Driving Innovation and Competitive Advantage," October 2007, IBM Center for CIO Leadership in collaboration with MIT Sloan Center for Information Systems Research (CISR) and Harvard Business School, http://www-03.ibm.com/industries/education /doc/content/resource/thought/3387462110.html.

CHAPTER THREE

CIO LEADERSHIP

Monday, March 26, 10:43 a.m. . . .

"I think it's a question of whether the five of us working alone will be able to accomplish what you have in mind," said Bernie Ruben, director of the IT department's Technical Services Group. The others around the table controlled their movements and facial expressions, but Barton could tell that they agreed. Ruben, at least twenty years Barton's senior, near enough to retirement to feel safe or simply old enough not to care, was the bravest of his direct reports. Ruben's voice contained no fear as he spoke, which differentiated him from the others in the conference room: Raj Juvvani, director of Customer Support and Collection Systems, Tyra Gordon, director of Loan Operations and New Application Development Systems, and Paul Fenton, director of Infrastructure and Operations; all younger, with more to lose.*

The meeting had not gone according to Barton's plan. First thing that morning he'd asked Jenny, his assistant, to find an IT department organization chart. With that in his possession, he'd ascertained who reported to him and summoned them via e-mail to a 10 a.m. meeting. He chose to assemble only his operating managers, not including Gary Geisler, a more junior manager with whom he planned to meet later in the week.

---

*See "IT Organization Chart" at the end of this chapter.

Once they had all assembled, exchanged greetings, and submitted brief status reports, Barton had floated his idea of an off-site management meeting to set direction for the department. Before the meeting, Barton would have been hard-pressed to imagine any reasonable objections to his plan. He'd expected quick acceptance followed by a session of planning for the event.

But he'd been wrong. No more than three or four minutes into his explanation of what he had in mind, Fenton interjected a question: "You want *just* the five of us at this off-site?"

"That's what I was thinking," said Barton. Fenton and Gordon exchanged knowing looks. Barton had not understood the question; he tried for clarification: "Why not just the five of us?"

Fenton shifted uncomfortably. He glanced in the direction of the others and saw that no help would be forthcoming.

"It's just that we'll only be able to go so far in certain discussions without other people involved," said Fenton. "For example, if we want to talk about security, I'd want to involve John Cho."

"John Cho?" said Barton.

The others nodded, their movements synchronized. Ruben spoke up: "Cho. You know him. Wild hair, purple streaks. Boots. Black tee shirts adorned with human skulls. Piercings."

"That guy," said Barton, nodding. "Been in meetings with him. Not sure I've been formally introduced."

"He's what's standing between this company," said Ruben, "and the armies of hackers who'd love to loot a financial services firm."

"Are we sure Cho is on our side?" Barton intended this as a joke, but it fell flat.

Fenton, speaking up for his employee, said: "Oh, John is definitely a white hat."

"A white hat?"

They all nodded, again in sync. Ruben smiled, said, "Although he wouldn't be caught dead actually wearing one."

Everyone laughed, which shattered the tension in the room. It was the effect Barton had been going for when he'd tried his joke. Ruben had realized it, done Barton a favor.

"What if we wanted to talk about security at a management or policy level? Would we need John Cho then?"

"John's really a nice guy, despite his attire . . ."

"It's not that," Barton interjected. "I'm not trying to avoid having John Cho in the meeting. I just think it makes sense as a starting point to have the five of us reach consensus on some things before we expand the circle."

"It really depends on what you want to talk about," said Ruben.

"I'd hoped we might talk about how things are going, challenges we see in the present and future, risks, and our vision of how we think IT ought to contribute to the success of the company. I also want to figure out where IT is being prevented from doing its best work by impediments in the way the rest of the company works. IT is more important now than it ever has been."

Barton stopped talking to avoid making a speech. He looked around the room, saw more deer-in-the-headlight looks. That's when Ruben made his "whether the five of us working alone will be able to . . ." remark.

It seemed to Barton that they were all making this situation much more difficult than it needed to be. He knew nothing about IT; these guys had been doing it their entire careers. Shouldn't they have enough expertise to hold a high-level planning meeting without involving their tech nerds? Shouldn't Fenton know a thing or two about security by now? Barton wondered if he was getting insight into the weak performance of the IT organization over the years. Maybe his managers were not very good. At the very least, they seemed to have fallen into some bad habits, such as unhealthy reliance on people whom they surely couldn't supervise properly if they didn't understand the details of the work well enough.

Barton recalled a definition of supervision that he'd liked well enough to memorize, although he couldn't remember now where he'd first heard it: *A supervisor's job is to encourage employees to engage in appropriate actions, habits, and behaviors, and to direct changes in those actions, habits, and behaviors when business conditions shift in ways that necessitate such changes.* How could these guys do this if they couldn't even hold a management conversation without consulting technical specialists? Did they, Barton wondered, have any idea what was going on in their own organizations?

"What do you think the five of us alone could accomplish?" asked Barton.

Eventually they settled on a tentative plan that met Barton's objectives of making his direct reports responsible for the activities within their own groups, but at the same time tapped external expertise where his managers thought they would need it. They would hold their meeting off-site but nearby. They would begin a discussion with just the five of them, then pull in three more key people from each area with whom to continue the discussion. Barton insisted that they finish the meeting with just the core five.

Thus ended the first gathering of the management team under Jim Barton, the new CIO of IVK, at 11:24 a.m.

Barton let the group disperse, then set off in the direction of Ruben's office. He found Ruben listening to his voice mail. He waved Barton into his office, but finished listening to the current message before hanging up the telephone.

"Have a seat," said Ruben, motioning to a chair stacked with paper. Barton moved the paper to an edge of Ruben's untidy desk and sat down. "What can I do for you?" Ruben asked, flashing an accommodating, apparently sincere smile.

"You seem to be the one in this group willing to stand up to me," said Barton, "so I was hoping you could help me understand a few things."

"I'll do my best."

Barton thought for a minute, at first trying to formulate his words carefully to avoid the possibility of offending anyone, then finally jettisoning that idea and deciding to shoot straight: "I guess I don't see why the IT department heads need to have their sidekicks present before they can have a productive discussion. I've done this lots of times in other organizations, and I've never run into this objection before."

Ruben seemed to gather his thoughts before answering. "Well," he said, "possibly we are simply wrong or don't understand what you have in mind. But possibly, just possibly, IT is different."

Barton snorted. "Everybody thinks they're special. Is IT really different or do IT managers just think it's different?"

"I don't know," answered Ruben. "But maybe I can suggest some of the reasons why it might be special, *if*, in fact, it is."

"Love to hear it," said Barton, sitting back in the chair and folding his hands on his lap to signal open-mindedness.

"You've been heading up Loan Operations for the past few years," Ruben said. "I suspect that makes you the most expert person in the building about the intricate details of Loan Operations."

Barton nodded.

"I suspect," continued Ruben, "that you can do the job of anyone in Loan Operations as well, if not better than, they can do it. Or if not, you could probably get back to doing it that well within just a few minutes or hours of starting to do it again."

"I suspect you're right about that."

"Well," said Ruben, "none of us in IT can say that. Technology moves fast. Our people, many of them, are specialists. I was once a programmer, but the kind of programming I did bears little resemblance to what our programmers do now. I get the gist of it, but the details left me in the dust a long time ago.

"Moreover, some of our people are quite a bit more talented in their specialty than any of us managers ever were. These are people who, in terms of absolute intellectual horsepower, are probably a good bit smarter than you or me, but who have little or no interest in doing the jobs you and I do. They like the deep details, and they work with them expertly in a way that we, as managers, can't see into very well. So we have to depend on them to tell us what's going on in the details. Our ability to independently verify what they tell us is rather limited. We can tell the big things, like 'are we done?' or 'does it work?' at least to some degree, but most of the things that go on from day to day are not those big things. The interim stuff is a lot harder to observe and evaluate. These are the simple facts of our daily reality.

"This would all be merely interesting if it weren't for the additional fact that in IT, the details often matter. There are all kinds of business issues floating around within IT, but they are generally wound around and in between technical issues. As managers we have to tease them apart, so we can make the kinds of trade-offs we need to make—like 'Should we spend more money to reduce our risk of exposure to hackers by a certain amount?'—knowing full well that we can spend an infinite amount and never completely eliminate that risk. To put dimensions on this trade-off and others like it, we need to see into the details better than any of us still can. It would be nice to think we can all keep up with the technical stuff, and a few remarkable individuals probably can manage it, but most of us mere mortals can't. So we depend on side-kicks to help us tease apart business and technical issues, and to put dimensions on trade-offs. Make sense?"

Barton nodded thoughtfully, said nothing.

"Even with the sidekicks, it's really hard," Ruben added.

Barton wasn't completely buying this explanation, but he didn't say so.

"Any chance," asked Barton, "you could give me a little primer on who does what around here? Obviously I don't understand what goes on in the IT organization, down inside it. I mean, I realize John Cho is an important guy here, but everyone seems to have a sidekick. I'm guessing you've got some in your own organization."

"Yes, in the database group, most notably Gita Puri. She's a whiz, though probably not quite as hard to replace as Cho.

"So, okay, let's see. Let me try to do a high-level walk through of the department, see where these people might live. Starting with my department: I have three groups that perform mostly staff functions of one kind or another. One group is all about process improvement, new IT approaches, and so forth. Think of this as a sort of internal consulting group. A group of very smart people, a couple with sky-high potential, but no one with such mission-critical smarts that they'd provoke a crisis if they left the company.

"The database group is a different matter. They specialize in making sure we have robust database designs underlying all of our systems. They have really technical expertise in database management systems. This kind of expertise is rare, and it's not just a matter of understanding the technology. There's a talent to database design. Gita is our reigning expert; easily the key person in my department. She'd be very tough to lose. Part of what makes people like Gita valuable, too, is their knowledge of the database designs already in place, and the history of decisions that determined why they're designed as they are.

"Finally, I have a group that focuses on infrastructure and vendor products, making sure that as new vendor products appear—a new model of laptop computer, a new server, that sort of thing—they all work with our existing architecture. This group works with vendors to make sure we have the information we need to support new equipment or software versions, and they pressure vendors not to drop support of installed, old technologies too quickly. Think of this as a vendor management group. That's what they do mostly. No irreplaceable assets in that group, although there are a lot of established relationships between our people and vendor personnel that would take time to rebuild.

"Take Raj's group next. As you know, they primarily support customer service systems, really important stuff because of the way it immediately cripples us if the systems go down. We can't process new applications or deal effectively with customer phone calls without those systems. His is primarily a business applications systems group, focused on the corresponding customer service–oriented business units. Unlike my group, say, which has the luxury of taking a longer and overall business view, his group is very closely tied to day-to-day business concerns. He has about three application developers, super coders or architects, although none of them quite as good as Ivan Korsky, the best in Tyra's group. Nevertheless, they'd probably be very difficult to replace; any one of them leaving would have serious consequences to our ability to deliver on promises to business partners and customers. I'm probably a bit out of date on Raj's area, so you should consult with him to be sure I've got this right.

"Tyra's group you know, because it faces off to Loan Ops the same way Raj's faces off to Customer Service. Hers is the biggest application group in the company, bigger than Raj's because it has become where we develop platforms for institutional clients—not just Loan Operations but a lot of related Web-based management services that clients really care about. You know all about this, though, because you managed the business side not so long ago. Ivan Korsky is her heaviest hitter, but I'd bet she has another five or so it would really hurt to lose.

"Finally, we have Fenton's group, the Infrastructure Management gang, also quite large. Paul's group is, in a way, an odd mix of very technical talented guys, and relatively low-tech guys with a lot of familiarity with existing ways of doing things but not deep skills. The very high-tech guys are the ones like Cho, or the very technical network engineers. Top-flight talent, very hard to replace. At the other end of the spectrum are the guys who every day schedule batch jobs—or rather make sure the jobs complete successfully, since scheduling is mostly automated—or who do other sorts of moving things around. Care and feeding of testing environments, moving an application from one place to another, that kind of thing.

"Fenton also has the facilities guys, the ones who make sure we don't run out of power when we add another server to one of the racks in the data center. That's mostly technical real estate work, making sure we have floor space, climate control, connectivity, power, physical security, and so on. I'd say Fenton has maybe five employees with deep dark technical talent. The risk of them leaving is a bit moderated because he's pretty technical himself. Of all of us managers, he's the guy who retains the most technical know-how that is still relevant. He's stunningly competent in what he does, so much so that we pretty much abuse him by making him work too much. But as you'll notice, he's probably, of the four of us, the least managerial in his orientation. Took him a while when he first landed the job to become a good manager, but I think he's got it down pretty well now."

Ruben stopped, having traversed the entire organization in rapid description. "That's pretty much it," he said. "Does that help?"

Barton nodded. "It helps. All those key people happy here at IVK? Like their jobs? Their bosses?"

Ruben looked at Barton quizzically, as if trying to discern what he was really asking. Then the older man shrugged and ventured what seemed to Barton an overly cautious remark: "They're all different; some of them grumble their fair share, but I doubt anyone's on the verge of leaving, if that's what you're concerned about."

"That's what I'm concerned about," Barton acknowledged. "How about Cho?" he asked, picking as a "for instance" the person who came most easily to mind.

Ruben's expression flashed surprise before returning to normal. "John? His talent for grumbling rivals his technical talent, but I don't think he'll leave us any time soon. Ask Fenton. But I think we've proven more willing to accommodate Mr. Cho's unusual working hours than another company might be."

Barton smiled. He suspected Ruben knew more than he was telling, but made a mental note and decided not to press. "I really need to think about all this."

"Indeed," said Ruben. "I would guess you have quite a bit to think about."

Barton smiled, added a diplomatic chuckle that wasn't very heartfelt and probably didn't seem so. He stood and moved to the door. "Thanks, Bernie," he said, transitioning to an entirely genuine sentiment.

"No problem. Come back any time, we'll talk more."

"I'm pretty sure," said Barton, "that I will."

Monday, March 26, 12:12 p.m. . . .

Back in his office, Barton held his green pen aloft, contemplating the statement on the whiteboard: "IT management is about *management.*" Beneath this lone statement he began constructing a list, adding a first entry: "Skill and talent mgmt/key skills, key contributors." He had no idea how to create a solution or system in this area yet, but after the morning's meeting and the discussion with Ruben, he believed this was an important subarea of IT management. He wasn't sure yet whether the problems Ruben had described—knowing who your key people are and being able to supervise them and know what they are doing—were separate and needed different solutions, or whether they were part of the same issue. At this point, the new item on the whiteboard was a placeholder. He'd have to trust and hope clarity would emerge in this area.

Before putting the pen down, he considered writing something about his encounter with the kid at Vinnie's Bar on Friday night, and maybe something from his subsequent encounter with Davies. But he didn't think those things were part of a system of management he might come up with. They were more like challenges, things to remember. Up in the corner of the whiteboard, Barton wrote: "KWYDK," his own private code for "Know what you don't know." Then, at the bottom right corner of the whiteboard he wrote Davies's challenge: "YWLOY." "You won't last one year." Good things to keep in mind, but not for others to understand.

IT management is about <u>management</u>   KWYDK

→ Skill and talent mgmt/key skills, key contributors

        YWLOY

Wednesday, March 28, 7:35 a.m. . . .

Stuck in traffic and running late for a 7:30 a.m. meeting with his executive assistant, Barton leaned over to fiddle with his Audi's sound system. The traffic started to move just as he landed the radio on a business story. Interestingly, it was about a CIO who'd had a major problem at a large hospital.[1] Barton listened attentively, but he'd come in at the middle and wasn't sure he understood what had happened. The story digressed into a mini-biography of the CIO, which made Barton feel incredibly inadequate. The guy was amazing. A critical care physician who still took his turn in the ER; PhD from MIT in bioinformatics; former entrepreneur who had started, grown, and sold a company (while completing medical school); and former student of a Nobel Prize–winning economist. He was also the author of four books on computer programming, and had written the first version of many of the hospital's software applications himself. Barton marveled, *I bet he doesn't need three technical experts with him to talk about IT management issues.*

Breaking free from traffic congestion, Barton guided his car into the IVK parking structure, which promptly interfered with his radio reception. Between crackles, he gathered that the hospital's computer network had been down for some days and required heroic intervention by a network equipment company. The CIO had earned kudos for the transparency with which he dealt with the crisis and, in an interview, highlighted his lack of networking expertise as the reason he'd failed to foresee the problem. He listed the areas of his expertise—a formidable list—but then pointed to a hole in his command of networking technology.

About that time, the radio completely lost the station.

Barton emerged from his car and walked toward the elevators, making a decision as he did it. Right after work he'd head to a bookstore, buy some books on IT subjects. There was no way he could become an expert like the guy on the radio, but he could do some reading, surprise some people, ask questions he already knew the answers to, just to see how people would interact with him.

He stepped into the elevator and pushed the "Up" button to begin his day.

Wednesday, March 28, 11:43 p.m. . . .

Barton sat on the floor beneath the halogen glow of a crane-necked lamp, amid piles of books opened and strewn randomly. Two dirty plates and several takeout cartons lay discarded at the periphery of the circle of light. He held one book on his lap, his eyes fixed at midpage. But it had been a while since he'd actually read anything.

He'd left work early to visit the huge bookstore nearby. He wandered through the vast computer section, picking up books, reading their back and front material, leafing through them, choosing many of them, and setting them aside in a pile for purchase. Books on TCP/IP, on router protocols, on firewall design. Java programming, Java servlets, PGP, PERL, Oracle DBA certification, Linux, Apache, SOA. Thin clients, project management, the "capability maturity model," Extreme Programming, and EAI.

After charging more than $1,200 to his credit card and recruiting two bookstore employees to help him get his purchases to the car, he set out for home with a plan to judge for himself the theory favored by his direct reports—that you can't know enough about technology to manage without a crew of nerd sidekicks. He picked up Indian food on his way home and called Maggie to warn her against calling him later that night.

He intended to be busy.

A few minutes later, he was on the floor of his condo, forking food into his mouth and studying the basics of IP addressing in subnets. When he began, the bright light of afternoon was streaming through the windows.

As daylight faded, Barton realized that his lamp alone burned amid the darkness, but he didn't mind. It would help him concentrate.

In retrospect, the first signs that his plan was ill-fated appeared in the earlier phone conversation with Maggie. He had expected her to be incredibly impressed, but she had been reticent.

"TCP/IP? BGP?" she said, after he read her a couple of the titles on top of the pile in the passenger seat.

"You betcha," he said.

"Well," she said. "Don't spend too much time on it. I think a general idea of what all that is all about will suffice."

"Don't try to protect me, babe," joked Barton, "I'm up for it."

"Okay," she said. But she didn't sound so sure.

By 9:00 that night, he perceived a problem. His mind was swimming. There were so many different layers. He had a book on data communications that talked about types of wire and voltage and stuff. There were seven "OSI layers"—except when there were only six—and each layer was complicated as hell. Most of them had nothing to do with delivering direct functionality to system users. He'd had no idea so much complexity resided "below the floorboards" of IT systems. By 10:30, no dots had even begun to connect: he'd learned a lot but he couldn't see any way that most of it would help him manage, except by accident.

Maggie called him just before midnight.

"How's it going?" she asked, but he could tell from the sound of her voice that she knew. She'd known how this whole thing would go from the moment he'd told her of his plan.

"I think I'm going to need to think a lot more about my assumptions," he said.

"Which ones?"

"The big ones. I think I might need to rethink my ideas about how management works. Who can know what. I thought I knew what I didn't know. I had no idea."

"How does that make you feel?"

"Horrible. It's a huge job, Maggs. I don't know if I can do it."

"If it helps any, I think you're reaching the right conclusions. And you've gotten there a lot faster than most. Some managers never get there."

"Whatever you say."

"I'm right about this."

"Yes, Maggie."

"Get some sleep."

"Yes, Maggie."

"I'm coming home this weekend. I'll make it all better."

Barton had forgotten that. Not everything was horrible, then.

"Yes, Maggie," he said, smiling.

REFLECTION

Do you think IT management is different from management of other functions?

What did Barton learn from his trip to the bookstore and late night of studying?

What depth of IT understanding must a CIO leader have to be effective?

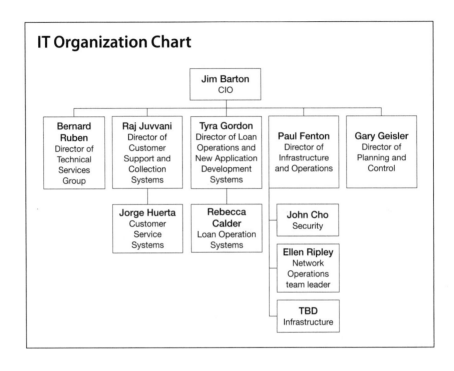

PART TWO

THE ROAD OF TRIALS

CHAPTER FOUR

THE COST OF IT

When Barton had been in his new position as CIO for four days, an e-mail arrived from the CEO to announce a series of meetings of the leadership team. They'd begin with a kickoff meeting of one hour and continue indefinitely with meetings of two-plus hours every Tuesday and Thursday afternoon. The stated subject of the meetings: *Review of costs and business operations, formulation of a plan to recover IVK growth trajectory.*

Different departments, the e-mail explained, would take the lead in each meeting. IT had been assigned Tuesday, April 17. This gave Barton some time to get his act together. He'd need, the e-mail told him, answers to a few questions. The key questions: "How much are we spending in your area?" and "How does the spending fuel growth or contribute to the bottom line (and how are we measuring this)?" Barton had expected the e-mail—and these questions. It was exactly how he would have begun if he were the new CEO.

In anticipation of just these questions, Barton had planned to spend the afternoon with Gary Geisler, the IT department's financial guru. Despite his modest rank (the most junior manager level at IVK), Geisler's importance was clear from the location of his office. Other managers at his level worked in cubicles in the open office area, but Geisler had a private office right next to the CIO's (empty since the departure of Davies—Barton had not moved into that space yet and wasn't sure that he would). Geisler reported directly to the CIO; unlike the other CIO direct reports, however, no one reported to Geisler.

Barton didn't know Geisler well, but had been present in meetings when Davies had turned to the financial wizard for explanations. Barton read the guy as a bit of a know-it-all; he spoke with a silent "of course" implied, as if expecting that no one should ever contradict him. Barton didn't relish the thought of dealing with the guy, but he was looking forward to diving into the numbers, to get a *management* handle on how things were going in the IT department.

Right on schedule, Geisler stepped into Barton's office and scanned the unfamiliar space for an appropriate seat. Gesturing to the chair opposite his desk, Barton started their conversation simply; he asked: "So, Mr. Geisler. How much are we spending on IT?"

Barton's question was the last simple thing to happen in the meeting.

"What do you mean by 'we'?" said Geisler.

Barton laughed, then realized that Geisler was not joking. He tried again: "How much does IVK spend on IT?"

"Ah," said Geisler, "that 'we.' It depends on how you count."

"Why," said Barton, impatience rising, "does it depend on how you count? It's a simple question."

"Well, as you know, the IT department formally controls none of the budget that gets spent on IT. The business units get budget allocated to them for IT expenditures, then we charge them for our services, using an internal pricing system.

"In some cases, they are also free to use IT budget to obtain services from external providers, although there have been limits placed on that in the past, to make sure that we offset all of the fixed costs associated with IT salaries and infrastructure. Basically, as long as our IT staff remains fully 'billed out' to business units, the business units can also choose to go outside for services.

"In addition, there are IT-like services, such as PDA service and support, which each individual department has procured on its own, some using non-IT budget. Your predecessor, Bill Davies, thought he ought to have some influence over those services, but he was unsure how to go about reining in the business units. Each unit has a preferred PDA technology, and in some units there are multiple technologies even within the unit. Of course, the fact that the services are not provided by IT and don't use IT budget doesn't stop the business units from seeking IT support when their PDA e-mail stops working."

"Okay," said Barton, processing this rapid-fire explanation. He was thinking about Loan Operations, realizing that his former group was one that had multiple PDA technologies, each from a different vendor. That hadn't seemed like a big deal when he was in charge of Loan Ops. But, as CIO, he would be held responsible for maintaining e-mail service to the business units, just as he had held Davies responsible for it. As more people relied on PDAs, the IT group would have less control over e-mail service. An outage at a service provider could shut down e-mail to PDAs as easily—even more easily—than a problem internal to IVK.

"Anyway, I assume you'd ultimately like to include all of that IT spending from non-IT budgets when you ask for a total spent on IT," said Geisler, returning to the original question. "We can always break things out into categories if that's helpful."

Barton nodded. He would, later, want things in categories, but he was still trying to understand the basics: "So give me a number, any one of those numbers," said Barton. "What ballpark are we talking about?"

Geisler removed a sheet of paper from the file folder he'd been clutching and handed it to Barton.* "Without the money being spent on IT services that is *not* from the IT budget—in other words, *not* including those PDA services and the like that aren't acquired using IT budget—that's the number I have here at hand—we spent just over $29 million on IT last year on a cash flow basis, about $18.5 million on an accrual basis."

Barton did a quick mental calculation. "About 8 percent of sales."

"Yes, although historically we have run lower than that. As you know, we've had trouble lately with revenue growth leveling off. The former rapid growth rate was causing us to spend more on IT each year to provide new services and the same old services to more and more customers. But we were always playing catch-up. Our spending lagged demand for services, and we were scrambling to add service capacity.

---

*See "Project IT Capital and Operating Expenses for Fiscal Year X" at the end of this chapter.

When the growth rate leveled off, IT spending on a catch-up trajectory couldn't level off as fast. Davies was working on ways of slowing down spending when—well, you know what happened to him. It's not going to be easy to bring costs back down. The percentage will probably go up before it goes down. We're not caught up in terms of modernization of the IT infrastructure. Others are more expert on this than I am, but I think we are in the middle of some major projects that won't be easy to cut back.

"Historically, I'd say we've run closer to 5 to 6 percent of sales on IT spending. Which, by the way, Davies thought wasn't enough to keep IT assets from degrading over time, in terms of general robustness."

"Hmm," said Barton. "So the IT department has no budget of its own?"

"That's right. We are essentially a service provider to the business units. Some hours we directly bill to them via the chargeback system; others, like expenditures on shared infrastructure or costs less directly related to services for a particular area, we charge out as general overhead, also within the chargeback system. We ultimately charge back all of our costs to the business units."

Barton remembered being puzzled by a largish item called "IT and telecom services" on his Loan Operations monthly budget reports. He'd paid little attention to it because his actions didn't seem to influence it. It went up a bit when he started major projects, but mostly it seemed not to change over time.

"The overhead component is pretty big, right?" Barton asked. "I don't recall having a lot of control over the amount I was charged for IT services when I was in Loan Operations."

"That's right. It varies by department, but I'd say most departments' overhead chargebacks are between 70 and 80 percent of their total amount. I can find out the exact number for Loan Operations if you like . . ." He began leafing through the pages of an imposingly thick black binder.

"No, never mind," said Barton. "Tell me more about the chargeback system. How does it work?"

"The direct billing part is just straight billing for hours—"

"I get that—"

"—but the overhead calculation is pretty complicated. It's a formula."

"Where did the formula come from?"

"It came to IVK with CFO Mark Lundy, who isn't here anymore . . ."

"Yes, I remember him," Barton said. Lundy had come to IVK from the financing division of an established manufacturing company. He hadn't stayed with IVK long. The theory in hiring him, Barton recalled, had been something about IVK needing someone who could bring more systems and controls to the company. But Lundy never had been a good fit; the fast-growing company's immune system had rejected him.

"In the original version of the chargeback system," continued Geisler, "we just added up all of the overhead costs and allocated them to departments equally, based on the number of telephones in use in that department. In that system, the only way you could, as a business unit manager, reduce the biggest portion of your IT chargeback was to take a telephone away from someone."

"Telephones?"

"Yes, it was an imperfect system to say the least. But that was the way they had done it at Lundy's old company."

"But we don't do it that way anymore."

"No. The number of telephones is still in there, but we've gotten much more sophisticated in recent years. The formula now includes things like number of e-mail accounts, number of accounts on various other systems, average number of concurrent users per business unit logged on to various systems at any point in time during the work day, number of new records generated in various databases per day, and so on. It's a much closer approximation to charging back the 'real cost' of resource used."

Barton felt a little dizzy. He considered asking Geisler to walk him through the details of the formula, but decided against it. "Where did the new formula come from?" he asked. He was imagining some sort of a committee commissioned to come up with the formula, itself an awkward compromise between business units. It would have been brutal, not a committee Barton would ever want to serve on, nor had he ever heard of such committee at IVK. But, as it turned out, a committee was not the source of the formula. Geisler explained the formula's origins with a broad smile and a single word:

"Me."

"You?"

"Yes. I've been working on it and adjusting every year for the last several. I feel that it's really getting good now."

Barton shook his head.

"Anybody else involved in determining this formula?"

Geisler became uncomfortable. "Uh, no."

"Anybody else know and understand the formula?"

Geisler thought, then answered: "Probably not, actually. Of course, I've designed the formula to represent economic reality, within the limitations of our ability to measure usage of IT services."

Barton made a snap decision not to fight the battle of where the formula came from right now. It didn't seem to be on anybody else's radar, and it probably made more sense as Geisler's invention than it would have if it had been the result of committee work.

"I'm going to need a one-page summary," said Barton, "that gives me the total cost number, including IT spending from non-IT budgets, broken out in major categories, and that explains in terms as simple as possible how those costs are being charged back to the business units. The formula, in other words." If he could get his peers to understand the formula—if he could understand it himself—then maybe later he could get them involved in checking and changing it.

"Sound doable?" asked Barton.

"Yes, it does. When will you need it?"

"When can you have it?" responded Barton.

Thursday, March 29, 4:25 p.m. . . .

Barton stared at his whiteboard, trying to figure out what he ought to include there about IT costs. He'd spent all afternoon either talking with Geisler or studying his cost numbers, but there remained huge gaps in what Barton understood.

He rose from his chair, walked to the whiteboard and wrote three things in a rough triangle: "IT costs," "IT services" and "chargeback." He drew an arrow from "IT costs" to "IT services" then wrote "mapping?" above the arrow. Then he drew an arrow from "IT services" to "chargeback" and another from "chargeback" to "IT costs."

He assumed that if his department could make that mapping accurate and explicit enough—so that costs could be assigned clearly to services and departments could be charged for the services they used in a way that made sense to them—this would be a good thing. But the earlier session with Geisler had demonstrated just how complex the mapping could be. Recalling Geisler's explanation of the Byzantine structure of the evolved chargeback system still made Barton's head swim.

A mapping too complex for managers to understand would be a poor input into decision making. Really, it would be a useless, needless complexity to manage. But Barton had no idea whether it had to be that way, or whether there might be a way of abstracting usefully to provide a business description of the mapping that was neither misleading nor too complex. Barton knew he suffered from huge gaps in his own understanding of what the IT budget paid for. He could read the names of projects in the budget documents provided by Geisler, but he didn't, he now realized, understand what the projects were acting on or adding to. He had no sense of the accumulated IT assets of IVK—the systems, software, databases, hardware, and other forms of assets.

Barton wrote a large "?" in the middle of the triangle he'd just drawn, then for the second time that day wandered down the hall to talk with Bernie Ruben.

"Me again," said Barton.

"Sure, sure, come in," said Ruben. Barton sat down and explained his problem.

"Well," said Ruben, "let me see if I can help some. Let me tell you a story about the evolution of the IT applications portfolio and infrastructure at IVK. To some extent, this is a general description. Most companies evolve their IT assets in a way much like this."

Ruben rose, moved to his own whiteboard, erased a big part of it, and began to draw a picture.*

"When we were a small company, back in the early days, we put together applications when we needed them for specific business reasons, without much of a sense of an overall application portfolio or underlying infrastructure. We didn't have much going on in IT relative to today, so that was just fine for that time and for that scale of operations. Most of our IT spending was on applications related to creating specific IT functionality in support of the business. The ability to originate a loan, to input loan request information, to process a loan decision, that kind of thing.

"This company was lucky to have been founded at a time when Web-based technology was becoming important. Because of that we don't have huge investments, as many other companies do, in older technology. Nevertheless, most of our operational systems run in overnight batches, rather than in real time. We outsourced payroll at first, so that helped us avoid some old technology investments in that area. We used a lot of e-mail from the beginning, and quickly jumped on using e-mail as a way of moving information, a sort of primitive workflow system for moving files around."

"Then," said Barton, trying to move the story forward faster, "we started to grow."

"Oh, yes," said Ruben, "did we ever. We grew, as you know and remember, quickly. As our IT operations gained scale, it made sense to invest in 'infrastructure,' common services that everyone could use. A robust database technology, security systems common to all our applications, and a big chunk of what gets called 'middleware' to manage interactions between different systems. We brought payroll in-house, and we acquired solid and robust systems for managing our call center operations. As we did all this, the distribution of IT spend shifted. We spent more on infrastructure, which meant less, as a percentage, on

---

*See "Ruben's Explanation of the Evolution of IVK's Applications Porfolio and Infrastructure" at the end of this chapter.

new responses to business needs, new applications—the only thing we'd spent on in the beginning."

"That doesn't seem like an entirely good thing," said Barton.

Ruben paused. "How do you mean?"

"Well, it looks like spending more money on maintaining, less on new ways of providing services to the business. The trend looks ominous. Does it mean eventually we'll spend all our money just on keeping our current functionality running and robust? Are we losing capacity over time to add new ways of competing using IT?"

"Excellent point. To some extent this shift of percent spend from applications to infrastructure is inevitable as we mature our approach to managing the increasing complexity of our systems, as we accumulate IT assets that need to be cared for. But you rightly point out that at some point our management attention should shift to trying to spend less, as a percentage, on maintaining, and more on adding new functionality and services."

"What's the right long-term percent spend for each?" asked Barton.

"I don't think there's any right answer to that," said Ruben. "I guess in the long run you'd like to spend as little as possible on maintaining, and as much as possible on new ways of providing services and using IT to compete. But realistically, I'd say it's going to be tough. It costs a lot to run a large operation, just to keep it up. And I'm reluctant to get into too much self-flagellation over a spend that goes mostly to infrastructure. It seems like just another club you could hand business managers that they could use to beat us with."

"I appreciate your candor and I see your point. Even as the business manager lingering within me longs to possess that club and use it to beat someone up."

Ruben laughed out loud. "But it changes things when you're likely on the receiving end of the beating, doesn't it?"

"It does indeed. So now we've got this very interesting question of how to divide IT spend over these two categories in the future. But I still don't have a good sense of what we'll be spending on. Where are we heading with our IT assets?"

Ruben finished his picture with a "future" diagram. "I'd say we are moving from supporting a hierarchical, traditional organizational structure to an increasingly networked organization that includes partners, such as customers and vendors. Technology-wise, we are moving more toward service-oriented architecture, more real-time operations, and expanding database structures more into data warehouses that we can mine for trends and other business intelligence."

"Service-oriented architecture? Business intelligence?"

"SOA is just a fancy way of referring to efforts to get more careful about decomposing IT services into small pieces so that they can be easily combined and reused to create useful applications and so that they can deliver larger services over a network. It involves working out standards for how information will be exchanged between services. Think of it as a way of investing in infrastructure that, if we get it right, will improve our ability to create new functionality and services that support business objectives. It might eventually allow us to shift some infrastructure spend to applications, and to get more functionality out of applications for less spend—also to deliver new functionality faster, which might be even more important. I've got a little blurb on this I'll send you.*

"Business intelligence is just a fancy way of mining all the data we have to better understand trends, customers, our competitors, and other things. If we can crunch the data we have in ways that yield great insights, we can achieve competitive advantage, potentially. If we learned something that allowed us to characterize the risk associated with a loan more accurately than competitors, for example, there are ways we can monetize that."

"Oh, yeah, definitely. So a data warehouse can do that?"

"*We* might be able to do it *with* a data warehouse. The warehouse itself just gives you the means to crunch a lot of numbers looking for trends. We still have to be smart enough to see the trends and determine whether they are real and worthy of pursuit."

"You mean they won't do our jobs for us, these computers?"

"Afraid not," said Ruben, grinning. "Despite all the sci-fi hype, it will be awhile before IT systems in companies eliminate the need for good managers."

***

*See "Will a Service-Oriented Architecture Help Your Business?" at the end of this chapter.

"Good news for us, I guess," said Barton.

"I guess," repeated Ruben.

Barton wasn't sure he could map costs to the picture Ruben had drawn, but he had undoubtedly picked up valuable new insight from their discussion. It was growing late. Tomorrow would be another day in his young CIO career.

REFLECTION

Are IT applications an asset or an expense?

What is the main purpose of allocating IT costs to user departments?

What is an appropriate percentage of the IT budget to spend on maintenance?

As a percentage of sales, how much should a company spend on IT?

Projected IT Budget Fiscal Year X

Capital		FY X
Capital budget purchases		
Development	$	132,000
Infrastructure/networking	$	279,800
Hardware	$	1,600,400
Software	$	956,000
Subtotal	$	2,968,200
Disaster recovery/business continuity/second site costs		
Telephone switch and IP support	$	1,148,500
Application licenses	$	481,450
Workstation technology	$	998,807
Networking/routing/firewalls-hardware	$	1,628,500
Servers (fax, Web, e-mail, database, application process, office management)	$	523,000
Other IT infrastructure expenditures (i.e., UPS, racks, spec. cabling, etc.)	$	660,800
Subtotal	$	5,441,057
Future Proposed Initiatives		
Security, compliance, customer service software	$	889,760
Security, compliance, customer service equipment	$	500,000
Re-eng project equipment	$	375,000
Re-eng project software	$	8,800
Common infrastructure equipment	$	2,350,000
Common infrastructure software	$	1,835,000
Business analytics (software and installation)	$	42,000
Budgeting and systems for Finance (software and installation)	$	220,000
QLP Project (equipment)	$	292,900
QLP Project (software and development services)	$	1,470,000
Subtotal	$	7,983,460
Total amortizable IT capital cost, FY X	$	16,392,717

The Cost of IT

Expenses		FY X
Network operations		
Network and operations	$	287,000
Internal support	$	480,000
Engineering	$	663,800
Network security	$	594,000
Information security	$	250,000
Administrative—technology and infrastructure	$	645,000
Planning and projections	$	6,500
Technology and infrastructure	$	12,500
Engineering—systems	$	602,000
Engineering—networking	$	567,000
Engineering—platforms	$	2,200
Subtotal	$	4,110,000
Applications and development		
Administrative	$	484,000
Applications	$	953,400
Business analysis and QA	$	606,500
Development	$	812,000
Presentation systems	$	597,300
Database management	$	854,000
Lending and guarantee	$	736,600
Customer service and ERP	$	363,000
Systems analysis	$	118,000
Project management	$	249,000
Architecture design	$	734,000
Middleware systems	$	1,302,500
Administrative—environment and compliance	$	7,600
Development and administrative compliance	$	363,500
Environment management	$	320,000
Quality assurance	$	78,000
Back-office systems	$	123,000
Subtotal	$	8,702,400
Total project IT expenses fiscal year X	$	12,812,400
Grand total IT expense (cash flow basis)	$	29,205,117
Amortization from Year X and previous years	$	5,712,874
Grand total IT expense (accrual basis)	$	18,525,274

Ruben's Explanation of the Evolution of IVK's Applications Portfolio and Infrastructure

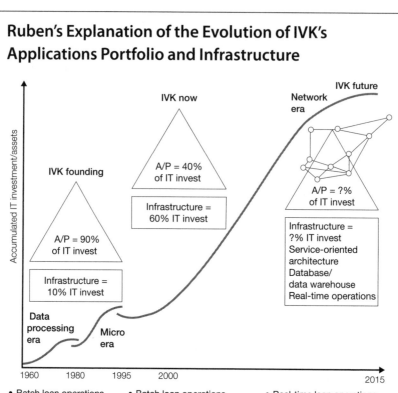

- Batch loan operations
- Internet e-mail for loan origination and customer service
- Call center
- Outsourced payroll

- Batch loan operations
- Legacy and duplicate copies for customers
- Web site and Internet e-mail for loan origination and customer service
- Call center customer service
- PeopleSoft payroll and HR
- Robust database

- Real-time loan operations
- Web site and Internet e-mail for loan origination and customer service
- Call center customer service
- Oracle payroll and HR
- Web 2.0

Article on Service Oriented Architecture

Will a Service-Oriented Architecture Help Your Business?

by Michael Rosen, Senior Consultant, Cutter Consortium

We know that technology alone doesn't solve business problems; at best it can act as an enabler. Some combination of technology, business, and organization is always required to meet business goals. Likewise, a service-oriented architecture (SOA) can enable a flexible enterprise where higher-level services are quickly and inexpensively composed from an inventory of more primitive business processes. But alone, an SOA is not enough; it must be accompanied by business design (i.e., a business model). The business model is critical to creating a set of services that can actually work together to provide higher-level value. You can implement an SOA without an overall business model, but you will end up with a pile of incompatible services rather than an agile, flexible enterprise.

An SOA describes how to build systems composed of services. More precisely, an SOA is concerned with the independent construction of services that can be combined into meaningful, higher-level business services within the context of the enterprise. Traditional application development is based on applications implementing one or more business processes in isolation. The individual applications do not expose any underlying services for other applications to use. In an SOA, business services are implemented to be available to any application, and enterprise applications are built "on top of" these business services.

SOAs are not new. There are prominent examples of enterprises that have successfully implemented SOAs and have realized their numerous advantages, including reduced costs and improved competitiveness. Some of the world's most successful applications are based on SOA, built on an underlying infrastructure such as CORBA.

Unfortunately, these examples are few and far between because implementing a successful SOA is hard—very hard. In the past, few organizations had the skill to overcome the architectural, technical, business, and organizational challenges required. And while many of those challenges still exist, several technologies, such as Web services and business process management, are converging to make SOA more obtainable to enterprises staffed by mere mortals. These technologies provide the following characteristics to assist SOA implementation:

- Web services provide the infrastructure to connect services together. Web services have several advantages over previous technologies:

- Web services naturally support service-based interfaces.

- Web services are not an implementation technology; they are an interfacing technology designed to bridge between the external service interface and the internal implementation.

- Web services are standards-based, platform-independent, and supported by all major players.

BPEL4WS (Business Process Execution Language for Web Services) is designed to work explicitly with Web services and provide coordination and integration of services into higher-level business services.

SOA has the potential to help enterprises become more efficient, agile, and competitive. In addition, it provides a much cleaner boundary between business concepts (expressed in the business model) and IT details (how that model is implemented).[a]

a. Cutter Consortium, www.cutter.com, October 29, 2003. Reprinted by permission.

CHAPTER FIVE

THE VALUE OF IT

Thursday, April 5, 9:30 a.m. . . .

Barton studied the one-page summary that Geisler had left in his box the night before. It was the third version he'd seen; this one was looking good. He was feeling increasingly confident in his ability to answer questions about the cost of IT. But a big hole remained in his thinking around the question of how much *value* IVK obtained from IT. In the early meetings of the leadership team, business units were providing either growth or profitability numbers for their specific areas to answer their own value questions. IT differed from these areas, though, because it was not a profit center, at least not within IVK. Unlike, say, Loan Operations, IT didn't bring in revenues from external sources, so it could not point to growth in revenues or profitability in terms of revenues less costs. The obligation for IT, it seemed to Barton, was to have something to say about how IT created value for its internal customers, the business units. But he wasn't sure how to come up with that. He was even less sure how to measure that kind of benefit. Geisler didn't offer much help; he'd never been asked this question before.

In requesting work from IT, to justify IT projects, business units routinely projected benefits from each project, but no one ever checked after the fact to see that benefits had been realized. One option for coming up with a value number would be to simply go back through the portfolio of approved and completed projects and add up the dollar value of the benefits claimed in project proposals. Barton wanted to have that number, but he wasn't sure it would be credible with his executive peers. Business units tended to claim that huge savings would result from anything they wanted to do in order to get the project approved, but everyone knew this was a game. Besides that, some business units might claim these savings as their own. If IT claimed them too, that would be double counting. If a business unit proposed an IT-enabled change and the change *did* result in savings, how should credit for those savings be allocated between the business unit and IT? Often the savings would have been impossible without IT, but it would be a hard sell to allocate all, or even some portion, of the value to IT.

Barton picked up the telephone and took a chance that Maggie might be available to discuss this. She was and, as expected, had interesting thoughts on the matter.

She pointed him first to a celebrated example of a company using IT to provide big value. Zara, a clothing retailer based in Spain, spent only 0.5 percent of its revenues on IT, and employed a similar percentage of its staff in the IT department.[1] But the way Zara used IT—to allow it to read demand signals for certain products at the point of sale and then to fulfill new orders for hot items less than three weeks later—created a capability that its competitors could not match. The capability led directly to higher profits, because hot items were stocked faster for customers to buy, and fewer unpopular items were produced only to be sold later at a steep discount.

Maggie also suggested he read a controversial article from the *Harvard Business Review* called "IT Doesn't Matter," in which the author, Nicholas Carr, used historical analogies to suggest that IT had become such a commodity that investments in IT could not generally be counted on to provide capabilities that were not also accessible to competitors.[2]

"Doesn't the Zara example directly contradict that?" asked Barton.

"Yes," said Maggie, "I think it does. So do a lot of other examples. Wal-Mart gets a lot more value from IT than K-Mart, for instance. When Carr gets pressed on that point, he usually concedes it, but says it's not the IT that's causing the competitive differentiation, but the way IT is used and the success with which it is adapted within the company culture. So, yeah, duh, but when is IT *ever* acquired without people having to figure out how best to use and introduce it? I guess you could say that Carr's arguments apply to, say, word-processing software—I don't know any company that achieves sustainable advantage over its rivals via its word-processing capability—but a lot of IT is not like that."

"But these kinds of debates do make it clear that the value from IT arises from its ability to confer on a firm some capability that separates it from its rivals."

"Yes, that's the way to think about it," said Maggie.

She also pointed him to a series of research articles by an MIT professor, Erik Brynjolfsson, which seemed to prove that firms achieved value from IT in a variety of different ways.[3] Maggie suggested that *Harvard Business Review* probably should have gone to Brynjolfsson, a careful thinker who'd been studying the question of IT value for years, rather than Carr, if they wanted the real scoop on whether IT "mattered."

"Some of Brynjolfsson's stuff is industry level," Maggie said, "but some recent work with Andrew McAfee has brought more of it to a company level.[4] Their research seems to say that firms that have invested heavily in IT deploy new business processes more quickly. If all the firms in a particular industry have similarly invested, then this would suggest that the value IT provides might be fleeting—one firm deploys a new process idea, then the others are able to quickly copy it. This shows up in their data as a lot of sales turbulence in industries with high IT investment, as firms implement new process ideas quickly and others quickly copy the ideas. But their study also shows that firms that have invested a lot in IT have increased market share a good bit, and that these dynamics affect firms primarily in industries with a generally high level of IT investment.

"The punch line seems to be that IT *does* matter; industries with a lot of IT behave very differently, competitively speaking, than industries with less IT. IT investments allow some firms to consolidate market share and assume a more dominant position in an industry. But the benefits from specific IT investment in high-IT-investment industries can be fleeting, as the services they provide more rapidly become commodities thanks to past investment in IT. Overall, the competitive trend for successful IT investors in IT-intensive industries is upward, even though there is greater volatility—wider swings, in the short run, above and below the trend."

"How does this help me when I think about IVK?"

"Maybe not a lot. But you can think about how quickly your competitors have been able to match your IT-enabled new capabilities, the ones that translate into growth and profit. The most value would come from investments in IT that give you an edge that your competitors can't copy.

"Sorry Jim, I've got to run. We've got a meeting starting here in a few minutes."

"No problem. You've helped a lot. You definitely earned your fee, Ms. Landis. I guess I'm taking you somewhere fancy tonight."

"If I'd known I was on the clock, I'd have talked slower," joked Maggie. "We still haven't gotten you to an answer yet, though, have we?"

"No," he conceded. "But we're getting somewhere."

Friday, April 6, 4:20 p.m. . . .

As the weekend rapidly approached, Barton's musings about IT value finally sent him down the hall to consult once again with resident philosopher Bernie Ruben.

"Not catching you as you're leaving early for a big weekend, I hope," said Barton.

"Not at all, come in," said Ruben. As usual, all the seats in the room were covered with piles of paper. By now Barton knew the drill; he simply moved a stack of paper to the floor and sat.

"Won't take long, I think," said Barton.

"What's on your mind?" asked Ruben.

Barton explained, giving him an overview of the progress of his thoughts on the issue of IT value.

"Carl is going to want to know our answer to this question," said Barton, "and he's going to want to hear our ideas about how to measure IT value."

Ruben didn't answer right away. He put his feet up on the desk and stared at the ceiling.

"It's a hard question," he allowed. "I don't really have an answer, but I do have some thoughts."

"Shoot," said Barton. "I'm just looking for a nudge in a productive direction."

"There are several things that complicate the matter," said Ruben. "Sometimes when we invest in an IT project, we do it without any expectation that it will give us an edge over the competition. Sometimes we do it because we have to if we want to stay in business. Maybe new legislation requires it. Or maybe if we don't do it, our competitors will obtain an unreasonable edge on us. Sometimes we invest in IT just because our competitors are doing it, to avoid what you might call 'strategic jeopardy,' a situation where they have an advantage on us. We don't get an edge from IT expenditures in this category, but it's a necessary cost in our business. In a way, you'd say this is very valuable, because we might not have a business at all without it. But because everybody also has it, we can't say it provides competitive advantage."

"A very important point," said Barton, "which I can certainly present as a plausible argument. Though, in a way, it dodges the question of measurable value."

Ruben nodded. "It doesn't seem right to say that there's zero value from those expenditures. But by some arguments, these investments provide zero competitive advantage."

Barton described the "IT Doesn't Matter" argument briefly, as well as the Zara case. Ruben was already familiar with both.

"Yes, Carr would say we get no competitive advantage from commodity IT areas. He'd recommend that we supply IT services in this category at minimum cost. Actually, I'm giving him too much credit. He says all of IT should be run this way. You can't get any competitive edge from it, so just do what you must at minimum cost and risk."

"What about the Zara example?" said Barton. "Suppose we *can* point to sustainable advantage from IT."

"I suppose then we could compare what *our competitors* are able to do with what *we* can; or, maybe, how much of it we would be able to do *without* the IT, hypothetically, with what we are able to do *with* it."

"So maybe," suggested Barton, floating an idea he'd been mulling over, "we ask the business units what allows them to win deals, or what helps them become more profitable or gain market share. A survey, or interviews maybe. Then we can look at the role IT plays in that."

"You've still got the problem of teasing apart what IT can claim and what the business unit will want to claim of that value. But there ought to be no doubt that IT has played an important role in those instances.

"It's more complicated than that, even. Sometimes our investments demonstrate clear value. ROI. Cost savings or, more rarely, increased sales. But other times we invest just to position ourselves for high ROI investments in the future. If we calculated the ROI from our initial ERP implementation, for example—if we did it honestly, I mean—we'd find that the damn thing didn't really pay for itself, at least not *by* itself. But it eventually allowed us to build systems on top of it that really earned big returns. In that case, if you'd tried to calculate ROI too early, before those other systems built on top of it were finished, you've have considered it a lousy investment. Eventually, though, the investment was a huge success."

"And," said Barton, "if we're going to be consistent with our past logic, it also depends on whether our competitors have also invested in ERP systems, and whether they've successfully built the same kind of systems on top of the ERP systems. If they have, then we've gotten no competitive edge from any of it."

"I agree with that in principle," said Ruben, "but in fact I don't think our competitors have equaled the capabilities we get from those investments. We have an edge, and our competitors can't match it. Not all of it, anyway. Not yet."

"So if we hired consultants, or asked our business units what we are better at than our competitors, and maybe how fast they are catching up or falling behind, that would help us get some rough idea of value, some of which might be attributable to IT."

Ruben nodded. "Reminds me of a categorization scheme that might be useful. You can usefully distinguish, not just in IT but in other areas too, between investments that are merely "Qualifiers" and investments that help you "Compete." Call it "Competes versus Qualifiers." A Qualifier investment keeps you in business. You have to qualify to run in the race, but Qualifiers only buy you a place at the starting line. A Compete investment gives you a potential edge over other companies in your industry. Competes help you win the race. We could go through our portfolio of active systems and ask which are primarily in each of these categories. It'd be interesting to know how much of the IT budget we spend to qualify versus how much we spend to compete."[5]

"And we could try to affect the distribution of expenditures across those categories over time," said Barton. "What do you think they are now? Scat-of-the-pants estimate, percentage-wise, how do you think it breaks out?"

Ruben laughed. "We might be horrified. If the way we are thinking is correct, systems that have been in the Compete category move into the Qualifier category as competitors manage to copy us. So, over time, the Compete category gets smaller, the Qualifier category larger. Unless, I suppose, we add new Competes faster than the old ones become Qualifiers."

"But as Competes become Qualifiers, we ought to change our philosophy of how to manage them. We ought to shift into cost minimization mode. If we can reduce costs for running Qualifiers, then even if their numbers increase, we might be able to reduce our total spend on them."

"That's a rosy vision," said Ruben, "but it sounds hard to do. Reminds me too of another, related, categorization scheme: McFarlan's Strategic Grid."[6] Ruben stood, walked to his whiteboard and drew a 2×2 grid.

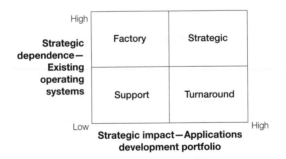

"As I remember it," said Ruben, "the vertical axis is about the operational dependence of the company on IT. The horizontal is about how much competitive differentiation the company obtains from IT. If you are in the bottom left corner, you don't depend much on IT operationally or strategically. Systems have to go down for a while before you are badly hurt, and you don't get much edge over your competitors from these systems, though they might be essential to have in your industry. If you are in the upper right quadrant, you get a lot of competitive advantage and you are very operationally dependent. We're definitely operationally dependent. If our data center went away, you'd be getting calls within thirty seconds from customer service. Competitive advantage from IT shows up on the horizontal axis. Rather than just separating systems in our portfolio into Compete and Qualifier categories, maybe we should also see how they fall out into these quadrants, and how we should think differently about them in terms of cost and value."

"I like the idea of taking a run through our portfolio of existing systems with these kinds of categories in mind. Any chance you'd be willing to take the lead on this? I'll get Geisler to help. Also, I'm meeting with some consultants next week, mostly on some organizational development stuff, but I think they might have people who can help us with this IT value question. I'd like you in on the OD stuff anyway. We need to hold an all-hands IT meeting; I'd like a chance to introduce myself to the department now that I'm the new boss, and I want people to have a chance to ask questions, offer feedback. I'd like you involved in the planning."

"That'd be very interesting. All of it. Shall I ask Jenny about day and time of the meeting?"

"That'd be great. I can't remember."

"I'll do that and get with Geisler to prepare for the value discussion. First thing Monday morning."

On hearing this, Barton remembered that it was late Friday afternoon. As usual, his date with Maggie would begin quite late in the evening, but Ruben might be keeping to an earlier schedule. Barton stood. "Thanks, Bernie."

"Always glad to help, Jim."

Friday, April 6, 5:12 p.m. . . .

Barton returned to his office, encouraged by Bernie's grid, but feeling still unsettled. The route to determining value from IT investments seemed so elusive. Each path he followed in his thoughts moved him deeper into a tangled forest of issues. He needed a new perspective, a view from above the trees. Maybe from a different, higher vantage he could see a way forward.

If IVK is the forest, thought Barton, *perhaps I should start with the value of IVK. Then at least I can establish an upper bound of the value of IT, and begin a more constructive conversation.*

Although he knew it to be a controversial measure, one estimate of a company's value is the price at which investors are willing to buy its common stock. He got onto his computer and obtained IVK's closing stock price for the day: $30.72. He then grabbed last year's annual report, turned to the balance sheet page, and found that there were about 63.5 million IVK common shares held by investors. A simple multiplication of share price and shares outstanding gave IVK an estimated market value of about $1.95 billion. Barton wrote these numbers along the bottom of his whiteboard. He placed a "?" after "IT value" to remind him of the question: How much did IT contribute to this $1.95 billion market value?

The flip side of this question was also important: how much did IT diminish this market value? If well-managed IT contributed to a company's market value, poorly managed IT could just as well hurt market value. Barton remembered celebrating the moment in August, year before last, when IVK's stock price passed $75, giving IVK a market value of almost $4.8 billion. Just one and a half years later, after investors reassessed the company's value following a disappointing financial result, IVK had lost more than half of its market value. What role did IT play in that loss?

He added a "+/−" next to the question mark. To capture more of the value issue, he added "C vs. Q" as a reminder of Ruben's "Competes versus Qualifiers" model and, from their previous conversation, he drew the 40 percent new applications on top of the 60 percent infrastructure that reflected the current distribution of IT spending at IVK.

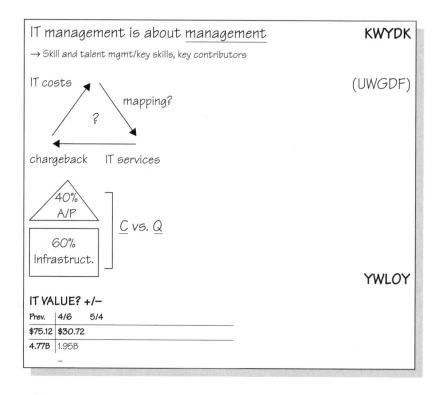

Barton still hadn't found a way through the forest, but he felt better going into the weekend with some thoughts concretely illustrated on his whiteboard. Perhaps the next week would yield insight. He was, after all, still rather new to all this.

Tuesday, April 10, 11:54 a.m. . . .

Returning from a meeting, Barton immediately noticed the two thin file folders that had appeared in his inbox.

"These just arrived from the CEO's office," said his assistant. Barton nodded, took them, and went into his office.

After his debacle with $1,200 worth of computer books, Barton had begun to wonder how Davies operated. How much of that stuff did he get? How much of a tech expert had he been, and how did he use that expertise as a manager? What did his employees think of him? How did they interact with him? Did they consider him an expert? It would be useful to know these things, because whatever Davies had done had gotten him fired.

After contemplating his experience with self-education, Barton had launched his own personal project called "Understand What Got Davies Fired." He'd written it in parentheses in the middle of his whiteboard, in coded block letters "(UWGDF)," just as he had written "KWYDK" and "YWLOY."

To begin the project, he'd called Carl Williams's assistant and asked whether there was anything in the files inherited from Kyle Crawford, the previous CEO, about IT. He explained it in terms of trying to maintain continuity of the IT function, but he was really hoping he might get some personnel evaluation files on Davies. A long shot, as usually personnel files would receive special protection, but worth it if he did get something that helped him understand how Crawford saw Davies and judged his performance.

As he glanced quickly through the two files, he realized that he had hit the jackpot with one of them. It contained a confidential report to Crawford from expert consultants—their assessment of the job Davies was doing as CIO.* It said a lot that Crawford had relied on expert outsiders for this assessment. But the report itself said even more.

The report characterized IT leadership in terms of three levels of maturity, from Type 1 to 3, Type 3 being most mature. According to this report, Type 1 leadership was about functional requirements and individual systems; the focus was operational. Type 2 was less about managing individual projects and systems, more about managing portfolios of projects and infrastructures, as well as playing a senior team leadership role; Type 2 leaders left the details of managing operational functions and individual systems to others, though they remained accountable for it all working. Type 3 evolved into a job of managing strategy and resources, leaving the details of management of portfolios and infrastructure to others.

The consultants rated Davies a Type 1 manager, struggling with transition to Type 2. They recommended sticking with Davies to see if he could make the transition to the next level, and then to the next level—

---

*See "Excerpts from the IT Leadership Consulting Report" at the end of this chapter.

level 3. They warned that it would not be easy simply to replace him; it would take a long time for a new person to become effective as CIO.

Barton though he might come up to speed a bit faster than their projection; he was not new to the company, just new to IT. But the warning sobered him. What "Type" manager was he? As the new CEO, Carl Williams gave no evidence that he was asking that question or even thinking in those terms. On the other hand, Williams and the board had been involved in the new CIO selection. Maybe he, Barton, was selected as a direct result of the board thinking about these different types of managers.

The report noted that Davies seemed to be respected by his IT staff, but had a big problem interacting with peers and those to whom he reported. He had a tendency, according to the consultants, to pull back into the confines of the IT world he knew well when faced with difficulty, especially conflict with an executive from the business side. They hoped he could overcome this tendency, with sufficient executive coaching and counseling help.

Barton thought to himself, while reading the report, that it would make a lot of sense to make contact with Davies, to buy him lunch. If nothing else, the need for thoroughness in his UWGDF project dictated as much.

REFLECTION

How do IT investments create value? Enable value creation?

How might we get a quantitative handle on the level of value provided by IT?

What light does the consultants' report shed on the matter of Davies' firing and the subsequent choice of Barton as CIO? What (if anything) does it add to the IT value discussion?

Excerpts from the IT Leadership Consulting Report

IVK corporation

CIO Assessment

William Davies, CIO

IT Leadership

Requirements for effective IT leadership change as the economics and scope of IT continue to change. As shown in figure 1, IT has evolved through three eras since it first appeared in companies during the 1960s.

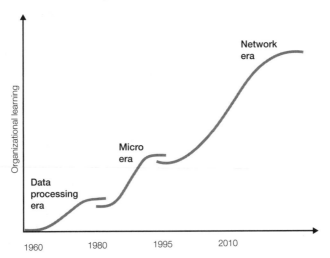

Figure 1
The three eras of IT growth

Each era is characterized by a dominant IT technology and an organizational learning curve that runs over multiple years. The first era, the *data processing* (DP) era, was characterized by mainframe computers used primarily for automating transactions. The second era, the *micro* era, shifted the dominant IT technology from mainframes to microcomputers, or PCs. Mainframes were still used, but were gradually replaced by microcomputers or arrangements of servers and clients.

What has been termed Moore's Law, which roughly describes the economics of computers, continues to result in new capabilities for information technology. In its simplest form, Moore's Law states that the cost performance of computers doubles every eighteen months or so. Another way of stating Moore's Law is that for the same computer performance, the cost halves every eighteen months.

The practical effect of Moore's Law is that applications of new technologies not economically feasible just a few years earlier become economically feasible. Accordingly, an important requirement for IT leadership is for the IT team to stay on top of emerging new technologies and the changing economics of the new technologies. In addition, an important IT leadership tenet is to build IT capability in a flexible manner to enable the incorporation of important new technologies as they become economically feasible. While this tenet is now quite obvious, it was not during the early IT eras. Consequently, many companies incorporated early technologies in an inflexible way and are now experiencing what has become known as the "legacy systems problem." IVK is experiencing the legacy systems problem in an indirect way with its third-party package for loan origination.

Companies are now embracing the *network* era, in which the dominant technology has shifted from stand-alone centralized computers loosely networked with PCs to integrated networks of literally millions of computers operating over inter-connected networks (including the public Internet). The network era is truly a sea change in the management of IT. Before the network era, companies had to build expensive networks, like American Airlines' Sabre systems, to electronically connect with customers and employees. Through the Internet, companies can easily and economically connect with their customers and partners using a publicly available infrastructure. As a result, IT in the firm can support both efficient transaction processing and direct customer interactions in real time.

The network era presents an incredible set of potential opportunities, but the opportunities come with significant exposure to risks, exemplified by the threat to IT service levels from computer viruses that have been unleashed on the Internet over the past few years.

IT Eras: Management Challenges and Opportunities

IVK has taken advantage of network era technologies and the Internet to serve customers. Indeed, IVK has taken advantage of this capability to gain a strategic advantage. However, IVK's packaged software, developed some time ago, is based on batch processing rather than real-time processing. An important IT problem for IVK is the reconciliation of its back-office batch technology with its newer front-office-real time technology.

IVK has a strategic advantage with its front-office systems, but is facing a key issue with re-architecting its back-office batch-oriented systems in order to sustain its current competitive advantage.

IVK IT Leadership: Transitioning from Type 1 to Type 2

Driven by changes in technology and economics, IT leadership continues to change through the years. Effective IT leadership depends on the specifics of a company and its situation: its size, strategy, growth rate, competitors, and industry. Three levels of increasingly sophisticated IT leadership can be identified, as shown in figure 2.

Figure 2
Evolution of IT leadership in the firm related to IVK Corporation

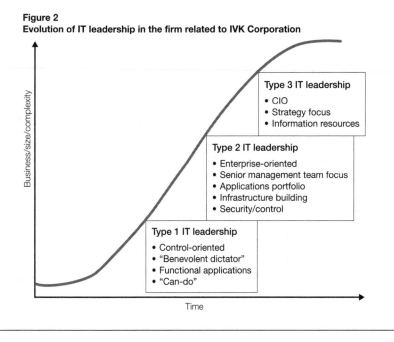

IVK's IT leadership is Type 1, the least sophisticated level, evolving into Type 2. A Type 1 IT leadership capability is one in which IT has built functional transaction-processing capabilities, enabling the company to realize an overall efficiency in operational business processes. IVK's Type 1 IT capability has resulted in the achievement of a great deal of loan origination along with the associated back-office processing.

Responding to the growing transaction volume, however, has stretched back-office systems. Rather than dealing with the novel requirements of different clients by using configuration changes, whole systems have been replicated and then customized for individual customers, creating immense complexity and a need to manage parallel systems. This approach helped solve short-term problems in delivering functionality to clients, but it has become a maintenance nightmare. Changes to core loan processing now have to be made as many times as IVK has major clients, with careful consideration to the special, customized features of each client system. Changes that work well for one client can potentially cause problems if identically applied to another client system. The ability of IT staff to manage this complexity is reaching its limit. Accordingly, there is an urgent need to re-architect the IT infrastructure to accommodate the business growth expected in the next several years.

IVK has begun to evolve to Type 2 IT leadership; this means moving from managing individual functional applications to applications portfolio/infrastructure management.

The existing IVK applications portfolio is dominated by operational systems. Poorly integrated spreadsheet applications are widely used for operational purposes, making data flows and transaction flows exceedingly cumbersome. The IVK IT infrastructure has bubbled up from the bottom and lacks architectural coherence.

IVK needs to address the need to implement Type 2 applications portfolio management along with the development of an IT architecture for the supporting infrastructure. To sustain competitive advantage through its use of IT, IVK also should be designing its application portfolio strategy and IT architecture with an eye toward Type 3 IT management as shown in figure 3.

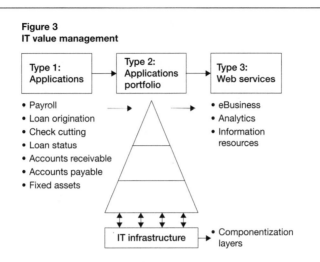

Figure 3
IT value management

Recommendation Concerning Current CIO

Good CIOs are hard to find. Even if you can find one, it may take as much as a year for a CIO new to the company to learn the company environment and become an effective leader. Your current CIO, who came up through the ranks of IT managers, is struggling to transition to Type 2 leadership. In our judgment, he may be able to complete the transition successfully. If IVK continues to grow, the issue will arise again when there is a need to transition to Type 3 IT leadership. If the transition to Type 2 is uncertain for the current CIO, the transition to Type 3 will be even more so. However, given (1) the difficulty of finding good CIOs, (2) the time it will take to bring a new CIO up to speed at IVK, and (3) the urgency of the need to update the IVK back office, we recommend:

- Retain the current CIO for at least another six months to a year, time enough to see if he will be able to transition to Type 2 leadership.

- Assist in this transition by providing executive leadership counseling for the CIO.

- Reassess in six months to see how this transition is going.

CHAPTER SIX

PROJECT MANAGEMENT

Wednesday, April 11, 2:35 p.m. . . . .

Barton's headache worsened. Sitting back in his seat, hands folded in his lap, he'd ceased trying to get into the conversation. What had begun as a project status review had deteriorated into open conflict. The combatants represented the company's two major IT subgroups, Loan Operations Systems and Customer Support Systems. At first the meeting had been orderly and polite; each person took turns walking through his or her list of projects in progress, explaining the reasons for "red," "yellow," or "green" status indicators beside each project. The lists showed a lot of green, some yellow, and a small amount of red. Oddly, Barton noticed, both departments seemed to have exactly the same proportion of green-, yellow-, and red-status projects.

The trouble had started when Rebecca Calder, a brilliant young fast tracker from Loan Operations Systems, had commented that one of her yellows might better be classified as a green. Jorge Huerta, an experienced senior analyst from Customer Support Systems, seemed annoyed by the remark and made a point of saying the same thing about one of his own yellows. In the course of the ensuing argument, it became apparent to Barton that many of the green and yellow projects on both lists were behind their original schedule and over their original budgets.

Although he found it educational to listen for a while, eventually Barton raised his hand and leaned forward, which both Calder and Huerta correctly interpreted as a signal to shut up. Then he asked a question: "Why is it that we are behind schedule and over budget on so many of these projects?"

Huerta was quickest to respond: "It's because we lack discipline in the project management process." Body language told Barton that Calder disagreed, as she had with pretty much everything else Huerta had said for the past ten minutes. Barton glanced in the direction of Calder's squirming, but raised a finger to keep her from interrupting. Barton turned back to Huerta: "Explain."

"It's simple, really," said Huerta. "We don't plan enough, and we don't establish project scope sufficiently in advance. We don't do a good enough job of obtaining a general agreement on what we are trying to accomplish with a project. Because of this, success is a moving target. We suffer again and again from scope creep."

"Scope creep?"

Huerta defined it: "It's the expression used by project managers under pressure to deliver in excess of what was originally agreed. Scope creep results from a failure to establish the clear requirements of business users. Scope of the original plan can start to move and continue to move. If the project manager is not alert, the requirements will constantly change. The project spends long periods of time on delivering nothing, continually reviewing and altering direction."[1]

This sounded like a reasonable answer to Barton. But he pressed Huerta: "And your suggested solution to this problem?"

"More planning," said Huerta, "and more discipline in decision making. We spend more time up front in formal planning activities, working with users to understand their needs and to help them understand what is possible in what we are planning to do. If we do this well, we'll be able to strike a firm agreement in advance on what the project will accomplish, which will provide a basis for a disciplined process for achieving those objectives. If it's not part of what we're trying to accomplish, we don't do it, no matter who's asking for it. There may be some things outside the scope that have to be added, but we can do that deliberately too. If we're going to expand the scope, we should take official notice that we're doing that and adjust our estimates of the time and resources it will take to complete the project too."

Barton was impressed. In just a few words, Huerta had presented a diagnosis and a prescription for cure, both of which sounded plausible. But Calder was still squirming. Barton turned to her.

"Calder, you don't buy this logic?"

"No sir, I do not."

"Why not?"

She sighed. "Jorge has just presented to you the solution that we've been trying to implement since the beginning of time; it never works."

"Why not?"

"Because the diagnosis is flawed. He thinks we should spend more time and effort making sure we understand the requirements up front. I don't think the users' requirements even *exist* in advance, and they are certainly not knowable in advance—"

"Ooooh, now we're getting metaphysical," ridiculed Huerta. Barton didn't like his tone.

"I didn't let her interrupt you," Barton said to Huerta, "so let her finish." Huerta shut up. "Go on," Barton said.

"Well, the difficulty is that we discover many of the important requirements only as we begin to try to create the system. Communicating intangible ideas is very difficult. Only as they start to interact with the system do users begin to see more concretely what is possible, and come to better understand the questions we are asking them. Only as our discussions begin to refer to actual system features do we really understand what they are saying they need. Of course, users change their minds about what they want as they come to understand better what is possible and as we come to understand their needs better. An approach that denies or even discourages such changes by claiming that it is more 'disciplined' to stick to the 'formal plan' is just denying reality."

Huerta couldn't help himself: "So we just launch off on a project, expecting to gather our requirements as we go . . ." Barton turned sharply as his words trailed off.

"No," said Calder, "we don't just 'launch off.' We spend some time in advance trying to figure out what we can of what the system needs to do, but at some point we need to start building the system so that we can discover the things we'll never discover if all we do is think about, talk about, and plan a hypothetical system. Jorge implies, along with a lot of other management gurus, that if we are just more careful and thorough, if we just spent enough disciplined time in the requirement-gathering phase, we could get pretty close to understanding what we need, and from there it would just be a matter of executing to plan. Their prescribed solution is more planning—more time spent studying and not doing anything. I don't buy it. Let's admit that even if we think *really* thoroughly about things in advance, we still won't anticipate important problems . . ."

"That's what contingency planning is for," interjected Huerta, quickly.

"Contingency plans are for problems you *can* anticipate. A big chunk of the problems with most projects are things you *can't* anticipate. If we buy into the philosophy of project management that considers unanticipated problems to be a result of flawed planning, we doom ourselves to repeat our failures. Every time you have a scope creep issue, you blame something you should have done on an earlier phase of the project. Never mind that the thing you supposedly should have done better earlier was impossible."

"It's *not* impossible!" Huerta practically shouted. Barton did not stop him this time. "A couple of years ago, we were developing a user interface with a notebook metaphor. On the screen, it looked like a notebook page, and there were tabs at the edges so you could flip to a different page. We had made an arbitrary decision to place the 'spine' of the notebook at the side, and that was built into the design of the underlying software infrastructure—the 'object classes,' if you want the technical term. When we showed it to users, they said, 'Looks great, but can you put the spine of the notebook at the top rather than on the side?' And we did it! We spent weeks making a change because we had not captured that detail in advance. We could easily, with a truly disciplined process, have picked up this requirement in advance. Or, alternatively, a good process would have labeled this change for what it is: scope creep. We would have said back to the users, 'No, we're not going to do that, it doesn't matter that much.' And we'd have been right. They would have gotten accustomed to the spine at the left rather than the top after less than an hour using the system. A disciplined process helps us avoid these kinds of problems."

"Not a fair example," said Calder. Barton settled back to listen and rest his eyes. His head was pounding. "Not all examples are like that. Last year I was working on a project where we had peak load problems. We would have had a tremendously difficult time imagining in advance that the load requirements would be so high; nobody foresaw the business events that caused such high peaks in load on the system."

"That could have been anticipated, with the right process . . ."

"Yeah, well maybe it could. In an ideal world without taxes, crime, or war. Maybe. But how confident are you that you can anticipate every problem, or even every important problem, on the large complex systems we work on all the time? You can't do it. You'd have to be prescient or superhuman to anticipate all of the possible emergent issues. The idea that a coherent and complete set of customer requirements can be captured in advance is pure fiction, at least in most cases. And it makes no sense to give advice that, in effect, says, 'We need you to be more superhuman.'"

"What makes no sense," said Huerta, "is to encourage people to just race off at the start of a project, like a bunch of IT cowboys, justifying their actions on the grounds that 'you can't anticipate all the important problems anyway, so we might as well race ahead so that we can begin making messes.'"

Calder did not respond immediately. This pause to think and change the tempo of the argument impressed Barton. Her argument had begun to, also. There was a welcome moment of silence, before she replied, quietly, "Actually, that's *exactly* how I see it. We should get on with making the messes so that we can deal with them sooner rather than later. You will inevitably have messes. Better to have them sooner rather than postpone them. Early messes on a project may not always be pleasant; they may look like management messes. But better early mess than late-breaking disaster. Fail faster to succeed sooner. Fail forward."

Barton stirred. "Is that it?" he asked Calder. "Is that your proposed solution? 'Fail forward'?"

Calder's expression displayed disappointment. She thought Barton was siding with Huerta.

"No sir," she said. "I'd recommend that we structure our projects to begin creating prototypes very early and to generate a rapid succession of prototypes. We should do some gathering of requirements before we get started, but in doing that we need to employ the 80-20 rule. At some fairly early point, you need to break away from the planning and starting trying things, or else you are just delaying the discovery of problems you'll never anticipate through mere contemplation."

"That's all well and good," said Huerta, "for things you can create prototypes for. But for most things you can't."

"True," acknowledged Calder, "you can't literally create a succession of quickly evolving prototypes if you are implementing, say, a large off-the-shelf vendor package. If it takes nine months just to install and configure it, it's hard to see how you can run a two-week prototype. But you can do some things that approximate prototyping. Like detailed walkthroughs of how the purchased system handles certain processes. You just need some sort of procedure that gets you into prototyping details, even if you can't literally produce a prototype. You can simulate a prototype on paper, sometimes—a paper prototype. Call it a 'conference room pilot test.'"

"That starts to sound a lot like a document of some kind. A lot like the documents I might propose in what I call a disciplined project management process."

"Maybe. But most project management documents don't prompt the sort of active attention to detail and discussion that you get out of a 'paper prototyping' process. Maybe that's what they were once intended to do, but I don't think they do that anymore."

"Be careful," said Barton, "the two of you just nearly agreed on something." Huerta and Calder laughed, warily.

"If I can summarize?" Huerta asked.

"Sure," said Barton.

"I think we need to stop perpetuating the myth that IT projects are somehow special. People manage building construction projects all the time and manage to anticipate the requirements well enough that they don't have the kinds of problems we have in IT—if they are well managed, anyway. IT needs to grow up. Becca says we can't, because we're special. Well, that may make sense when you are just out of school, fresh from hanging out with ivory-tower types. But it's just not good enough when we are making decisions about major capital investments."

Calder responded: "Jorge thinks I'm living in an ivory tower when I say an IT project is different from a construction project. Saying it makes me less than a hardheaded business macho dude. But I think he's the one living in a dream world by maintaining on principle, and despite evidence to the contrary, that we *ought* to be able to define customer requirements clearly in advance, even though we never do."

A silence settled over the room. Barton broke it: "It sounds to me like we need some new thinking on project management around here. We'll get to that. However, I don't think that we've achieved today's original objective of reviewing the status of active projects. So I need each of you to go back to your departments and adjust these lists so that the reds, yellows, and greens are accurate and honest. I don't want to see a negotiated settlement where both of you have the same proportion of reds, yellows, and greens. Judging from what I've heard today, I'm under the distinct impression that some items labeled green ought to be labeled yellow or even red. When we reconvene this meeting in a few days, I want to hear accounts that have a strong connection to reality. Understand?"

Calder and Huerta nodded.

"Good. Now let's get out of here. I have a terrible headache."

Thursday, April 12, 5:49 p.m. . . .

Done with meetings for the day, Barton opened the bottom drawer of his desk and removed a musty book that he'd retrieved the night before from the back of the self-storage unit where he kept a lot of old junk. The meeting with Calder and Huerta had prompted him to go in search of it. It had taken him a couple of hours to find it; by the time he did he'd lacked the energy to open it.

Titled *Project Management,* the book dated back to a course he'd taken in college. For the first time in more than two decades, he opened it and began reading, skimming the table of contents, jumping around as chapter titles caught his interest.

He read about Gantt charts, PERT analysis, and CPM. In essence, these were planning methods. They broke down projects into discrete tasks with stated durations (and, in later chapters, possible variances—

a task might be 5 days, plus or minus 2 days), keeping track of which tasks had to be completed before others could begin. The project tasks could then be graphed out with dependencies between them explicit. The longest duration line of dependencies could then be identified as the "critical path;" that is, the path along which any delay meant an overall project delay. These tasks on the critical path deserved extra scrutiny during the management of the project, since they were so important to keeping the overall project on schedule. The book also spent many pages on planning the allocation of resources, such as key people or machines. By using the methods described in those pages, you could be sure not to make plans that required a single person to be in two places or doing two jobs at once. Useful stuff. Much of it, Barton was sure, had been incorporated by now into project management software packages; he suspected that computer software now did the calculations that took up so many pages in the book.

In the end, the book seemed more about how to plan projects than how to manage them. It provided some advice about actual in-progress managing, but most of that was pretty straightforward. Be *sure* you don't forget this. You *must* do that. The sort of exhortation that dodges questions about why people in real life *do* forget things they shouldn't or *don't* do things that they must.

Barton put the book aside and turned to his computer. Searching on project management and IT-related keywords, he came across some information about the Software Engineering Institute's Capability Maturity Model Integration, which included an approach to project management. This was more helpful. It seemed to provide advice about how to actually do the work of keeping a project on track. But it too seemed to primarily emphasize planning.

Barton had nothing against planning. He was a huge fan of planning. But he suspected that Calder was right that, no matter how much you planned, some unexpected things would still happen on something as complex as a big IT project. It nagged at Barton that most of the advice he was reading seemed to focus mostly on preparing for the expected, not managing the unexpected. Calder's critique rang true: the authors' assumption seemed to be that if you experienced something unexpected, then you hadn't planned well enough. Thorough planning would help you identify a problem that you might not have anticipated without doing such thorough planning—that was obvious. But it was just as obvious that you couldn't count on anticipating every problem. So project management, Barton reasoned, had to contain some advice about how to manage the unexpected. Or maybe that was a crazy idea? How can you manage something of which you have no prior perception?

A bit more searching led him to an article called "Agile Project Management: Principles and Tools" by a consultant, Jim Highsmith.[2] Barton grew interested as he read the following:*

> APM practices thrive in projects that are exploratory in nature, ones that push the envelope of schedule, risk, and rewards. As such, these projects don't conform to the traditional plan-build mode of operation, but progress by exploring and adapting. The speculate phase generates a hypothesis about the future, not a detailed deterministic plan. Agile project teams "expect" the plan to be wrong; they expect changes—often very large ones. Therefore, the monitor and adapt phase names what happens when variations are found. Traditional project managers talk about "corrective action," which implies that the plan was correct, and the actual results, if different, must be in error.

Barton didn't completely understand everything he read in the article, but he liked the way in which the author made realistic assumptions about the need to deal with the unexpected. Standing up from his desk, Barton went to the whiteboard and wrote headings for two columns. The first: "Managing Problems You *Can* Anticipate." The second: "Managing Problems You *Can't* Anticipate." He wasn't sure what specific management measures should be listed under each, but filling in those blanks, that was the task at hand, he thought. He wrote "planning techniques and methods" under the first heading. By that he meant Gantt charts, PERT, CPM, and resource scheduling methods. Under the second heading, he wrote "exploring, adapting, course-correcting techniques and methods." Then he put down the pen and sat back down to contemplate what he had written.

---

*See "Excerpt from 'Agile Project Management'" at the end of this chapter.

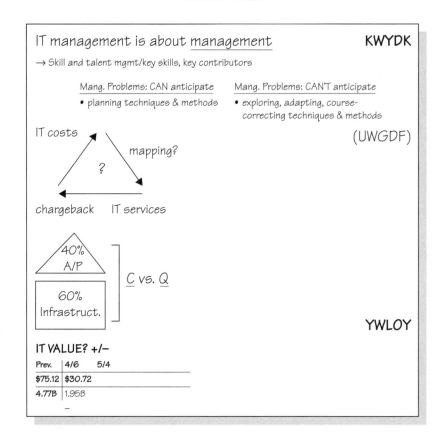

He had no idea, he realized, what "exploring, adapting, course-correcting techniques and methods" were. Highsmith had some suggestions, but Barton lacked the expertise to know whether they were any good. Nevertheless, the direction seemed promising.

Reaching back into the bottom drawer that had contained the old textbook, Barton removed a file folder marked "Project Status Review" in Davies's handwriting. Davies had jotted notes in the margins and changed some numbers. You could see the numbers changed in red pen; then in later versions of the document the red pen numbers became official. It appeared that Davies was in the habit of doubling, roughly, the estimates made by his own people for how long it would take to complete a project. He'd take an IT internal estimate, then mark it up by 25 to 100 percent. The amount of the markup appeared to be related to entries in a column labeled "Estimate Confidence." If the estimate confidence was "High," the markup would be small, usually. If the estimate confidence was listed as "Low," Davies marked up the estimate by a lot. The rule wasn't exact. Barton guessed that Davies knew who had generated each estimate and confidence entry, and was adjusting based on his own knowledge of the reliability of the estimator's estimate and the estimate confidence.

ct	IT Internal Estimate (Per. Mo.)	Estimate Confidence	
ystem	12	Med	~ 16
TS	10	High	14
	6	Low	14 R.J.
m	14	Med	Tyra-24
ial	18	High	ok
	7	Med	12
ation	10	High	14/12
	6	Med	12
opment	22	Low	32
rs	20	Med	28? ask Paul
	10	Med	14
	8	Low	priority?
	24	Med	40/ start +1yr
CAP	3	High	ok
em	18	Med	26
	16	Low	32
ect	23	Med	30
Y	12	High	14

Barton recognized the temptation to mark up the estimates. This was a big part of the way Davies had managed the unexpected. He added enough slack into every estimate so that he had a reasonable chance of bringing projects in on schedule, even if the unexpected happened.

But Barton could also see a problem with the approach. As he looked through the other project status documents before him, it was clear that few (if any) projects finished ahead of the marked-up estimates. In other words, project teams pretty much always took all the time indicated in the marked-up estimates. Barton guessed that there were numerous reasons for this. Sometimes the unexpected did happen and the marked-up estimate was more realistic. When nothing unexpected impacted a project and it was running ahead of schedule, resources were likely diverted from it to projects in greater trouble. Then there was "Parkinson's Law," the truth of which Barton firmly believed. It stated, "Work expands so as to fill the time available for its completion."[3]

One thing Barton liked: the estimate confidence seemed like a useful thing to capture. In essence, it expressed the likelihood of an unexpected problem arising on a project. A "low" estimate confidence said "We're pretty sure we'll have problems we haven't anticipated on this project," while a "high" estimate confidence said "We're pretty sure we *won't* have unanticipated problems." This information, reflected Barton, might be used to help decide between what Highsmith called "traditional" and "agile" project management approaches.

Barton searched the Web some more, exploring the subject of project estimation. There was a ton of material out there on the subject, but most of it was about estimating the cost or duration of software development projects. The usual method, as best he could discern, called for somehow gauging the "size" of a development project in terms of lines of code or something called "function points," and then using different methods and adjustments to derive from the project size its cost and duration.[4] The biggest problem with all of it from Barton's perspective: very few of the projects in the IVK portfolio were software development projects. None of them, really. Some of them contained components that required software development. But that was not the major part of the project. Usually any development in an IVK project had to do with fitting a purchased package of some kind to existing IVK systems, creating the interfaces between two systems, that sort of thing. For the kind of projects IVK usually had to do, there was no obvious way to estimate size, so there was no place to start with the estimating models. And anyway, the estimates developed by these models had huge ranges of error, plus or minus 50 percent or more; how useful was that? It was too bad, really, but the science had not caught up with management practice.

"Does it ever?" Barton asked no one in particular. He looked at his watch. It was time to call it a day. Replacing the file folder and book in his desk drawer, he packed up and headed for home, still thinking about methods for managing the unexpected.

Friday, April 13, 8:49 p.m. . . .

Barton walked in to Vinnie's. Immediately he noticed the kid seated at the bar, sipping a Coke and eating a burger.

"How's it going?" said Barton, taking a seat beside him.

"Well, well," said the kid, "the great manager returns! How goes the new job?"

Barton ordered his own burger and Coke before answering. "Pretty well, I think. Starting to get my bearings. Still trying to be sure I know what I don't know."

"Good man," said the kid. "What's the hot issue this week?"

"Not sure there's just one. But if I had to pick it would be project management."

"Hmm," said the kid. "That's a tough one."

"Is it?"

"A classic area where managers don't know what they don't know. Some of them don't really care that they don't know what they ought to, I think."

"What makes you think that?"

"I look young, but I'm a survivor of many 'death march' projects. Way too many."

"Death march projects?"

"Yeah. Term comes from a book by Ed Yourdon.[5] Or at least he's the one that made it really famous. A death march is a project with a bad plan that managers are determined to stick to. The primary management tool is yelling a lot and making people work longer and longer hours. Managers leading a death march don't want to hear about unexpected problems, and workers understand that. So everybody just sweeps problems under the rug; it's the de facto management policy. People on the front lines, the smart ones anyway, take steps to make sure they're not standing too close when the whole thing collapses under its own weight. They all keep their heads down and mind their own business. Lots of burnout, morale stinks. Catastrophe in the end, usually. Death march."

"Does that really happen so often?"

The kid didn't even answer, but Barton could read the expression on his face.

"So," asked Barton, "what's the alternative to death march management?"

"I'm not sure the alternative has been perfected yet, which is one reason there're still so many death marches. It's the fallback approach. The fundamental problem is that it's the guys on the front lines who see a problem first. If you're holding those guys accountable for schedule primarily, then they have an incentive to avoid realistic assessment or communication of those problems. Often they're just overly optimistic. You know, 'Yeah, that's a problem, but I think we can adjust quickly and solve it by doing this or that.' Only this and that have little chance of saving the day.

"In managing an IT project, the boss has the difficult task of getting the workers to behave in a fundamentally irrational way. You need the frontline guys to be willing to bring bad news to the boss. The boss often can't detect the bad news alone. So the best project management policies are those that promote open flow of information up and down the project hierarchy. On death march projects, there's almost no information moving upward—no reliable info, anyway. Everybody understands what they're not supposed to tell their managers."

"So what are the policies that promote better flow of information upward?"

"Hey, you're the manager. Speaking from my experience, the managers I'm most likely to talk honestly with, the ones I provide with early warning of unexpected problems, are those I talk to a lot and like. Who seem to want to understand what I'm doing and ask me about it. I'm a bit too talkative anyway, when approached—as you might have noticed. Get me talking, and I'll blurt out all kinds of things that I should have thought about before I said them. A lot of people like me are like that, I think. It's a dysfunctional learned behavior for us to censor what we tell our managers."

"What do you think of the 'agile' approach?"

"Iteration is good. If you structure it right, each iteration prompts an important conversation. If you set things up right, you get early warning on most problems, and iteration lets you see opportunities to create value you didn't see at first, value that isn't in the plan."

"If you start too soon, you might go down some dead-end paths, though."

"Sure. Get over it. It costs you some of your project budget to learn what you need to do to succeed. If you insist that every hour or cent moves you in a direct line closer to the next milestone, sooner or later you'll be on a death march. Sometimes you have to back up to get around an obstacle. Plus, I believe in working code, above all else. I think you'll find that most people like me do. Working code beats half-baked or un-executed plans any day of the week. Iteration gets you to trying to implement quicker. Yes, that can be inefficient sometimes, when you start in the wrong direction and a bit more planning would have worked better, but it can also save you time by showing you that an assumption you made in planning wasn't even close to correct."

The kid had finished his meal and was paying the bill. "Got to go. I've got a date in Second Life. She's totally hot. Her avatar's hot anyway. Who knows what she looks like in real life?" The kid winked. "Then again, I'm not six feet of tattooed, leather-clad muscle, am I? Speaking of which," he joked, "what's a guy like you doing here on Friday night alone?"

"Girlfriend's out of town. Too often."

"Ahhh," said the kid, standing. "That's where virtual dating beats the terabytes out of real-world dating. No out-of-town hassles. Think on that."

"I will." Barton smiled, "So, you ready to come to work for me yet?"

"Not yet," said the kid. "But let's talk again next time."

The kid left. Barton motioned to the bartender. He needed another Coke.

REFLECTION

Which side would you take in the debate between Huerta and Calder?

Does it really make sense to jump directly into project coding and early proto-types in order to discover "messes" (unanticipated issues) early—that is, "to fail fast to succeed sooner"? Can this advice be implemented in a practical way?

How can you manage, or prepare to manage, what you cannot anticipate and do not expect? What do you think of the approach that Davies seems to have used (as revealed in the documents discovered by Barton) to manage uncertainty in IT projects?

Excerpt from "Agile Project Management"

Agile project management (APM) complements traditional project management (TPM) in many ways.[a] Project managers should understand the basics of setting up project organizations, budgeting, critical path scheduling, and myriad other established project management practices. However, project managers should also know when and how to apply agile practices. There are three broad situations in which APM should be considered over TPM:

High exploration–factor projects

Projects in which customer responsiveness is paramount

Organizations with innovative cultures

The APM Lifecycle Framework

The lifecycle framework includes five phases:

- Envision—determine the product vision, who is going to do the work, and how the team will work together.

- Speculate—develop a feature-based release, milestone, and iteration plan.

- Iteratively deliver features—deliver tested features in short time frames.

- Monitor and adapt—review the delivered results, the current business environment, and the team's performance—and adapt as necessary.

- Close—conclude the project, wrap up loose ends, and celebrate.

The names of the phases are different from traditional ones to reflect the focal points of agile project management. "Envision," for example, indicates the critical nature of a clear product vision in a project.

APM practices thrive in projects that are exploratory in nature, ones that push the envelope of schedule, risk, and rewards. As such, these projects don't conform to the traditional plan-build mode of operation, but progress by exploring and adapting. The speculate phase generates a hypothesis about the future, not a detailed deterministic plan. Agile project teams "expect" the plan to be wrong; they expect changes—often very large ones. Therefore, the monitor and adapt phase names what happens when variations are found. Traditional project managers talk about "corrective action," which implies that the plan was correct, and the actual results, if different, must be in error.

TPM approaches allow for a variety of development lifecycles, although in practice, they are heavily biased toward sequential, waterfall lifecycles. APM takes exactly the opposite approach; it is decidedly short-cycle, iterative, and feature-driven. Agile teams deliver in short iterations—weeks for software projects, longer periods for industrial products. For industrial products, teams get as close to actual features as possible, using simulations or models to give the customer something tangible to review.

Nine Principles of APM

The core components of APM are the tools and principles. Principles guide actions; they breathe purpose and dynamics into tools. Without principles, team members won't understand "how" to use the tools, nor how to adapt them when needed. Conversely, principles without tools are lofty phrases devoid of concrete meaning. The nine principles of APM are:

- Deliver something useful.

- Cultivate committed stakeholders.

- Employ a leadership-collaboration management style.

- Build competent, collaborative teams.

- Enable team decision making.

- Use iterative, feature-driven delivery.

- Encourage adaptability.

- Champion technical excellence.

- Accelerate throughput.

APM Tools

Tools implement, or instantiate, principles. Developing a product vision box helps a team focus and deliver something useful to their customers. A project data sheet helps a team grapple with the scope boundaries of a project. Estimating a project's exploration factor helps a team quantify, to some extent anyway, the uncertainty surrounding a project. Feature cards provide a tactile, low-ceremony, easy-to-use tool for project planning. Daily team integration meetings are a critical piece in creating collaborative teams, as is a collaborative decision-making tool. These and other tools help teams implement APM.

Conclusions

Some people may think APM isn't all that different from TPM. Some may already practice their own version of APM. Some may think it heretical. I think APM differs from TPM in several significant ways.

First and foremost, APM is principles based and tools instantiated. The nine principles of APM are the drivers; they help us interpret how to use tools. Second, APM focuses on delivery, not compliance activities. Because of this, customers and products, rather than stakeholders and activities, become the focal points. Third, when we focus on customer needs and problems and then build products to solve those needs and problems, we recognize that exploration, innovation, and adaptability are key to success.

These values define agile project management. APM may use some of the tools of TPM, or vice versa, but the fundamental philosophies differ. For more and more of today's projects—those that have high exploration factors, require active customer responsiveness, or take place in organizations with innovative cultures—APM should be strongly considered.

a. From Jim Highsmith, "Agile Project Management: Principles and Tools," Arlington, MA: Cutter Consortium, March 9, 2004. Reprinted by permission.

CHAPTER SEVEN

THE RUNAWAY PROJECT

The coffee tastes particularly good this morning, Barton thought, as he settled in behind his desk to catch up on things he'd been neglecting. Monday and Tuesday had been a blur, getting ready for the IT review in the senior leadership meeting on Tuesday afternoon. Barton, aided by Geisler and the other direct reports to the CIO, especially Ruben, had been scrambling to make sure all the *i*'s were dotted and the *t*'s crossed before Barton went into the big meeting.

All the hard work had paid off. The IT group, using a framework based on "Compete" and "Qualify" categories, had wowed Carl Williams. All the other groups in the departmental reviews conducted thus far had used simple metrics, such as revenue or profitability growth, for demonstrating the value of their work. With some exceptions, it was hard to show that specific activities of a department had caused growth in sales or profitability, so most had rushed past the value question to analysis of costs, which had occupied most of the meeting discussions.

But if customer-facing departments had trouble showing causality between their activities and favorable financial results for the company, the difficulties of the IT department were even more profound. IT was not customer facing. IT sold nothing to customers directly and only rarely interacted with IVK customers. Almost everything the IT department did was in support of other departments. So, with very few exceptions, drawing a line between something the IT department did and increases in sales or profits—well, that was very difficult indeed. Even if Barton had been inclined to do it, he'd risk claiming credit for benefits that other departments had already said were the result of their own activities. Consequently, he'd risk having such claims challenged by department heads in the meeting.

This had led Barton and his team to flesh out the "Compete" and "Qualifier" (CQ) framework and estimate in various areas the gaps between IVK capabilities and competitors' capabilities as a result of IT functionality. Each IT-enabled capability they identified was categorized as either a "Compete," meaning that IVK intended to move ahead of its competitors using that capability, or a "Qualifier," meaning that IVK did not expect a competitive edge from the capability but nevertheless needed it to do business. For Compete advantages, the IT team had also estimated the *sustainability* of the advantage: not only how far ahead of competitors they were in months, but also whether IVK was extending or losing its lead in that area. Of course this methodology inevitably identified areas where IVK trailed competitors. It was a tribute to Davies and past IT management that relatively few of those impacted customers. Partly, Barton suspected, this was because powerful managers outside IT demanded that customer needs be met first, and Davies, not a very strong proponent of alternative views, generally gave in. Nevertheless, the facts presented an opportunity for a congratulatory word or two about Barton's predecessor. No one had seized that opportunity in the senior leadership team meeting, but Barton commented to that effect within his own team, congratulating them on their past good work.

By the end of the IT review, Williams had ordered each of the other areas to apply the CQ analysis in their own areas and to return to a future meeting to revisit the value side of their own departments' activities. Barton concealed his pleasure at this outcome because his peers took the CEO's instructions as a reprimand. Another dynamic surprised him as the meeting broke up: Barton picked up a vibe emanating from the others that bordered on resentment, a "Why don't you IT guys go back to the basement where you belong?" sentiment. They were dead wrong about this, and surely they knew it. Solid analysis was solid analysis, whichever department it came from. Wasn't this the reason they'd encouraged him to take the IT job in the first place? To bring the quality of management that had been practiced in the business areas into the IT department?

It was, Barton reflected, his first big win as the new CIO, accomplished less than a month after taking the job. Maybe this job wouldn't be as hard as he'd feared.

Williams had also asked Barton to prepare an update to the board of directors sometime in June. The CEO's enthusiasm for the CQ framework had provoked this command; Williams wanted Barton to use the framework as part of the update. But a report to the board would also need to include an assessment of the current state of IT and recommendations about what to do about what was perceived as "the IT mess." June was still pretty far out on his planning horizon, but Barton would begin to discuss it with Ruben and Geisler.

The only sour note in the IT review had centered on the infrastructure replacement (IR) project, which stood out as the single largest item in the IT budget. Barton knew what it was, but had not prepped on it as much as he should have. Others on the leadership team noted that the project had consumed more than $3 million already, and no one could think of any business benefit that had yet materialized from it. When asked why and what was going on, Barton did not have a good answer, but promised to investigate. Williams requested an update in a meeting scheduled for two weeks later.

"Is that enough time?" Williams had asked.

"I'll make it enough," said Barton. As a turnaround CEO, Williams did not have a reputation for patience. Barton suspected that Williams considered two weeks roughly equivalent to eternity. But Barton resisted the urge to offer to do it more quickly, since he had no idea what investigating would involve. And in the area of IT, he understood already, things often turned out to be more complicated than he would at first expect.

So it was to the IR project that Barton first turned his attention, as he sipped coffee and cleared his desk of some minor matters that Wednesday morning. It was too bad that he'd not prepared sufficiently for the questions about this project from his colleagues. But, on the other hand, perhaps it presented an opportunity for another triumph.

The Road of Trials

Friday, April 20, 1:34 p.m. . . .

Barton leaned back in the chair and propped one leg across the other knee as he listened to Tyra Gordon. Her Loan Operations and New Application Development Systems unit comprised the largest portfolio of systems in the organization, although Raj Juvvani's Customer Support and Collection Systems portfolio had grown in recent years to a size that nearly rivaled that of Loan Operations. Many of Gordon's systems did back-end processing, the heart and soul of the enterprise, but these had less direct customer impact than Juvvani's systems—unless they didn't work, in which case the entire IVK business would screech to a halt.

Barton had asked Gordon to set some time aside for the two of them to review status on the IR project. Though the project touched all areas of systems in the business, its biggest impacts would be on the back-office systems that were under Gordon's care. For this reason, Gordon was the IT department's point person on the project, although she was not the project leader. In compliance with the advice of consultants in the not-so-recent past, a business (not IT) manager led the IR project. Jay Palmer, a senior manager who reported to IVK's top sales executive, was the official leader of the IR project, though Barton had a hard time imagining him taking a very active role. Palmer was a sales guy by training, a deal maker, very good at what he had worked his way up doing. He was a conscientious person, but not very detail-oriented. Barton suspected dysfunction; it was unclear how Palmer would lead a huge IT project.

Barton's concern about the IR project led him to Gordon's office, where moments earlier he'd entered and asked, simply, "So what's the story on the Infrastructure Replacement project?"

"Well," said Gordon, "it's had its difficulties, but I wouldn't say it's way off the rails."

"That's good," said Barton. "I got asked about it in the leadership team IT review the other day, and I didn't know as much about it as I wanted to. Can you give me the short version of the background on the project?"

"Sure," responded Gordon. She stood and moved to a file cabinet. Searching, she quickly located a file folder, which she opened on her desk as she sat back down.

"Here," she said, handing a single page to Barton. "This is the consultant's summary report, which launched the project. As you can see, the recommendation that led to the IR project is first on the list."

Barton read a section labeled "Obsolete Systems Issue":

Begin a project to replace middle and back-end systems. Form a cross-functional team composed of equal parts business and IT staff, led by a senior manager on the business side, who should have hands-on responsibility for this project. Put your best people on this project. Do not pull them off for short-term urgent reasons. Cost Estimate: 3% of current revenues. Recommended timing: VERY SOON.

"Hmm," Barton said. "Three percent of revenues—that's some serious cash. Is this it?" He waved the single page in the air.

"No," said Gordon, "that's just the summary. Should be some more detail . . . here." She handed him several more sheets of paper, all stapled together, opened to an early page.

Barton read this page and the page and a half that followed it in silence.* At the same time, Gordon refreshed her memory from an extra copy she'd kept in her folder.

"Hard to argue," observed Barton, "with the logic behind the need for the project." Gordon nodded in agreement. "When was this done?"

"Let's see." Gordon paused to remember. "It's been about a year and a half now," said Gordon. "We jumped right on it after the assessment. Project leader, as I'm sure you know, is Jay Palmer."

"How's that been going?"

"You mean Jay's leadership?"

"Yes."

"Fine."

Barton said nothing, waited for Gordon to elaborate. Gordon saw that she was not going to get away with a one-word response.

"He was really energized at first, put a team together and did a lot of good work with a process consultant, current state versus desired state analysis, that sort of thing. Pretty detailed. But at that level of detail, the

---

*See "Excerpt from Consultant's Report" at the end of this chapter.

size of the project is overwhelming. They finished their first cut in about three months, as I recall. The consultants handed them a huge document, then nobody quite knew what to do next. Jay was instrumental in landing the BtJ deal about then, and—how can I say this?—he became motivated to think more broadly about his goals in life."

"You mean he made a truckload of money on the deal and became less motivated in his day-to-day activities."

"Yes, that's what I mean. Plus, I do think it really was difficult to know what to do next. All that detail documented, what do you do with it? The team did take a next step. They hired NetiFects, the systems integration firm we are still working with on the project."

"The firm we're still paying every month."

"The same."

"That's what brought it up in the meeting. We've spent quite a lot and no one could name any concrete benefits from the work."

"That's a reasonably accurate assessment. There have been issues."

Barton sensed reluctance, a political issue lurking behind Gordon's general statement.

"Tell me more," said Barton, "and don't leave out your own opinions of what has happened." This last bit he added with more sternness than was perhaps called for. But he didn't want the official version; he wanted the lowdown.

Gordon sighed, then nodded. "The project leadership team, Palmer and the other members, are mostly *not* IT people, in keeping with the recommendations of the consultants. This worked well in the early stages. But when it came to evaluating systems integrators, we had—this is my opinion—a problem. NetiFects was very smooth, gave a great presentation. I was there. They made a big deal about their resources in India, how they would work on our project across continents and time zones. I raised an objection. To me, it seemed likely that we would rely to a considerable extent on packaged software for the new back-end infrastructure. Guys in India are likely to be useful for a lot of custom development of software, but I wasn't then and still am not sure how much custom development we'll do in this project. Some, of course, but the bulk of it is likely to be getting packages configured, installed, and running. We're not going to rewrite our own loan origination systems. So it seemed to me they were making too much out of the India developers thing."

"But that appealed to the IR project team."

"All of it did. We—IT—had a couple of people on the team, good people, and I went to most of the meetings, but I'm not all that confident that we asked as many hard questions as we should have."

"It's been over a year since we started paying them. What do you think of their work?"

"There's a bigger issue. They didn't make a lot of it at vendor selection time, but it turns out that a lot of NetiFects expertise is in Unix/Linux, Oracle, and Java technologies. Historically, we have had heavy reliance on Microsoft technologies: Windows, SQLServer, Visual Basic, dotNet. These are two competing technology platforms. No sooner did we hire NetiFects than they put on a full-court press trying to get us to switch to their favored platform for our next-generation back office."

"Any merit in the idea?"

"Sure, they're good technologies, solid. The problem is that our entire base of IT experience is in a different set of technologies, which are also pretty good. If we're going to switch to a new technology base and retrain everyone as that would require, I'd like to have a better reason than 'It's more convenient for our systems integrator.'"

"Is that the only reason they're recommending it?"

"The main reason, I think, though they'd never admit it. For them it's a very practical issue. They have tons of Java- and Oracle-qualified resources, not so many dotNet or SQLServer experts. Even if they have the ability to deliver on this very challenging project, they may not be able to do it in technologies they don't know well. They know this is going to be hard, so they're trying to gear the playing field to their strengths, to reduce their risk of failure."

"Reasonable enough. We don't want them to fail either."

"Yes, but we might have been better off choosing an equally qualified vendor who had a lot of experts in our technology base. Again, the non-IT composition of the project team came into play here. I think they didn't realize what a big deal it was; they believed the vendor reps, who were inclined to downplay the problem."

"They believed the vendor, not their own IT department?"

"You bet. It almost always goes down that way. A classic problem. The vendor wants to win the contract, so they tell the business people what they want to hear. The internal IT guys raise concerns, become the naysayers. 'This won't work for that reason, that won't work for this reason.' The business guys interpret the nay-saying as lack of expertise within the company because they want to believe what the vendor is saying. Of course the vendor changes tune as soon as the contract is signed. The problem from the vendor perspective shifts then from winning the project to managing the overblown expectations created by claims made while trying to win the deal. Choosing between a vendor and your own IT department, you business guys never choose us."

"Actually," Barton reminded her, "I'm now an IT guy."

"Oh, I know. Just venting a bit."

Barton smiled. "So what has NetiFects been doing?"

"A few things. They're walking the project team through the packaged software selection process. Not surprisingly, they have a bias in favor of packages based on their favored technologies, not the ones we're most comfortable with. They've also been writing a lot of interface code, which will be needed to link systems built with their technologies to our systems, legacy systems that won't be replaced. Much of which would not be needed at all if we stuck with our favored technologies."

"Sounds like we're going sideways."

"Basically," agreed Gordon.

"We pay them a fat retainer every month, plus a lot of extra billable items. The invoices come through my office for a signature."

"It's not only their fault, to be fair," Gordon allowed. "We have a substantial degree of analysis paralysis going on. This kind of project is just too big. You get all psyched up to tackle it, then you start to look at it in earnest and it just looks impossible. For a few months now the project team has been running hard up to the project and bouncing off of it."

"Couldn't it be split up into smaller chunks?"

"That's probably the right thing to do, but figuring out what the chunks should be is really hard work. You're replacing an infrastructure that's an immense tangle. There are no obvious places to cut the infrastructure apart so that you can work on just a subpart. There are places that look like logical places to cut, but when you look closer you see that there are all sorts of vital nerves and blood vessels running through that juncture. Cutting it apart without killing the patient is hard to do."

"Should the IT department be in charge of this project?"

Gordon shook her head. "I don't know. It's been a joy to watch the non-IT members of the IR project team taking responsibility for business process decisions that are all too often left, inappropriately, to the IT department. But the lack of technical expertise in the majority of the team members has landed us some serious problems."

Barton realized that this was about as far as he could push Gordon. He didn't want to give her the idea that he blamed her for problems with the IR project. She had been admirably free from defensive inclinations during the conversation; Barton wanted to preserve that aspect of their rapport. He shifted to a few other subjects, then was gone from her office before 2 p.m.

Tuesday, April 24, 1:43 p.m. . . .

Barton was annoyed. He sat across a conference room table from Carlton Leopold, the NetiFects manager for the IVK account. To one side of Leopold sat Ash Srinivasa, the technical lead on the IR project. Barton kept trying to talk to Srinivasa, and Leopold kept answering. It was pretty clear that, by prior arrangement, Srinivasa was keeping his mouth shut, which was exactly what Barton did *not* want.

Barton was trying to get them to admit the project was going sideways, because once that was out on the table they had a chance at formulating a recovery plan. He could see in Srinivasa's eyes that he agreed. Barton had also asked some questions about the technology platform, and whether it was such a good idea that IVK switch to an entirely new (to IVK) set of technologies. Srinivasa appeared eager to answer these questions too, but Leopold refused to admit that things were going badly, and the conversation never, in Barton's view, veered toward productivity.

"I think we are on track," Leopold said. "If you'd like we can schedule a time for a full presentation of our progress. Would some afternoon this week work on your schedule? We'd probably need two to three hours to do the job properly."

Since the day Barton had been appointed CIO, NetiFects—specifically, Leopold—had been trying to get a three-hour block of time on his calendar. Barton had no intention of acceding to this request, as he was certain the plan was to hit him with a full-blown marketing pitch. NetiFects, or Leopold anyway, had clearly decided that their best chance of impressing the new CIO was to set out their case in full. Barton wondered too if they'd decided they could snow the new guy since, as everybody knew, he wasn't a techie. In the comfortable context of their PowerPoint presentations, Leopold would be able to dazzle Barton with technological bullshit. Or, anyway, that would be the idea.

In honest moments, listening to Leopold go on and on, Barton admitted to himself that he just didn't like the guy. He reminded Barton of the worst kind of biz-dev con artist, the big talker, the kind it took you many precious hours to figure out was clueless.

Finally, Barton gave up. He recalled, suddenly, another meeting he was late for and excused himself, promising to set up a three-hour appointment if Leopold would only call his assistant. The first thing Barton did upon leaving the meeting: walk to Jenny's desk and tell her that under no circumstances should she schedule a meeting with Leopold.

He did it just in time. Before Barton left her desk, Leopold had called to request the meeting. Jenny deftly dodged the request, saying she'd need to speak with Barton and that Leopold should call back in a few days. As much as he disliked the guy, Barton had to hand it to Leopold; he was certainly prepared. He had located Jenny's number and called her from his cell phone before he'd even left the IVK conference room.

.

Friday, April 27, 10:32 a.m. . . . .

"I'm thinking of firing NetiFects," said Barton.

Bernie Ruben, who had been about to head off to a meeting, froze in his tracks and dropped back down into his chair. Barton had wandered into Ruben's office without warning, caught him just as he was due at a meeting of his group. The two had been making arrangements for Barton to return later when Ruben asked for a preview of the subject of the conversation.

"Maybe we'd better talk now," said Ruben.

"Okay."

"What's the rationale?" asked Ruben.

"The project is going nowhere. It needs a shakeup. They seem to me to be mostly collecting their fees and working on things we wouldn't need if we had a vendor with different technology expertise." Barton sat down too.

"All true," acknowledged Ruben. "But you'd have to pay a ransom to get free of the project. I'm sure there's a termination fee."

"I figure they'll try to get us to pay another million or so. I might refuse."

"Hardball."

"If they try to get tough back, I'll claim they haven't delivered value. Maybe some of their other clients would be interested in what I mean by that."

Ruben nodded. "Are you sure firing NetiFects is your decision to make?"

On Thursday, Barton had spent some time with Jay Palmer and floated the idea. Palmer had seemed relieved that someone else might be willing to take the initiative on the project. He clearly had no deep affection for NetiFects, at least none that got in the way of his relief. *Undoubtedly*, thought Barton, *he's met Leopold*.

"Palmer won't make a fuss. He'll be happy to get out of the line of fire."

"You'd be stepping into the line of fire in his place."

Barton nodded.

"Just as well that someone take over from Palmer, though," said Ruben. "He's moved on to other things. His head's not really in it."

"He told me yesterday he's thinking of taking some time off to do a long executive program at a business school. Said he'd already talked to Carl about it."

"Figures," said Ruben. "He hasn't been fully with us since the BtJ deal."

"I think," said Barton, "that IT should now take over the IR project."

"Risky," said Ruben, "It's a big project. Complicated. Good chance of failure—or perceived failure—no matter how well it's managed."

Barton nodded again.

"It'll set the timetable back. You'll have to go back to vendor selection. Members of the current project team will see it as disregard for the work they've already done. But it *is* decisive action. Might have the shakeup effect you're looking for. Who in IT?"

"I was thinking you or Tyra should take charge of it."

"Tyra would be ideal," said Ruben.

Barton grinned. "Under IT guidance, with business involvement, we can make sure the hard work of dividing the project into smaller projects gets done. I'm not criticizing the work already completed, not by our people anyway, just acknowledging the difficulty of the task and the need for a careful approach. But I have no intention of signing off on a huge dollar amount. We're going to do this thing in smaller pieces."

"That *is* hard work," said Ruben. "And many of the software packages we've been looking at aren't very modular. The software vendors don't like that question: 'Can we implement in pieces?' They prefer the all-at-once approach."

"That way, they get paid more sooner."

"Yes, but also because they understand better how to install the software in the way they've most often installed it. You know, NetiFects is a pretty good firm, on the whole. There is the technology platform issue, but you might find you don't like the alternative firms a lot better. They all come with baggage and complications. The references we collected on NetiFects were very good. Their tech lead, Ash Srinivasa, is very, very good."

Barton felt doubt seeping into his psyche. But he pushed it back, hard. "The bottom line for me," said Barton, "is we've paid them over $3 million, and we've got little to show for it yet."

"They'd say this was partly our fault. I'd probably agree."

"Nevertheless, it's *their* problem as our vendor. And what we're doing now isn't working." Barton stood. "I'm going to let you get to your meeting."

"Do you need anything from me as you consider this decision?" asked Ruben.

"You just gave it to me. I wanted to bounce this off of you, get your reaction."

"You've got it."

"Thanks," said Barton.

Tuesday, May 1, 2:16 p.m. . . .

"I've decided," Barton said, providing his update on the IR project to Carl Williams and the rest of the leadership team, "to fire our systems integrator." Williams looked surprised but vaguely pleased, Barton thought. Most of the others around the table were not surprised. Palmer had already mentioned it to a couple of them, and the news had traveled. Barton didn't mind. It was not his intention to surprise them.

He explained that there might be some cost to extracting IVK from the relationship with NetiFects, and that the timetable for the project would need to be revisited. Williams did not object. "But," said Barton, "we will not be paying even one more hefty retainer, and I'll put a stop to billable work right away. There will be no more '$3 million and no results to show for it.'"

Williams smiled. The others nodded in agreement. *That guy is a damn good manager*, Barton thought their expressions seemed to say.

"What's next on the agenda?" Williams asked.

REFLECTION

What root causes lead to the need for a major infrastructure replacement project?

What makes such projects so difficult?

Do you agree with Barton's decision to terminate the agreement with NetiFects?

Can projects like the IR project be avoided?

Excerpt from Consultant's Report

The immediate need to begin redesigning middle and back-end systems was apparent in many ways during our assessment. Many business and IT staff members stated their conviction that this must be done soon. Some of the reasons to initiate this project include:

1. The large and increasing number of "kludges" in the current middle and back-end systems necessary to support diversification of product types and client services creates increasing risks of service outages as the complexity of these "duct tape and bailing wire" schemes grows.

2. Integration between middle and back-end systems is not sufficient; in particular, financial systems are not well integrated with loan systems, which results in inadequate financial controls and vulnerability to internal security threats.

3. Data structures and lack of real-time functionality in middle and back-end systems inadequately support flexible pricing, reporting, and the need for management metrics (e.g., queue management in credit decisions, marketing analysis by product). The problem will grow worse as the company's need for such reports and metrics grows.

4. These middle and back-end systems are inferior in important ways to those of competitors; an absence of imaging capability is one important shortcoming of systems relative to competitors. Such shortcomings seem inconsistent with IVK's strategy, which proposes outcompeting rivals by having superior capabilities that result from the company's focus on particular market segments.

This project is not something that can be delegated to the IT department. The project's impact on the business will be such that business people must take a lead role. We suggest that you take four to six key business people representing the major business areas at IVK, team them with an equal number of senior IT staff, and make this project their primary responsibility. These should be people you can't imagine taking out of their current roles in the organization. You will need to rely on others within the business areas to step up into important business roles. Resist the urge to return these people to their non-project-related roles to deal with short-term crises. External consultants will probably also be needed as members of your team, to provide expertise and additional resources during implementation.

Within this team, make sure responsibilities for project tasks are shared. Business staff should share responsibility for technical tasks, and technical staff should do the same for business tasks. Assign some business tasks to IT staff members and some technical tasks to business staff members. By the end of this project, the business people will have received a formidable technical education, and the IT people will similarly have a much deeper appreciation of business issues. If other such projects we have seen are any guide, this project will be an important professional development experience for project team members; the understanding of the business and its IT systems that staff members will gain on this project will continue to be valuable to the company for many years.

We attach to this report a Harvard Business School case on a major systems replacement project at Cisco Systems, which was done at a time when that company was growing very rapidly.[a] Many of the actions Cisco took to assure the success of its project should be adopted by IVK. Specifically, success factors at Cisco included:

- Assigning best people to the project ("If they're easy to give up, they're the wrong people.")

- Business people involved, not just IT

- Top management attention and commitment (successful project completion was one of the CEO's top seven objectives for the year; all executive bonuses depended on successful project completion)

- Iterative, adaptive approach that recognized the importance of developing prototypes or else manually walking through how the system would work in great detail, to discover problems that could not be foreseen any other way, and to make midcourse adjustments

- Minimizing the changes to purchased packages where possible

- Speedy implementation (the project was not "career diverting" for business staff)

- Strong vendor relationships

- Project steering committee that also included senior executive members from vendors; excellent high-level business contacts between Cisco and vendor executives

This project will be difficult, and you will need to plan to make changes and adjustments throughout its life span. It probably cannot be completed before your peak volume period next year, so you will have to simultaneously take actions to limp through another high-growth year before this new infrastructure is in place. We believe the time to begin this project is now; it will be difficult now, but it might be impossible later. You may get through one more year with the current systems, but we do not think you will make it through two more years.

a. Robert D. Austin, Richard L. Nolan, and Mark Cotteleer, "Cisco Systems, Inc.: Implementing ERP," Harvard Business School Case no. 699-022 (Boston: Harvard Business School Publishing, 2002).

CHAPTER EIGHT

IT PRIORITIES

Once again, Barton found himself in a seemingly interminable meeting with Gary Geisler. But he had only himself to blame. The most recent leadership team meeting had included a discussion of the company's approach to allocating resources and maximizing return. Each department, the team had decided, would assess its current approach to resource allocation and propose improvements to increase return on investment. In IT, this meant understanding and improving processes for figuring out which projects deserved investment—which required that Barton again dive into the numbers with Geisler.

But Barton had something else on his mind as the meeting began. He'd just come from lunch with Paul Fenton, whose large and important Infrastructure and Operations domain included IT security. Fenton had mentioned a concern that the notorious John Cho had expressed.

"I hate to bring this back up," Fenton said, "but Cho is pretty concerned about it. He's seen some unusual activity on the IDS logs. I don't want to be unduly alarmist. John thinks it's most likely nothing important."

"Can't he tell for sure?" Fenton acted as if Barton knew about this issue already, but he didn't remember discussing it.

Fenton sighed, shook his head. "It's not that easy. You're looking at huge streams of transaction data and trying to notice systematic irregularities.

Most things that you see, that set off intrusion detection alarms, turn out to be false alarms. Perfectly normal, explainable activity that we are seeing for the first time in the immense complexity of packet flows around the network. A misconfigured router, or one that has a slight but functionally inconsequential problem arising from the manufacturer's design, can generate what might look like odd traffic patterns until you understand it. And there's a lot more of that kind of thing going on than we have time to explain. You get a feel for it, what to worry about. Cho's the guy on this; he's got the radar."

"So he *doesn't* think something bad is happening? Or he *does*?"

"He thinks it's unlikely, but possible."

"If it's happening, what's happening?"

"An intrusion, maybe. Someone wandering around in our data that's supposed to be secure. Possibly customer data."

"That would be bad," said Barton. "What can we do?"

Fenton seemed hesitant. "That's why I said I hated to bring it up again. We can close those security holes Cho is most worried about with an upgrade project."

"Why don't we close all the security holes?"

Fenton smiled patiently. "It's not possible to be sure that you have no security weaknesses. Or, rather, it would require an infinite amount of expenditure. So we target the high-likelihood or high-consequence holes first, and work our way down the list."

"Sounds reasonable. So let's do this one."

"That's just it," said Fenton, "we've tried to get it funded twice now, without success. Cho and I were talking this morning and thought maybe you should decide whether you want to take action on it. As the new CIO. Davies never could make much headway."

"Why not?"

Fenton looked uncomfortable. "I'm not sure," he said. Barton thought he was leaving something unsaid. Maybe he didn't want to say anything bad about Davies.

"Who would know?"

"Geisler probably has the most complete picture."

"I'm meeting with him after lunch. I'll take it up with him. Dovetails with some work we're doing in the leadership team meetings, actually."

That's where that conversation ended, although the lunch went on for a few more minutes. Fenton was proving to be a very solid manager in his deeply technical area.

Later, in the meeting with Geisler, Barton started their conversation with Fenton's security issue.

"What can we do about this?" Barton asked Geisler. "If Cho and Fenton are worried, I'd like to get this project done."

Now Geisler looked uncomfortable. What was going on? Nevertheless, Geisler had a suggestion.

"We could go to the slush fund for it," he said.

"Slush fund?" asked Barton, not smiling.

Geisler stumbled forward: "We have a few slush funds. For when we can't get important projects approved. Accounting lets us bill back operating expenses, but when it comes to incremental, project-based stuff that we need to do within IT, we have to figure out a way to sneak that into the overhead chargeback. It's not a lot of money. We like to keep it in reserve for crises, but there might be enough to make some progress on Cho's project."

"Why can't we get our projects through the same decision processes we use for business unit projects?"

"We can, sometimes, but we have trouble getting some projects approved. Especially the deeply technical ones that don't provide direct customer benefits. Cho's project is a preventive maintenance thing, as I understand it. No direct benefit, just prevention of future, hypothetical harm. It was in the proposed project list; it just didn't get funding."

"That sounds nuts," offered Barton. "Didn't they understand what was at stake?"

Geisler looked down at his binder, tabbed it open to a particular section then traced down the page with his forefinger. "Okay, here we go. Here it is. 'Network consolidation.' Back a couple of years, when we merged with People's, we kind of just 'glued' their network to ours. They used a different technology, and we could get the two to interoperate, but maintaining both—as I understand it—exposes us to additional risks. We put this project through the general project-approval process for two years in a row, and each time it got killed."

"So somebody thought doing this was not as important as the things that we did fund?" asked Barton. He often attended the last round of those prioritization meetings, and he recalled being impatient with the number of projects that seemed to be about technology for technology's sake.

"That's one interpretation," said Geisler. "But I think Davies, and especially John Cho—you know John, right?"

"Purple hair, skull T-shirts, security guy, yes."

"Right—well, John thinks there's a security hole in the technology that People's was using, so he's worried about it. But it's more a professional opinion than a specific threat that we're able to anticipate right now. So the project aimed at plugging this hole keeps losing out when we take it through the usual process."

"That's nonsense," said Barton. "If there's a security risk, we ought to be able to get it funded. Did Davies present it? I might have been at the meeting."

Barton thought Geisler grew pale: "Davies presented it. He laid out the argument, as John prepared it, but it was technical and didn't go over very well. Security is a pretty technical area."

"Did he make it clear that not doing the project put the company at risk?"

Geisler was definitely looking piqued. He squirmed: "Yes, we thought he'd said that. Those of us who were there from IT."

"We shouldn't have to use slush funds or play budget games to get a security risk addressed," opined Barton. "In the future I'd like to take these kinds of projects right into the process, state the case justifying them clearly and forcefully, and face down anybody who refuses to see reality."

Geisler nodded weakly.

"So what happened to this project?" asked Barton

"Which time?"

"I don't care," said Barton, yielding to anger. "The last time."

"Well. The project had vocal and influential detractors. Another project with a favorable and more certain customer impact got funded instead. That's what it came down to."

"Who argued against this project? It just seems like common sense to me."

Geisler said nothing. Barton waited, stern-faced.

"Well," Geisler said, indignation slipping into his voice, "as I remember it . . . *you* were the biggest critic of this project. One of your Loan Operations projects was funded instead."

Barton contemplated this. He had no specific memory of the meeting, but he had often complained about the way IT presented its project proposals.

"What did I say?" Barton asked.

"You were displeased with the technical nature of the explanation. You said they should come back when they could speak English. As I recall it, the phrase you used to start the discussion of the project, right after they'd presented their case was: 'Habla inglés?' It got a big laugh, and we all knew then the project was toast."

Barton remembered. He and other business unit managers had laughed about that line for days. Davies had flushed bright red and said very little else in the meeting after that. Now Geisler's recounting of the events on that day made Barton's own face warm. It was an unaccustomed feeling for a person usually confident of being right about most things. Embarrassment rarely penetrated Barton's self-assurance.

Geisler sat silently, carefully directing his line of sight into a corner of the room, curling his legs together around a metal leg of the chair in which he sat.

"Well," said Barton, recovering weakly, "that was unfair of me."

"Cho thought so. He almost left the company."

"Oh," Barton said. "I didn't know."

Geisler didn't answer but raised his eyebrows as if to say "No kidding." Barton suddenly realized just how diplomatic Fenton had been in their conversation about Cho's security concerns.

"I'm guessing," said Barton, "that I'm probably not John Cho's favorite person."

Geisler snorted: "You *could* say that."

The choice of new CIO at IVK would not have been good news to Cho. Barton would need to follow up on this. The company needed John Cho. Yet another reason why this upgrade project would *have* to be approved this time around.

"Anyway," Barton said, pulling himself together, regaining command, "we may need to change some of the way we're doing things around here. Maybe we need to get better at presenting our cases to justify IT projects."

"Maybe," admitted Geisler.

"Two objectives," said Barton, resolutely. "First, I want to find a way to fund this—an aboveboard way, not involving slush funds. Second, I want us to review the process we use to decide how to allocate out IT budget dollars, how we decide what priorities to fund. And, as this situation demonstrates, we need to improve the process. I want your recommendations. I'll send out an e-mail to my direct reports too, asking for their thoughts."

Geisler was assiduously taking notes. Barton thought about asking Geisler to prepare a short write-up on what had gone wrong with this particular infrastructure upgrade project, to use as a basis for getting recommendations back from his IT managers. They would, Barton suspected, provide richer advice in reaction to this case than to the idea in the abstract; and the example offered Barton the opportunity to demonstrate leadership. He'd admit that he'd been wrong when he'd killed the project as head of Loan Operations.

It was a great idea, except for one thing: This was about security. If something security-related ever happened, it might not be a great idea to have evidence of dysfunctional past processes laying around, just waiting to be discovered by plaintiffs' lawyers in shareholder lawsuits. Given the problems of the past few months involving the last CEO at IVK, shareholder lawsuits were no longer an entirely distant issue. For now, discussion of this particular security project would have to remain mostly spoken, not written down.

Friday, May 4, 7:35 p.m. . . .

Barton took another bite of his *salade aux foies de volailles* and sipped the full-bodied, slightly bitter California red that the waiter had recommended. The combination of flavors added to his general sense of well-being. Maggie, sitting across from him, was savoring a portobello mushroom appetizer. Having her in town for the weekend put Barton in a positive frame of mind, and the food and drink were fabulous, but it was not just these things that pleased him. The week had gone well. He'd been CIO for over a month, and the wheels had not yet fallen off. Also, he thought he'd reached an important decision. He broke one of his long-standing agreements with Maggie—not to talk about work on Friday night—because he wanted to get her thoughts on a decision he was near making.

"I've decided to ask Carl for control of the entire IT budget. Right now, IT controls none of the budget; it's all at the discretion of the business units. This has been causing problems. We've neglected important infrastructure investments. I've got a business background. I can see things from both sides of the fence. I'll make IT investment decisions in full collaboration with the business units, but I want control. I want the final say."

Maggie's pause before answering told him that she had noted the breach of their no-talking-about-work policy. But she could see that it was important to him.

"Will the others go along?"

"I think I can convince Carl, and if he buys in, so will the other members of the leadership team."

"Will they really buy in, or will they just shut up because Carl agrees?"

"Some of both. But if I have control of the budget, I can fix some of the problems with the priority setting, and I can keep the IT staff from getting jerked around when priorities change for bad reasons. Right now, some of my guys get their priorities rearranged pretty much weekly, if not more often. They can't get anything done. It's just thrashing. One week Project A is urgent, the next week it's Project G. It needs a steady hand."

Maggie considered it. "You might be right. Do you see this as a permanent arrangement or a transitional one?"

Barton hadn't really thought about that. He'd conceived the idea of taking over the IT budget as a way of fixing the immediate problems with prioritization, like the problem Fenton and Cho had surfaced. Barton wanted to protect the integrity of the process from the influence of the kind of problem that he had caused when he'd been head of Loan Operations. He had to admit, too, that he wanted to demonstrate, mainly to John Cho but also to others, a willingness to reverse himself, to do the right thing. Barton explained all this to Maggie.

"So this is personal. You're righting past wrongs."

"I'm not sure that's the main thing. I'm pretty worried about the security risk Cho has identified. But yes, I suppose so. In my opinion, my past actions in this matter hurt the company, and I'd like to remedy that. Besides that, I was a jerk. I'm just sorry Davies isn't around anymore to hear my apology."

"There are definite downsides to the action you're proposing. Have you thought those through?"

Barton smiled. "I think I have, but that's why I'm talking to you about it. What don't *you* like about the idea, Maggie?"

Just then the waiter arrived with their main courses. Barton polished off his salad and set the plate to one side so that the waiter could place before him an elegant variation on the traditional *steak au poivre*. Maggie had chosen roasted hen, which also looked really good. Barton stuck with his red wine, but Maggie chose a new white to go with her dish. By the time all was settled, Barton couldn't remember what he'd asked Maggie. Fortunately for him, she had not forgotten.

"There's not one best way," she began, between initial bites, at first confusing Barton, who did not realize she was back on the subject of IT priorities, "but what you are proposing runs counter to advice I sometimes give. I can think of objections on a number of levels, but the first has to do with what I like to call the 'one-neck-in-the-noose' problem."

Barton laughed, almost choking. "What's that you call it?"

Maggie didn't laugh. "One neck in the noose," she repeated. "Here's the argument: To do a good job in IT, you need help from people in the business units. They're the ones who know best how they want to do things, how processes should work, what risks and reward trade-offs they're willing to make. Ideally, you'd like them to work conscientiously until they've understood all the alternatives, all the pluses and minuses—then you could all come to agreement about what positions you're taking. Which risks you've agreed to accept, and which ones you've decided to mitigate. In the example of your John Cho problem, this hasn't happened. Ironically, in this case *you* were the one, in your role as head of Loan Ops, who didn't do the conscientious work to understand the trade-offs. But it could have been anyone. Organizations and managers are imperfect, and IT trade-off decisions can be very hard to understand. So getting everybody to understand and agree is usually an aspiration, an ideal, not always realizable in practical reality."

"So far," said Barton, "you're making the case in favor of my decision to take over control of the IT budget. I can conscientiously represent the business *and* IT point of view."

"Except for one thing. If you get people to understand the trade-offs and participate in decisions, then something goes wrong—say a risk you all decided to live with generates some serious consequences—then you are all in it together. You all decided. You took your chances, placed your bets, and you lost. That hurts, but it hurts you all together. Everyone had his or her neck in the noose and everyone can feel it tightening.

"You take over the IT budget, though, and you're effectively letting them take their necks out. *You're* the one who makes the trade-off decisions. When something goes wrong, *you'll* be the one who feels the noose tightening. You alone. They may feel something, but their reaction to their own pain will probably be to turn around and tighten the noose around your neck."

Barton considered this. Maggie was right, he thought, and it annoyed him. Up to a point. "But if the alternative is not realizable," he asked, "is it a real alternative?"

She shrugged. "Maybe not. I've seen it work fairly well and, more often, very badly. Probably depends on your assessment of what's possible within IVK."

"So what would the alternative look like? Can you tell me what you've seen other places?"

"I read somewhere about a system they were putting in place at a car company. Volkswagen of America, I think. Have your guy—what's his name, Geisler?—Have him look it up for you. He'll find it if he searches for 'Volkswagen America IT priorities.'[1] But they didn't have everything working right either. As I remember the story, they put this very careful and logical system in place, and then everyone complained about the investment decisions that resulted."

"So, what, they set up some sort of a committee-based process?"

"Yes, I think that's basically it. IT facilitates the process, but the business units decide the priorities. It's a consensus process. Even if you don't love the outcome, you agree to stand by the results. All necks in the noose."

"Business units control all of IT spending?"

"Actually, no. I think in the Volkswagen system, IT retained some portion of budget on their own discretion."

"That in itself would help matters."

"So maybe that's a less radical fix to the current problem. The simplest summary I know of how this ought to work, in theory, is by a bunch of business school professors. They argue that priority-setting processes ought to have three basic characteristics.

"First, the process ought to be *owned* by the business units, not the IT department. Each business unit contributes a representative who has decision-making authority. That at least starts to solve the necks-in-the-noose problem. It keeps the IT department and the CIO from being held solely responsible for outcomes that IT can't fully bring about or prevent from happening. It matters a lot to the behavior of managers in business units if they know their own necks are in the noose. You take a very different attitude toward solving problems when your neck is in there too.

"Second, the process ought to exhibit *extreme transparency of process* and *exaggerated visibility of decision consequences*. The people in the business units ought to be able to look into the process and see clearly how it works, how decisions are arrived at. By implication, I guess, they need to think it looks like a process that makes sense. It probably means it has to be a reasonably simple process, and there can't be any steps where it disappears mysteriously into the IT department. No black boxes. The related idea, exaggerated visibility of decision consequences, means that you go out of your way to make it clear when decisions have been made and what decisions have been made, and the resource implications of those decisions. If you've agreed to move Susie to Project G from Project A, maybe you move a Post-it note on a wall from one box to another. Things like that make it impossible for anyone to credibly claim that they were not aware of a trade-off decision. People can't selectively, conveniently, or politically remember only what helps their own projects. You know the problem: 'I don't remember agreeing that we would not work on Project A . . .' and so on. The ideal here would be to put all your current-state resource allocations up on a giant wall chart that everyone can understand. Everyone can see all the time what everyone has agreed to. There it is, just look, right on the wall. Of course this gets a little complicated in larger companies with multiple locations.

"Third—and this is really just a way of addressing the primary issue you've been raising, of meeting it head-on—the participants in the process agree and are reminded to maintain some degree of *continuity and within-project focus*, to prevent thrashing. Every time the group is tempted to shift people or money resources around to deal with the crisis du jour, they formally weigh the losses due to switching, and from taking the resource off the project you are deciding to give less precedence to."

Maggie fell silent and Barton let the silence remain. Now he was actually angry. She was talking sense, he knew that, but it unsettled his confidence in a decision he'd pretty much already made. And it all sounded so . . . idealized. A bunch of business school professors, ivory-tower types. Geez. And Maggie, as crazy about her as he was, well, she was a *consultant*. Not the same thing as a line manager in a real company. Not at all.

Barton took another bite of his steak and changed the subject. He didn't want his inner seething to ruin the rest of their evening. There was good reason for the policy that ruled out talking shop on Friday nights, which they both inevitably realized every time they violated it.

Tuesday, May 8, 10:05 a.m. . . .

Geisler stuck his head in the doorway of Barton's office and said, "Found something on the Volkswagen of America system for managing priorities."

Barton waved him into the room. "Give me the short version."

"It's pretty interesting," said Geisler. "An annual three-step process, involves reps from all the business units in big workshops over a period of a couple of months. The overall objective is to align IT spending with the company's strategy."

"Does it work?"

"Unclear. It seems really logical and reasonable, but there are lots of complaints about it, mostly from people whose projects haven't been funded. Worth looking at in detail, though, as a possible model to play around with."

"Do you think their experiences are a good analogy to ours? Should we model ourselves on an auto company?"

"Good question. They aren't really an auto company, more a car-importing sales and marketing company. They don't do manufacturing; they leave that to VW AG, the parent company. But they do have some unique things going on. A lot of outsourcing of IT in their history, a lot of new programs, a severely constrained IT budget."

"Their process is an annual one?"

"Yes, seems to be. Must include some sort of ongoing element to address when priorities shift during the year, but we don't have much info on that."

"Does it help them align IT activity and investment with strategy?"

"I think it might. One of the most interesting things about it is the categories they use for projects. They categorize projects a few ways. In terms of how they justify the investment, for example, they use three categories. One is what we'd call 'mandatory,' meaning we have to do it because of legislation or something. Though they seem to make use of this category for infrastructure upgrades the CIO thinks are really important, things like our John Cho issue."

"So the CIO has some discretionary budget."

"In effect. The business units decide most priorities, but there's definitely a category of projects, a pool of funds, that the CIO controls. Labeled mandatory, maybe not quite accurately."

"Maybe that's the deal they strike with the devil to get some discretionary budget for the IT department. Maybe inaccurate, but maybe also very practical."

Here, again, was the alternative that Maggie had suggested. Rather than ask them for total control of the IT budget, he could just ask for total control of a portion of it, and leave the rest to the current, though likely to be modified, process.

Geisler was speaking again: "Their other categories, one of them is just ROI—projects that have high ROI. But they also have a category they call 'option-creating investment,' which I find pretty interesting. OCI projects are those that don't necessarily have high ROI, because some of the benefits are too speculative or too much in the future. But OCI investments create possibilities for future beneficial projects. Having this category seems to imply that if you just use mandatory and ROI, you won't fund big-picture 'vision' projects."

"I think that's true," said Barton. "Most good executives would agree, in my opinion. You want to know the ROI. You want to see the calculation. But it's not the only factor in how you should decide what to invest in. 'It's the way we want to do business' is a pretty good reason sometimes."

"Yes, well you'll like some other stuff I found too, then," continued Geisler. "I also encountered a lot of material on a related problem in product development, about what they call 'aggregate project planning.'* We'd call it something more like 'application portfolio management.' Same thing, though. Turns out that it's pretty well accepted in product development circles that if you use only ROI types of project justification to decide where to invest, you'll end up mostly doing incremental extensions to existing products, never going for breakthroughs or investments in new categories. One thing I read described how a review of the project portfolio at one company, whose stated strategy was to always be the product technology leader, revealed that it had not invested in a project with potential to lead in product technology in over three years. Its investments in product development had drifted out of sync with its intended strategy. I thought that seemed pretty similar to what IT gets accused of all the time."

Barton nodded. "So the Volkswagen of America process takes a look at what they are spending in each category and asks a high-level question: Is this well aligned with our stated strategy?"

"Well, it's not as explicit as that in the account I read, but it would allow them to do that."

"That would give you a check on whether your process, working through the details, has somehow, for some reason, drifted off course."

"A nice feature."

"You've got some stuff for me to read?"

---

*See "Excerpts from materials on prioritization of R&D (not IT) projects" at the end of this chapter.

Geisler handed over a thin sheaf of papers. "I tried to limit it to just the best stuff."

"Thanks. Let's talk more about this later, after I've had a chance to digest it. I'm thinking about proposing some changes soon. We'll have to hammer those out."

As Geisler exited, Barton reached for his green pen and went to the whiteboard. He made a note: "IT spending should be aligned with IVK strategy." He followed this statement with Geisler's priority categories: "Mandatory (i.e., security)," "ROI (incremental)," and "OCI (breakthrough)."

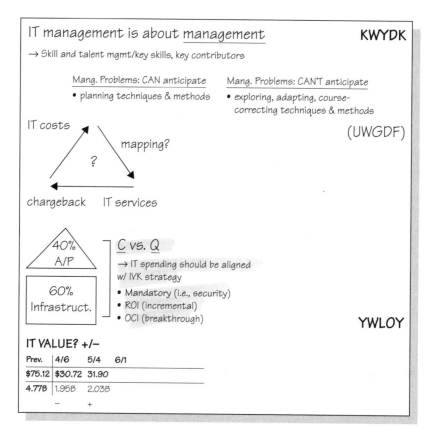

Barton paced around his office a few times, then sat. He grabbed a blank notepad on his desk and sketched out what he now thought were three alternative proposals he could make to the leadership team.

1. He could propose that he take over the entire IT budget. Williams would go for this, he thought. Barton was well positioned to represent the interests of both the business and the IT department. Also, having declared Barton the fixer, Williams would be inclined to give him plenty of rope to do the fixing. But that rope could also, as Maggie had suggested, become a noose with only his neck in it.

2. He could propose that before any of the prioritizing or IT resource allocation take place that he get a percentage of the IT budget—exactly *what* percentage could be discussed—to keep under his discretion. This might avoid some of the problems Maggie described, but it struck Barton as sort of an incremental solution, a more timid move.

3. He could try to fix the current committee-based system. This would be in keeping with the theoretical ideal that Maggie had described. But it also described fairly well the dysfunctional arrangement that was the status quo. If the second option was timid, this one bordered on doing nothing. Barton worried that there was insufficient splash in this option to motivate any real changes.

There was a leadership team meeting that afternoon, and on Thursday, two days later. Barton wondered when he should bring this up.

Thursday, May 10, 1:45 p.m. . . .

"I'm not so sure I like this idea," said Niels Hansen, the new head of Loan Operations. Barton had just made his case: he wanted complete control of the IT budget. Despite Maggie's concerns, despite the risks, which he fully acknowledged, Barton wanted to move fast. The pivotal issue, the thing that decided it for Barton: the urgency of the network consolidation project. Security was nothing to mess around with. With control of the budget he could begin Cho's upgrade immediately.

As he explained to his peers and Carl Williams, this would be only temporary—to get some things done quickly. Later, he'd propose a better and more inclusive framework for investment decisions and bring it back to them for discussion. But at the moment, he was asking for total control. Some of his peers didn't like it, but Barton was watching Williams, who was buying it. Barton would get what he wanted, for better or worse . . .

REFLECTION

What processes need to be in place to effectively establish IT project priorities?

Is assigning control of IT budgets to user departments an effective mechanism to establish IT priorities? Who should control the IT budget?

Given his disagreement with Maggie and his peers, do you think Barton is wise to ask for IT budget control? What consequences (positive or negative) do you foresee?

Excerpts from Materials on Prioritization of R&D (Not IT) Projects

Step 1: Strategic Goals & Objectives

- The R&D portfolio–creation process must start with a clear articulation of the company's overall strategy:

  - What customer/market segments?

  - What distinctive advantage are you seeking in your products or services?

- The strategy should also inform you about the overall investments in R&D:

  - R&D investment is set as a percentage of sales

  - Amount varies by industry and by market goals of firm

Step 2: Classification of Project Types

- There are different types of projects, for example:

  - Major breakthrough

  - New product or service line

  - Refinement/enhancement of an existing product or service

- Classification allows you to think about your project opportunities in a strategic manner

Step 3: Create an Aggregate Project Plan

- Using your *strategy* as a guide, determine the percentage of resources to allocate across project types:

  - Breakthroughs: _____%

  - Platforms: _____%

  - Derivatives: _____%

- Given your total R&D budget, estimate the *maximum number of projects* you can undertake within each category:

  - Need to have a handle on resource requirements for *each type of project*

Step 4: Commit to Specific Projects

- Compare project proposals *within* categories—not across:

  - Platform ideas compete with other platforms

  - Derivative project ideas compete with other derivatives

- Use different criteria across categories:

  - Derivative: ROI or NPV

  - Platform: impact on future options in the market

  - Breakthrough: longer term capabilities/options

- Senior management's job is to actively manage the process:

  - Shape the menu of choices, don't just passively select what's presented

Source: These notes are adapted from teaching case files in the Technology and Operations Management department at Harvard Business School, and adapted from the original material in *Revolutionizing Product Development: Quantum Leaps in Speed, Efficiency, and Quality,* by Stephen C. Wheelwright and Kim B. Clark (New York: The Free Press, 1992).

CHAPTER NINE

⊃ THE BOARD
⊃IRECTORS

ı ıu ʜoᴛ ···· ᴼʳder we've got these in," said Raj Juvvani. "Maybe we should list 'Underinvestment in IT' first. That way we hit them with the biggest, most important thing at the outset."

"I disagree," said Tyra Gordon. "That'd be like starting by accusing *them* of causing IT difficulties—it's their fault because we haven't spent enough."

"It kind of *is* their fault we haven't spent enough on IT," countered Juvvani.

"Yes," conceded Gordon, "but that doesn't mean we should start there. It'd be like shoving a tin cup under their noses in our first moments with them."

Juvvani considered this. "Maybe you're right," he said.

Barton had convened his direct reports to finalize the presentation to the board of directors scheduled for Thursday afternoon. Every member of this group had been involved in creating the presentation. Barton was pleased by how his team had come together. They'd achieved the quality of interaction to which Barton had aspired in that first off-site meeting in March, the one that they'd all so fiercely resisted attending without their various technical sidekicks. Now with just the five of them—

Barton, Gordon, Fenton, Juvvani, and Ruben, plus Gary Geisler—it all seemed completely natural.

They had designed a presentation in five sections:*

1. History of IT at IVK—Informal management

2. Moving to more formal management

3. Results already attained

4. Strengths and weaknesses

5. Opportunities and risks

Barton would review the slides with Carl Williams after lunch, so they were down to final touches. Williams would probably make suggestions that would send them scrambling, but Barton wasn't worried. They'd handle it. The whole thing was coming together. He'd be very surprised if Williams spotted any egregious shortcomings.

Barton's thinking had moved on, from the detailed content of Power-Point slides to the big picture, the overriding themes he wanted to emphasize during the presentation and subsequent discussion with board members. He had four issues in mind.

First, he wanted to make it clear that management of the department in the past had been too informal. This problem was common throughout the company, a consequence of rapid growth from a small firm to a large firm, a side effect of success in the marketplace. The entrepreneurial inclinations of the current set of firm managers, their tendencies to act as if the firm were much smaller, offered benefits: agility, "can-do" attitudes, and willingness to innovate, for example. But informality was also a source of risk. Big companies needed more coordination, more management systems, and—especially—more *controls* than small companies. This was particularly true in IT. Barton had begun instituting procedures, systems, and controls that would reduce risk without sacrificing agility or innovativeness. Some of these changes were simple, things no one had gotten around to in the past; based on his knowledge of Loan Ops and using his new vantage as CIO, for ex-

*See "Board of Directors Presentation" at the end of this chapter.

ample, Barton had instituted better integrated procedures between loan origination and finance, to make sure checks and fund transfers could not be initiated without proper approvals. Building those controls into IT systems, by better integrating the systems that supported each activity, would take more time, but Barton had launched an effort looking into that and other opportunities to better enforce financial procedures. He'd also ordered the implementation of an array of new metrics, each of which gave managers fresh insights into IVK operations and performance.

Second, Barton needed to convey that the IT infrastructure had not received the attention and investment it required. Since the company's revenues had leveled off in recent months and Williams had come on board as a turnaround CEO, it was inevitable that everyone would be asked to tighten belts a few notches. Barton wanted to express willingness to do what was right for the company, but also to point out that IT had some very important projects under way that could not stop on a dime without wasting the already considerable investment in them. Furthermore, it had become clear to Barton that an even bigger project was looming—the back-end infrastructure replacement—so investment would need to continue. Without new investments, the company would eventually face unacceptable levels of risk. He wanted to be sure the board understood that trade-off.

Which lead to the third major theme: governance.[1] Barton wanted the board and the senior management team of the company involved more deeply in decision making about IT matters, especially where there were opportunity and cost, or risk-reduction and cost, trade-offs. He wanted the responsibility for such trade-offs to be borne jointly by the business units and the IT department, not just left to the techies. To accomplish this, the attitude of joint responsibility had to come, Barton thought, from the very highest levels. He'd be asking the board to take greater responsibility and become more involved in IT decisions.

Finally, Barton wanted to emphasize a strategic partnership role for the IT area within IVK. He had become aware that many of his senior management colleagues would be most delighted if they never had to deal with IT—if IT would "stay in the basement where it belonged." Barton himself remembered feeling that way when he was head of Loan Ops, but this didn't keep him from being a little surprised that his peers seemed to continue to think this way even after he—obviously a business guy—took over in IT. Most managers wanted IT to listen to ideas from the business units, then go make them happen. Barton imagined a more involved role for IT—coming up with ideas, helping close sales. He wanted IT to contribute to revenue growth. IT could, he believed, be part of how the company recovered its aggressive growth trajectory. In initial conversations with some of his peers, they had resisted the idea. The sales organization in particular hated the idea of having IT participate in client meetings. Given such resistance, this role for IT also needed the active and visible support of the board of directors.

It was a lot to accomplish in one thirty-minute presentation. Barton knew getting across these themes would likely be a long-term effort, especially the last one. He had been disappointed to see, when the agenda for the board meeting had been distributed, that his presentation came at the end. If the meeting was running long, as was likely, he might have even less than thirty minutes to get his points across, so he wanted to be prepared for that possibility too.

"I think this is getting pretty good," said Ruben. He turned and spoke directly to Barton. "Do you want to keep refining, or should we get back together tomorrow, after you've spoken to Carl?"

"Or this afternoon," said Juvvani. The others all nodded. Barton smiled.

"Yes, let's call it quits for the moment. I'll let you know what Carl says, and we'll get back on this tomorrow. Keep your calendars flexible."

The feeling of confidence in the room was palpable. These managers were proud of the presentation. More important, they were proud of what it said, of the plans it expressed. Confidence was a feeling Barton had not often encountered in this team when he'd first taken over as CIO. Now that had changed, and he rather liked it.

Thursday, June 14, 4:47 p.m. . . .

"This is outstanding, just outstanding," said Francesco Carraro, an IVK board member. Barton had just completed his presentation, a compressed version because they had indeed been short of time at the end of the meeting. He looked around the room and saw signs of agreement. Sally Lee, sitting next to Carraro, was beaming and nodding. The two of them, both outside directors, tended to have a lot to say in board meetings. Lee's reputation, in particular, was enormously influential. But Carraro, as it turned out, was the most IT-savvy board member. Barton had been surprised by the extent of his past experience in IT. Carraro had served as a CIO once, and had been a COO responsible for IT in another company. When both of these people were nodding after your IT presentation, things were going well indeed. Oddly, Williams, at the far end of the conference table, wore an expression that Barton could not quite read. But there was no time to dwell on that; the questions and suggestions came rapid-fire.

Carraro went first: "I have some examples of controls, procedures, and metrics that I'd like to send to you," he said. "From the looks of what you've shown us here, they'll probably not add much. It's clear to me that you plan to go far beyond my old organization, but maybe there will be something helpful in there."

"Sounds great," said Barton. "Do you want to e-mail them to me?"

"As soon as I get back to the office," said Carraro. Barton caught a glimpse of an oddly strained look from Williams. "Let's also exchange some thoughts on how you can accomplish some of your governance objectives and get your area more focused on innovation."

"Great," said Barton, now definitely picking up a disconcerted vibe from Williams, but seeing no other appropriate response to Carraro's offer.

Carraro turned to the rest of the board: "I suggest we set up a committee at the board level that would focus on IT governance. It'll help with a lot of the objectives we've heard this afternoon. It'll also help us control the risk associated with the current state of the company's IT infrastructure. Boards can potentially face huge liabilities from lack of involvement in IT. In the future, 'I don't know much about IT,' will be no better a defense against criticism of a board of directors than 'I don't know much about accounting.'"

"Can you say more," Lee asked Barton, "about the risks related to IT?"

Barton nodded, "I'll try. It's hard to be very specific, because the risks are largely a function of the evolved complexity of the infrastructure. You can't make any system as complex as an IT infrastructure completely bulletproof, not without infinite investment. The problem is not any single factor you can easily point to, it's the emergent result of countless incremental and individually harmless decisions. Decisions to take a shortcut in how a program accesses a database, to make response time better after the customer service department hits a new peak processing week. Decisions to leave until later standardization on a particular networking technology, to glue two network segments together into a workable kludge, rather than to do the design work, buy some new equipment, and make it right. We get away with these things all the time, but over time they add up to risk."

Carraro was nodding: "Some of these things look like housekeeping items. Investments to reduce the complexity don't get made because they are hard to justify in terms of customer benefits."

"IT risk," Barton added, "is mostly invisible to managers—and board members—until the you-know-what really hits the fan."

"Which is why we need to be more involved, why we need a committee for IT oversight," said Carraro.

Barton could see, from his vantage at the front of the room, that board members who had just moments earlier followed Carraro eagerly, now seemed less certain. Probably they were imagining being asked to serve on a board-level "IT Oversight" committee. Probably they were having a reaction to that thought not unlike Barton's reaction to being chosen as the new CIO. They'd have to get over it, Barton thought, just as he had. But it might, he knew, take them a while. And Carraro, Barton could see, had overplayed his hand.

"Let's put it on the agenda for a future meeting," proposed Williams. Board members other than Carraro leapt aboard this lifeboat, nodding emphatically, glancing at watches. "We've just about run out of time here, and many people have other places they need to be."

Barton nodded and began collecting his things. Overall, the presentation had been a spectacular success. *I'm on a roll*, he thought to himself. *Can't wait to tell my team.*

The meeting began to break up, fragmenting into separate conversations. Some people left right away, rushing off to other engagements. Carraro stopped to shake Barton's hand before he departed. In the course of a brief chat, Carraro proposed that the two of them should have lunch sometime, an idea Barton quite liked. They parted company after agreeing to exchange e-mail on several more subjects. Barton had not counted on having such a strong ally on the board, but he could see only good in it.

Moments later, as Barton turned to leave the room, Carl Williams stepped away from a conversation he was in to whisper: "Great job. Stop by my office before you leave today, I want to talk briefly." Barton nodded, and Williams ducked back into the conversation he'd been involved in before. *Hmmm,* thought Barton. *Guess we'll find out what was bothering him during the meeting.*

Williams had provided almost no feedback on the PowerPoint slides in his meeting with Barton on Tuesday afternoon. But now he was clearly stirred up about something. Barton would find out what it was soon enough.

Thursday, June 14, 5:38 p.m. . . .

Barton stuck his head through the doorway to Williams's office. "You wanted to see me, Carl?"

Williams looked up from something he'd been reading. "Yes, Jim, come in." Williams stayed in his command chair, behind the enormous desk, and motioned Barton into a chair opposite. Barton considered this odd. Williams had always used the table in the room for past conversations with Barton. Moving to the table said, "Let's talk as equals." Remaining behind the desk said, "I'm the boss and you work for me." Barton tried not to think too much into this choice, but it was hard not to notice the departure from a past norm. Maybe Carl was simply tired. A board meeting could be stressful.

"You did a great job in there," said Williams.

"Thanks, Carl. I had a lot of help getting ready, of course."

"Understood. You are happy with your team, then?"

"Yes, they're very good, actually. I had anticipated needing to replace one or two of my direct reports, maybe reorg the department. But that hasn't seemed necessary. Not yet, anyway. We have some holes and problems further down in the department, but with your help and a few key hires, we'll deal with those eventually."

"That's great," said Williams, not seeming to have even heard, transitioning to what was really on his mind: "I want to talk about how we manage Carraro."

"Manage him?" said Barton.

"Yes, he's very enthusiastic, but we need to make sure he understands that the CIO job is yours. I don't want him to complicate things for you."

"I appreciate that, Carl. I hope we can make him a supporter and ally more than someone who is inclined to interfere."

Williams nodded but frowned. Barton realized that he was not reading something going on here, something important to the CEO.

"Well, to make sure he doesn't insert himself too profoundly, I'd like you to copy me on e-mails and other conversations between the two of you. I'm sure you'd be inclined to do this anyway, but I wanted to make certain. I've turned around several firms, as you know, and my experiences have made me understand how important it is to keep a handle on relationships with the board."

Ahhh, Barton thought. *Of course. He's worried about being left out of the loop. He's worried that Carraro and I seemed to hit it off too well.* The odd looks in the meeting, they were about control of communication with the board. The presentation had gone so well that Williams was feeling threatened.

As Barton thought it through, the pieces fell into place. In the meetings to reshuffle the management team, Barton had been discussed as a possible COO. Now he was doing spectacularly well with a difficult assignment as CIO. This made him a potential rival to Williams. Barton felt that he had been dense not to see this coming.

"Carl, I'll make absolutely sure you stay briefed on every communication I have with *any* board member. If Carraro sends me something and doesn't copy you, I'll send you a copy. And if I have lunch with him—he invited me after the meeting today—I'll brief you on it right away."

"He invited you to lunch?" asked Williams. But he seemed reassured.

"Yes, but who knows if it will even happen."

"How about if we set it up through my office?"

"That'd be ideal," agreed Barton.

"We'll strategize together before, about what we want to accomplish. And we can debrief after."

"Sounds perfect, Carl."

"Great. Thanks Jim. Like I said, great job out there today."

"Thanks." Barton stood and exited, contemplating this new complexity in his management situation. He'd been so focused on the IT department that he had missed this important dynamic in his relationship with the CEO. Going forward, he'd make a point of thinking much more about his relationship with Carl Williams. It was flattering to realize that Williams considered him a rival at some level, but there was also immense danger in this fact—danger that would need Barton's attention.

REFLECTION

Why do you think the IT presentation at the board meeting was scheduled as the last agenda item and given only thirty minutes?

What are the board of directors' responsibilities in respect to IT oversight?

Why do you think they seemed eager to delay forming the IT Oversight committee until the next meeting?

What should Barton do about "managing Carraro"? Managing Williams?

How is Barton doing after almost three months as IVK's CIO? What is your assessment of his performance?

Slides for the Board of Directors Presentation

Historical Background—IT at IVK

Informal and ad hoc—Few plans, policies, procedures, controls, or metrics

- No formal IT planning or priority-setting process
- Ad hoc systems for tracking progress against plans
- Invent-as-you-go policies, even in areas such as information security (no high-level framework or review, no senior management involvement)
- No mandatory operating procedures
- Few operational metrics or standardized reporting

Underinvestment in IT

- Industry benchmark of 9% of revenue spent on IT
- IVK has spent less, sometimes much less (although current spend is roughly consistent with benchmark)
- Cumulative effect of underinvestment: pieced-together systems

IT underserving clients and business needs

- IT has been internally focused with no external client interaction
- Projects not delivered, promises not kept, delays have had customer impacts
- Historical projects on-time-delivery rate: 35–40%

Moving to More Formal Management

World-class management systems and practices

- Developing an IT planning process for aligning with and enabling business strategy
- Revisiting IT governance practices, priority setting, and project portfolio management
- Implementing metrics for managerial transparency

Linking IT to competitive advantage

- Leveraging Internet on several initiatives; many more opportunities
- Developing a platform for mining our extensive data for customer benefit
- Greater reliance on vendor platforms rather than in-house application development to reduce time-to-market

Assuring IT performance

- Building new infrastructure to ensure reliability and disaster recovery
- Implementing capacity-planning discipline to forecast and lead demand, thus supporting business growth
- Implementing a technology vendor–management process to assure that we are getting value from vendor partners

Organizing and resourcing IT for success

- Conducted staff review to identify staff capability, organizational needs, and deficits
- Considering reorganization to maximize IT's business responsiveness and impact
- Instituting procedures, better controls

Results Already Attained

Defined an IT strategy and implemented major elements

- Developed a formal IT strategy
- Implemented a new project-prioritization process
- Fired a nonperforming IT vendor

Delivered business results and earned client credibility

- Improved project on time delivery (80+% in last three months)
- Took concrete steps to improve communication and credibility with business units

Gained control and mitigated immediate risks

- Defined and implemented 25 controls, 50 tests, and 4 major operational reviews
- Achieved regulatory compliance in accordance with Sarbanes-Oxley
- Performed a penetration review with outside security experts and took several steps to mitigate security risks
- Conducting formal IT risk assessment, starting late this month

Strengths of the Current IT Organization

Alignment with organizational growth

- Playing catch-up but able to hold our own
- Will be hard to maintain without investments to follow through on current projects

Partnership with key clients

- IT systems help lock in clients and provide differentiating benefits to customers
- In some cases, IT systems capabilities have produced additional revenue streams from clients (clients willing to pay for better IT systems capability)
- Much more potential to leverage IT for growth and additional revenues

Improved delivery, reliability, security

- Project on-time delivery much improved (need to assure these results are for real)
- Availability monitored by system, average is 99+% (addressing issues with a few laggards)
- Peace of mind from security review with external experts

Weaknesses of the Current IT Organization

IVK underresourced in key areas

- Network management
- Information security
- Project management

Key systems groaning under the strain of their own evolved complexity

- Need to reengineer entire back-end infrastructure
- Key to further security risk reduction, operational complexity reduction, long-term reliability, IT agility
- Need many "care and feeding" investments with little or no direct customer impact (sometimes you have to replace the brake pads and the oil in your car)

Opportunities

Continue to align IT with board and senior management objectives

- Enable strategy, business agility
- Identify new ways of connecting with and retaining customers
- IT capability as a deal closer in acquiring new business
- Identify and/or execute acquisitions, partnerships, etc.

Streamline IT governance

- Institute concise decision-making body
- Make decisions quickly

Improve cycle time of project delivery

- Plan and execute rapidly across all functions

Consolidate control of all technology

- Reduce risk and cost
- Improve reliability

innovating business solutions

Risks

Information security risk to reputation and competitive position

- We have established formal policies, executed penetration tests, closed known "holes" in our defenses
- However, some risk remains
- Can never be completely safe (without spending an infinite amount of money)
- Most serious risks arise from antiquated, evolved infrastructure—cannot be replaced/reengineered quickly

Unforeseen disasters

- Natural disaster or human-precipitated catastrophe (e.g., 9/11)
- Building out back-up data center to maintain operations without primary business sites
- Back-up and disaster recovery infrastructure in place, but need to make a business decision about how much disruption the business can take to "practice" disaster readiness and response

PART THREE

THE HERO'S ORDEAL

CHAPTER TEN

Thursday, June 28, 9:24 a.m. . . .

Barton was enjoying an unusually slow morning, finishing an elegant breakfast at a Hilton in midtown Manhattan, when the first call indicating trouble came in.

He had come to New York for an early afternoon meeting with Wall Street analysts. That Williams had chosen him for the meeting was a sign of just how well things had been going lately for IVK—and for Jim Barton, CIO. In the past three weeks, IVK's stock price had begun to rise, lifting spirits throughout the company. Optimism percolated through the offices and hallways. At the same time, Barton had been scoring victory after victory. A recent all-hands IT department meeting had gone extremely well; he'd fielded a few tough questions, but people seemed pleased with his answers and the department's overall direction. Even John Cho had nodded in response to some of Barton's remarks. His resolute actions had also gained him the confidence of the company's senior leadership. In meetings of that group, Barton's views now swayed Williams more readily than anyone else's. And why not? This was a guy who knew the IVK business inside and out and had apparently mastered the mysterious world of IT in just three months.

Sending Barton—former Loan Ops VP, now chief IT guy—to New York on the crest of a wave of recovery, Williams had explained, sent exactly the right message. Under a new CEO, IVK had woken up to a realization of its current size and the consequent need for a new style of management. The company would *mature* into a grownup financial services firm. What had been a freewheeling, improvisational approach to management would become more professional. Without sacrificing organizational agility, the company would institute more formal systems and controls. IT was, of course, key to achieving this. An expression Williams and Barton had begun to use in conversation to describe where they were headed captured their joint vision of the future: "a lean service factory." It was only natural that Barton would explain all this to Wall Street.

He'd been sipping coffee, going over his notes, making some last-minute adjustments to the presentation for the afternoon meeting, when his cell phone rang. The phone display told him it was Bernie Ruben. Barton guessed that the call might be last-minute advice about how to tweak the analyst presentation.

He was wrong.

"Hi Bernie, what's up?"

"Hi Jim. I'm afraid we've got a problem, and we felt we should get to you with an update."

"My laptop is upstairs. Is it something I need to change in the presentation?"

"Nothing like that. We're experiencing an outage this morning, for about the last forty minutes. Customer Service is down. None of the call center systems are working, and the Web site is locked up."

"Oh. Damn. I assume we're executing recovery procedures?"

"Such as they are."

This confused Barton. He'd heard, time and time again, about the call lists and emergency procedures that assured business continuity in a crisis. "What do you mean, 'Such as they are'?"

"Sorry. That's my cynicism coming through. The fact is, those procedures are pretty badly out of date. I don't think we realized quite how out of date until thirty minutes ago."

This made Barton angry. "Wish you'd flashed that cynicism a little sooner. I've been taking everyone's word on this. I thought we were prepared for an outage."

Ruben, hearing the tone of Barton's voice, pulled back. "We're not completely unprepared, just not as prepared as we'd like to be. We've got great people on it. But the truth is that outages don't usually happen in a predictable way. Inevitably, we have to wing it a bit."

"And why are *you* calling to tell me?" Ruben's area had no operational responsibilities, thus would be involved in an outage only peripherally. Barton imagined his team voting on who the bearer of bad news would be.

"Because everybody else is kind of busy, frankly," Ruben answered. "Fenton and Cho are right in the middle of this. Ripley is at the data center, rebooting things. Juvvani and his team are trying to figure out what's wrong with the Customer Service systems."

"Cho? Do we think this might be some kind of security event?"

"I was coming to that." Ruben paused, as if to steel himself, before continuing. It was very unlike Bernie, that pause, and it communicated the gravity of the circumstances more than the words that followed it. A bolt of panic stirred the eggs Benedict digesting in Barton's stomach.

"We're receiving a continuous flow of e-mails at our Customer Service address," continued Ruben, "about three per second, each with no text in the body of the message and a one word subject line that says 'Gotcha.'"

"Gotcha?"

"Yes. It's like 'Gotcha, gotcha, gotcha, gotcha.'"

"What the hell does that mean?" Barton channeled his frustration into an exasperated hand movement, which promptly toppled his coffee cup. Hot liquid flowed from the table onto his lap.

"We don't know," said Ruben. "It could be a coincidence that Customer Service systems are down at the same time that we are receiving these e-mails, but . . ."

"But it doesn't sound coincidental, does it?" Barton stood, motioning to a waiter to indicate the spill and request his check.

"No," conceded Ruben. "This is the concern."

"Bernie, I need more information," Barton said. "I don't want to take people off their urgent duties, but at some point in the next hour or so I need a full update. Williams will get wind of this soon . . ."

"He has already . . ."

" . . . and I need to know what to tell him."

"I'll pull a group together, and we'll call you. How about 10:30?" Barton looked at his watch. It was 9:37 a.m. "Make it 10:15. There's no telling when Williams will call me. I'll hold off calling him until I hear more."

"I'm on it," said Ruben.

Barton hung up the phone. The waiter, rushing over to control the spill, also perceived the urgency of the call. He hurried the check to Barton, who quickly signed it and dashed out of the restaurant.

As Barton awaited the elevator that would take him to his floor, another call came in, this one from Graham Wells, IVK's VP of Legal Affairs and General Counsel.

"This is Jim Barton."

"Jim, we've got to reduce our legal exposure here." Wells's voice was an octave higher than usual.

"What do you mean, Graham?"

"We have to take dramatic action, signal that we've done everything we can."

"We *are* doing everything we can, Graham." The elevator arrived and Barton got on it. He pushed the button for floor 23. Two children got on too, with a woman apparently their mother. To Barton's horror, the two small boys pushed seven or eight buttons between the ground floor and floor 23 before the woman intervened. Barton immediately stepped out of the elevator, waited for the door to close, then pushed the up arrow again. All this time, Graham was speaking, not entirely coherently. Barton tuned into him again:

"Can we shut off power to the computer systems? Or cut the wires that go to the Internet?"

"We could, Graham, but I doubt that would be smart."

"Smart doesn't matter. What matters is what we can say in a deposition."

The elevator arrived, but Barton moved away from it to sit in a nearby chair.

"A deposition? What the hell are you talking about, Graham?"

"If this is a security incident," he continued, "we may be looking at legal implications. Customer lawsuits, shareholder lawsuits, government penalties, you name it."

"Because our Web site is down?" Barton said. But even as he said this, he knew it was more than that. His remaining optimism drained away, consumed in the heat of Wells's fear.

"If this is hackers—if hackers are stealing customer data—this is going to be *bad*."

"We don't know that yet, Graham."

"That's why we need to take drastic action. Listen, I just got off the phone with Carl. The last words he said to me were, 'Call Barton, make sure he understands the legal ramifications.' That's what I'm trying to do. And my official legal opinion is that we should shut down every computer in the place until we know what's happening. Can we turn off power to the entire company? I will now call Carl back and let him know that you and I have spoken."

Barton was shaken. "Thanks, Graham," was all he could manage. An elevator arrived and Barton dashed across the lobby to catch it.

Moments later he was back in his hotel room. His leg hurt where the coffee had burned it. It was a little after 10 a.m., not quite fifteen minutes until he'd get an update on the situation back at IVK. And he had no idea what to do. There were a dozen people he badly wanted to call, but all of them would be busy, and a call would only distract them. For a moment, he considered a call to Maggie then decided he didn't have time before 10:15. He shed the ruined pants and ran cold water over the coffee stain. For the analyst meeting, he'd have to wear pants from the day before.

At precisely 10:06 a.m., his cell phone rang again. It was, Barton could see from the display, Carl Williams. Barton took a deep breath and answered it.

"Jim Barton."

"Damn it, Jim, what's going on?"

"We're trying to figure that out, Carl," Barton said. He was trying hard to meet Williams's anxiety with calm confidence. "I've got a call with my team in . . ." he glanced at his watch ". . . eight minutes to get the latest."

"I just heard back from Wells. He said you were nonresponsive."

"Nonresponsive?"

"Look, never mind. Graham seems to have lost his mind. What do we know?"

"Well, call center systems are down."

"No kidding, those guys are just hanging out down there, chatting, drinking coffee. Costing us money."

"The Web site is frozen. And we're receiving suspicious e-mails. There are many possible explanations for the first two problems, some of them not very sinister, but the e-mails add a troubling aspect to the problem."

"Makes it seem like someone might be doing this to us?"

"Exactly."

"How can they? Don't we have a firewall?"

"Of course. We have many, but there's no such thing as perfect security."

"I don't want to hear—" Williams controlled himself. "I want an update as soon as you get a better idea, sometime in the next thirty minutes."

"Okay, right after my call in . . ." looking at his watch again, ". . . six minutes." Barton heard commotion in the background. Somebody was talking to Williams.

"Fine," said Williams. "I've got to go. Graham's calling again."

Barton closed his phone. He felt good about how that had gone. Unexpectedly, the interaction with the CEO had restored his confidence. The CEO had, in a backhanded way, expressed confidence in him. Now he just needed some good news from his team.

At exactly 10:13 a.m., Barton's phone rang again. He assumed it was the call he'd been expecting from his people, but when he looked at the phone display he saw that it was Williams again.

"Oh, boy." Barton had no idea why Williams would call back so soon, especially knowing that Barton was likely in a meeting, but he had a feeling that it would not be good news or helpful advice.

"Jim Barton."

"Hi, Jim, it's Carl. I've got Graham on the line. We've got another problem."

"What is it? I've got an update coming in two minutes . . ."

"I know, that's why we're calling now. We're not sure you should participate in the update."

"Huh? Why not?" Had they decided to replace him in the middle of a crisis?

"Jim, you've got a meeting with analysts this afternoon."

"Yes, I know, but that's not until after lunch."

Wells spoke then, explaining. "Jim, we've got disclosure issues if you talk to analysts in the aftermath of an event like this. Right now, you don't know what's happened. You don't know for sure, for example, that this event is security-related. Or that's what you told Carl, anyway."

"That's right," said Barton, not appreciating the implication that what he'd told Williams might be anything less than truthful.

"So," continued Wells, "we need to think about what we want you to know going into the analyst meeting. It might be best, if it's a security issue, that you don't know that yet when you talk to analysts."

"Carl, what kind of crazy, convoluted logic is this?"

"It's a legitimate concern," said Williams. "This may turn out to be nothing serious, or it might be very serious. We need to think about the representations you'll be able to make this afternoon without getting yourself and the rest of us in trouble. You're going to be on the hot seat. It might be best to have you go into it innocent of what's happening right now, or at least as innocent as we can make you."

"So you want me to just relax, enjoy the city, maybe take in a show?"

"Is there anyone you can delegate crisis response to?"

Another call was coming in on Barton's phone. It was 10:15 a.m. There was no time to think through what Williams and Wells were saying, but it felt wrong. Every fiber of Barton's being pushed back against what they were suggesting.

"The call from my team is coming in right now," said Barton.

"Don't answer it," said Wells.

"Don't answer a call from my team in a crisis?" Barton was aghast.

"Don't answer it," repeated Wells.

"Carl, this is wrong," Barton exclaimed. "This is my area of the company, my problem, and I need to be responsible for it. We can figure out how to manage the analyst meeting later. I can do that. I can handle it. Right now, my job is to fix this. Let me do my job."

"Graham?" said Williams.

"I advise against it."

Williams was silent. The digital alarm clock near the hotel bed clicked over to 10:16. Barton's phone beeped persistently as his team continued to try to reach him.

"Fine," Williams said finally. "Answer your call."

"Thanks, Carl," said Barton. He was about to switch over, but Williams wasn't finished.

"Make no mistake," said Williams, suddenly much angrier, "your butt is on the line here, Barton. I'm not a bit happy about this happening, not now, not at this time." He was venting. "Your timing could not be worse."

"Understood," Barton answered. For the second time that morning, he was shaken. Williams had said, "*Your* timing could not be worse." As if Barton had caused the outage. He gathered his wits and switched to the other call.

"Jim Barton."

"Hi Jim, it's Bernie. We've got you on speaker. Also present are Paul and Tyra. John Cho is down at his workstation, but he's with us on the line, as is Ellen Ripley, who's over at the data center, joining us by cell phone. Raj is with his guys working on Customer Service systems, so he's not with us; we can call him on his cell if we need to, though."

"Great, what do we know?"

Paul Fenton spoke up. "There are several things going on. You know about the e-mails, I think."

"Yes."

"The Web site is locked up because of what appears to be a rather sophisticated denial of service attack. We have software to defeat ordinary DoS attacks, but this one is coming from many locations and is attacking with a pattern of traffic designed to defeat our countermeasures. We are working on that and think we will be able to neutralize the threat in the next few minutes. The Web site should be operational after that.

"The thing that has us most puzzled is the Customer Service systems shutdown. We don't know what's causing it. Ellen tried rebooting everything that has anything to do with those systems, but it hasn't helped. Transactions against the database are returning an error code. We can't add new or retrieve existing customer records. That could mean there's something wrong with a transaction that's got everything jammed up behind it. Or it could mean the database is corrupted."

Barton interrupted: "Do either of those possibilities indicate that an intrusion has occurred?"

"Not necessarily. If it's a problem transaction, that is most likely an internal software problem. If it's database corruption, someone could have caused it, but it could also have happened without any malicious involvement."

"John, what do you think?" Barton braced himself for the possibility of anger in Cho's response.

Reuben spoke for Cho: "John thinks it's malicious, but that's his predisposition. He thinks someone has exploited the security hole he's been worried about." Cho, though supposedly on the line, did not elaborate.

"The security hole," said Barton, "that we've proposed addressing with a fast-track upgrade project." The project Barton had shot down while he was head of Loan Operations.

"That's correct."

"So what do we do?"

Fenton appealed to Ripley, his network operations team leader: "Ellen?"

"We can probably deal with the database corruption issue by going to a backup. But it might happen again. And we'll lose some data from yesterday afternoon if we revert to a backup. We'll have to re-enter all that data. Also, going to a backup may not solve our problems if they are due to an intruder. If it's a hacker and he's left malicious routines on our computers, they are likely also present among backup files.[1] The problem might just recur."

"Can't we tell if there are files on our computers that shouldn't be there?"

"We should be able to," a new, deeply annoyed voice broke in, "but we can't." Barton recognized it: John Cho.

"Explain."

There was a silence, then Cho started again. "We're supposed to keep careful records of all files introduced into production. But we haven't."

"Why not?" Barton asked.

"Because sometimes idiots in the applications groups rush changes in without going through the proper procedures—"

"There are good business reasons to do that sometimes," interrupted Tyra Gordon. "And it's not like others are not on board when we do it. Everybody knows what we are doing when we do that."

"I *never* agree to it," said Cho.

"It must be nice," Gordon said, "never to have to operate under pressure from a customer . . ."

"That's a load of crap," said Cho, "I advise you to come down here and try this kind of pressure . . ."

"Hey!" Fenton shouted. "People. Let's stay on point here."

"So," concluded Barton, "somebody in Tyra's group put in a change without following procedures?"

"Raj's group, actually," said Gordon, "it's his systems having the problems."

"But the rush-a-change-into-production thing is not unique to Raj's group," said Fenton. "It's been a sore point for years. We have careful procedures, but when a big customer screams for a change, procedures sometimes get circumvented. Outside IT, change control procedures tend to be viewed as a form of bureaucracy. Business unit managers sometimes force through quick changes that circumvent change control."

"Like, for instance," interjected Cho, "the VP of Loan Operations." Barton had a vague memory of browbeating Davies into such a quick change in the not-too-distant past. *I deserved that*, thought Barton, deciding to let Cho's not-so-subtle barb pass.

"I get it," Barton said.

Fenton continued: "As Tyra rightly says, we all know it goes on, and we all acquiesce. In the minds of many on the business side, this is justified if it makes a customer happy. It's a business trade-off, in effect."

"The bottom line is that we don't know if bad guys are involved," Barton concluded.

"That's right," said Fenton.

Barton heard a commotion in the background, some quiet talking. Fenton came back on the line: "The DoS attack is under control and the Web site is back up."

"Well, I suppose we can call that some kind of progress. Is there any other way we can tell if bad guys are involved?"

"Maybe," said Fenton. "It depends on how careful they were, if they were there at all. John's working on it."

"No smoking gun yet," said Cho, now speaking in more measured tones. "If it's bad guys, they're very, very good."

There was more commotion in the background. Barton heard a cell phone ring. Fenton answered it. Barton couldn't quite make out what was being said, but Fenton came back after less than a minute.

"Raj's people have figured out what the problem is. We'll have Customer Service back up and running in about ten minutes."

Barton felt relief that he knew was not yet justified. "Great. What was the problem?"

"Apparently a database index file had been somehow renamed, and another substituted in its place. All they have to do is rename the files back to how they were before, and we should be fine."

"Files renamed. Can that just happen?"

"I don't know," said Fenton.

"Not likely," said Cho.

"Let's be careful here," said Gordon. "There's danger in overreacting as well as underreacting."

"Okay," said Barton. "I've got to update Williams. I want us to meet again in sixty minutes, say, at 11:15 a.m. I need two groups, working on two different tasks. Paul, you, John, Raj, Ellen—I need your best sense of whether there's been an intrusion, and what we need to do about it, whether we're sure or not sure. Bernie, you and Tyra and whoever else you think might help who isn't working on what's happened here, I want you to develop some advice for me on how to handle the analyst meeting, which is at 2 p.m. Okay?"

"Can you cancel the analyst meeting?" asked Ruben. "Say you've come down with food poisoning?"

"Might seem suspicious, especially if word of what's going on here has leaked out. What if someone preparing for the meeting this afternoon has been having trouble accessing our Web site this morning? Or what if some call center employee has called a friend or sent an e-mail about what's going on? Word might be out already. But everything's on the table. If you think canceling the meeting is a good option, explain why. Okay?"

"Will do," said Ruben "Anything else?" All lines were silent; no one said anything. "Signing off, then." Barton snapped his phone shut.

Barton immediately called Williams with an update. Williams listened, said little. Barton hung up and ordered coffee from room service. He pulled on yesterday's pants. Then he sat down to put together his own ideas about what he might say at the analyst meeting under various scenarios. His leg hurt a lot, but his head hurt even more.

Thursday, June 28, 11:21 a.m....

Paul Fenton had just finished his update. Juvvani, Gordon, Cho, and Ripley were also on the line. The meeting to recommend an approach to the analyst meeting had been moved back fifteen minutes, to give that group time to send Barton some PowerPoint slides. Gordon, part of that group, was sitting in on this meeting to make sure she had the latest information on what had happened, as an input into what to say at the analyst meeting.

The facts so far: There was still no smoking gun that indicated an intrusion, although Cho was convinced that was the explanation. If it had been intruders, they had been deep enough into the IVK production computers to rename database files, which meant they could have also stolen customer data or corrupted it subtly. Loan applications asked for credit card numbers to be used in credit checks, but, fortunately, IVK did not retain that information. Unfortunately, the company's databases did retain Social Security numbers and other information useful to identity thieves.

"I think we need to disclose that something has happened," said Cho. "I think we're legally obliged to, in fact."

"We should get legal advice on that," said Fenton. Barton thought of Wells's incoherent state when last they spoke. Fenton continued: "My interpretation of our obligation is that we have to disclose if we know we've lost customer data."

"Actually," said Cho, "it's if we *suspect* we have."

Juvvani weighed in. "So what does that mean? You suspect we have, John. Maybe I don't."

"So you think those files just renamed themselves?" Cho asked.

Gordon came to Juvvani's defense: "We don't know what people do on the night shift. We don't know a hundred other things. Just because we can't think of another innocent explanation doesn't mean there isn't one.

How often before have we seen something happen that we think can't happen, only to discover some complex, idiosyncratic explanation?"

"Yeah," said Cho, "but renaming database files—that's pretty specific. How would that happen innocently?"

"Like I said—" Gordon began, then stopped.

"Might it be an inside job?" asked Fenton. "Could someone with approved access have done it? Is this somebody's idea of a joke that got out of hand?"

"I don't know," said Cho. "And I've been going over the logs pretty carefully. I don't think we're going to know. I have to admit, it seems implausible to me that someone could have done this without leaving any sort of a trail. But renaming a database index file . . . that's just not the sort of thing that happens by accident."

"So," said Barton, "what you're telling me is that we are not going to know whether this is a security event by this afternoon. That we may never know."

"Never is a long time . . ." said Fenton.

"That's what *I'm* saying," said Cho. "Unless we stumble onto something that tells us. I'm going to keep looking, but I've looked in most of the obvious places already."

"What do we recommend doing in the aftermath of this event?" asked Barton. "Williams is going to want to know what we're planning to do to avoid a repeat of this."

"Well," said Cho, "obviously we accelerate the security project we've got in motion. Maybe add some more to it—I've got a wish list of stuff. Maybe Williams will sign off on what we really need now. And, of course, we've got to begin following our procedures better. Maybe in the aftermath of this problem, people will understand better why we force procedures on them. Ellen's got a recommendation too, that I totally agree with."

"Ellen?" said Barton.

Ripley sighed, then launched into an explanation. "There's an additional concern. We can take the actions John is proposing, and that will close a lot of the possible holes in our security that we know about. But if—and as we've been saying, it's a big *if*—bad guys have been inside our production systems, what we've experienced so far might not be the full extent of nastiness they have planned for us. We can't tell what should be on our systems and what shouldn't be. So there might still be some bad code on our machines. Closing the holes in our security doesn't help with anything bad that's already on the inside."

"Okay," said Barton. This sounded like bad news, but so far he'd heard no recommendation. "And so that means we should . . . ?"

Ripley sighed again. "I think we need to shut down our production systems for a period of time, say three or four days, wipe production servers clean, and rebuild the production configuration from development files. It's unlikely, though not impossible, that the bad guys, if there are any bad guys, reached into our developers' machines. We should be able to put our production systems back together with only what *should* be there, and then we can keep tight control on them thereafter by following our change control procedures better."

"By shutting down our production systems," Barton asked, "you really mean shutting down the company's operations for that long?"

"Yes," conceded Ripley. "Mostly. We could take calls and do some things manually. But there's no doubt it would be a big deal."

Cho spoke: "We dust off and nuke the entire site from orbit. Eradicate any nasties left on our production servers. But it's really the only way to be sure."

"Can we," asked Barton, "set up parallel systems built from development files, *then* switch over to those before we take down our production systems? Wouldn't that help us avoid a shutdown?"

"Yes," answered Ripley, "we could do that. It would be expensive, because we'd have to buy or otherwise acquire additional space and equipment. And it would take time. Which is the biggest problem with that idea. If the bad guys have more difficulties planned for us, that's time—definitely days, maybe a week or more—in which their plans can execute. Waiting might mean we have more problems."

"Just so I've got this clear," said Barton, "You want me to go to Williams and tell him we need to shut down production computers as soon as possible, and keep them down for, what, three to four days?"

"That's about what it would take," said Fenton. Barton realized that his team had discussed it already and agreed on this plan of action.

"You realize that this is not our decision," said Barton. "It's Carl's decision. And I've got to tell you, I don't think he's going to like it. Nobody outside IT is going to like it."

No one said anything.

"Any ideas," Barton asked, "about how we frame this shutdown from a PR standpoint? What we say to our customers and the public about why we're shutting down for four days?"

Still no one said anything. It was Barton's turn to sigh. "Okay," he said. "Let me think about it."

He flipped his phone closed and opened an e-mail from Ruben that contained a PowerPoint slide attachment, a plan for how to handle the analyst meeting.

He looked at his watch. It was already 11:44 a.m. The meeting was in a little more than two hours, and he still had to get downtown.

REFLECTION

How should Barton handle the meeting with the analysts? What questions should he be prepared to answer and how should he answer them?

How vulnerable is your company (or a company that you know) to a denial of service (DoS) attack or intrusion? What should be done about such vulnerabilities?

Why can't perfect IT system security be achieved? If security can never be perfect, how should you manage against malicious threats?

CHAPTER ELEVEN

DAMAGE

"You're recommending that we shut down the entire business for how many days?" Carl Williams did not conceal his incredulity.

"Not the entire business," said Barton, "just parts of it, for three or four days total, which, if we did it on a weekend, interrupts the business only a couple of days. And I'm not yet saying we *should* do it. It's one of several options already identified." Barton wondered if he'd been too forthcoming in laying out for Williams everything known about the event so far. *Wrong way to brief the CEO*, thought Barton, *or this CEO, anyway*. He made a mental note. He hadn't had much time to think through the finer points of how he'd present to Williams, who had yanked him out of a meeting with his IT team.

"One of several options," repeated Williams.

"Yes."

"The one that most of your staff prefers," he said.

Barton squirmed. "That's right. At the moment."

Barton recalled the last time he'd been *this* uncomfortable in *this* chair: the day Williams had sprung the new CIO job on him. Barton now wondered if his boss might be about to take that job back. Barton wasn't far from just handing it over. He hadn't slept very well the night before.

As in that earlier meeting, the CEO now stared out the window, refusing to sit. Barton, on the other hand, was captive in a chair that suddenly reminded him of an interrogation seat, behind a table that had become unnecessarily long. He wanted desperately to get back downstairs; he needed more time with his team, to help them come up with a full slate of options.

At that moment, Barton could see the attraction in spending most of his time downstairs. As he looked at Williams, he was pretty sure the CEO would be happy never to have to talk about IT again. Probably, Barton realized, Williams had slept badly also.

"Carl," Barton said, seizing the initiative and succumbing to an irresistible urge to get on with doing something, anything, "let me get back to you in a couple of hours with all the options. We still have more work to do before we can make a real recommendation."

"I thought you just made one," said Williams.

Moments before, Barton had said that shutting down the business was *not* yet a recommendation. Now the CEO had, Barton assumed, moved on to expressing frustration. It would be a bad idea to respond in kind. Instead, Barton opted for calm: "No, Carl, what I just gave you was an update. I let you know some of the options we've been discussing. I especially wanted you to know about the *least palatable* option we've considered. I thought letting you know of that possibility now was preferable to surprising you with it later."

Williams turned toward Barton and nodded. Barton could see that he had scored points with these words, though not nearly enough to make up for the points he had lost in the last twenty-four hours.

"Nice job on the analyst meeting, by the way," Williams said. "There was no discernible impact on the stock price yesterday afternoon. We'll see when the market opens in a few minutes, but my guess is that you navigated that minefield successfully."

More points scored, Barton thought. "I think so too," he said.

Gordon's team had suggested playing it cool at that meeting, not even bringing up the attack unless someone else did. If it came up at all, Barton was to acknowledge it, note that denial of service attacks are extremely common, and that the company's security measures had handled the attack after a short delay.

During the meeting, Williams and Graham Wells called in and listened, not letting any of the analysts know they were present.

At one point during the meeting, also at his team's suggestion, Barton had laid the groundwork for future security measures, including a possible company shutdown, by reemphasizing the firm's commitment to security. "We think we're in pretty good shape," Barton had told analysts, "but, as the new guy, I can't rule out taking some very significant additional steps—including steps that might, say, shut us down for three or four days, for a maintenance outage—to reach a higher standard of service for our customers."

"Williams would go for that?" asked one of the analysts.

"Yes," said Barton, "I believe that he would, if I recommend it. Although," he added, "we don't have reason at the moment to think that would be necessary. I just don't want you guys to be surprised if we decide to do something like that."

Barton had added that last part mostly for the benefit of the lurking Williams, who at that time had not heard about any options involving a company shut down. But it was an effective moment in the meeting. It conveyed to analysts that the CEO entrusted much to his new CIO. Barton couldn't help wondering whether this was a past, more than present, situation.

He'd stuck to a general line of argument throughout the meeting: "We're in good shape already, but we want to be even better." The question he had dreaded—"Do you have any reason to believe today's event was anything more than a run-of-the-mill DoS attack?"—never came. Nothing about the attack came up. Barton spent most of his time sticking to a script he'd prepared before the attack.

Emerging from the meeting, Barton went directly to LaGuardia Airport and was back at his desk by early evening. But there wasn't much he could do to help. Cho and a couple of other security people continued to examine intrusion detection logs, but they'd found nothing yet. Fenton, Gordon, Juvvani, and Ruben had stayed around, awaiting Barton's return, but only Fenton and Juvvani could really help with the technical details. Everyone wanted to be supportive, but at some point too many managers just got in the way. Barton chose Gordon and Ruben to lead a complete review of the business continuity and emergency response measures, the ones that they'd discovered were out of date. Then he sent them home for the evening. Fenton and Juvvani sent most of their people (those not from or useful to the security group) home; the two of them and Barton were gone half an hour later, with a plan to begin early the next morning. By then, they hoped there would be more information about what had happened. It made little sense to charge ahead with the really big decisions until they had better information.

Barton was back at his desk by 6:30 a.m. Cho still had nothing. He and a small group had been working all night. When Gordon, Fenton, Juvvani, and Ruben arrived, all by 7:15, they'd begun talking through a list of issues.

First, they needed to identify the remedial security measures they wanted to implement to reduce the risk from future attacks. Along with knowing the security measures themselves, Barton wanted to know what they would cost. Cho's upgrade project would be accelerated, of course, but Barton wanted them to figure out what else they could do to avoid a repeat of the events of the day before. As long as they were going to ask for more money, might as well ask for enough.

Second, they needed to decide what should be done to make the company secure against additional mischief from the attack that had just happened. They had no smoking gun to tell them that there had been intruders, but neither could anyone think of a way a database index file could become renamed without someone meaning to do it. And then there was the matter of the "Gotcha" e-mails. It could have been a coincidence that those came in at the same time that the database problem occurred. It could be a coincidence that they arrived at the same time as the DoS attack. But that seemed unlikely to Barton. Others varied in their opinions, especially about whether the renamed database file was part of the attack. Gordon was far from alone in observing, "Just because we can't think of how it happened, doesn't mean somebody did it. In my IT career, I've seen a lot of weird stuff happen that seemed impossible at first, but that nevertheless proved to be quite possible under certain not-easy-to-imagine conditions."

Third, they needed to figure out what to recommend to Williams and the rest of the leadership team about what, if anything, they needed to disclose outside the company, and to whom. The risk of *under*reacting, by not disclosing something they should, which might then come back to haunt them, had to be balanced against the risk of *over*reacting, confessing too much, especially without hard evidence of intrusion. Without accurate information on what had happened, there was no way to know what "over-" or "under-" reaction even meant. Barton and his team were left arguing conjectures. What was most likely? What was second most likely? No one could agree, and Barton had no knowledge basis on which to form his own ideas.

This last issue was, to Barton, the real nightmare, the one with which Williams would have the greatest difficulties. If IVK managers decided they needed to announce to the world that information on their customers had been stolen, who knew what might happen? This was the issue most likely to get people fired, the issue most likely to spell an ugly end for IVK.

As he sat in the unpleasant morning meeting with Williams, in that unpleasant chair, behind that unpleasantly long table—as he wrapped himself in the sanctity of a policy of *always* letting his boss know of the "least palatable" options and possibilities—Barton realized that he was actually breaking his long-standing personal rule by not bringing up the disclosure issue. It was in his interests to do so. The longer he went without raising it, the harder it would be to discuss. Wells was probably harping on the issue already in his own conversations with Williams.

Barton had left the meeting without mentioning anything about disclosure. Before he returned to the meeting with his team, Barton stopped in his office to write on his whiteboard: "Always tell your boss the bad news first; tell him as soon as the possibility is known; don't put it off until you know it for sure." Then he added—and underlined— "But SYH2DP." *Yeah*, he thought, *sometimes you have to duck a punch.*

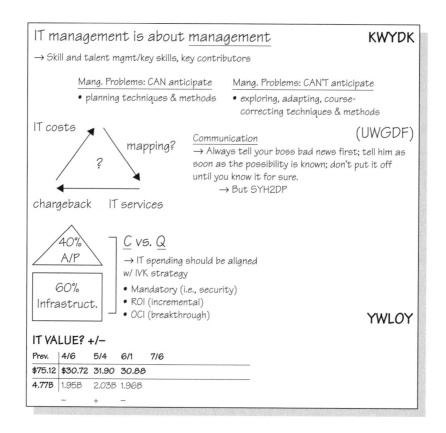

IT management is about <u>management</u>   **KWYDK**

→ Skill and talent mgmt/key skills, key contributors

<u>Mang. Problems: CAN anticipate</u>   <u>Mang. Problems: CAN'T anticipate</u>
- planning techniques & methods
- exploring, adapting, course-correcting techniques & methods

IT costs

mapping?

<u>Communication</u>   **(UWGDF)**
→ Always tell your boss bad news first; tell him as soon as the possibility is known; don't put it off until you know it for sure.
→ But SYH2DP

chargeback   IT services

40% A/P

60% Infrastruct.

<u>C</u> vs. <u>Q</u>
→ IT spending should be aligned w/ IVK strategy
- Mandatory (i.e., security)
- ROI (incremental)
- OCI (breakthrough)

YWLOY

IT VALUE? +/−

Prev.	4/6	5/4	6/1	7/6
$75.12	$30.72	31.90	30.88	
4.77B	1.95B	2.03B	1.96B	
	−	+	−	

Friday, June 29, 3:47 p.m. . . .

By Friday afternoon, options were shaping up. Cho still hadn't found evidence of intruders. He had, in fact, declared it unlikely that any such evidence would ever be found, whether or not there had actually *been* intruders. Fenton, with Barton's permission, then sent Cho home to sleep. The guy had been awake for nearly forty hours. But he planned to come back in later that night.

Gordon and Ruben would work on "future event avoidance" on a less urgent timeframe, but the other two issues, recovery from the attack of the day before and what to disclose, had to be dealt with now.[1] Concerning the attack, three options were shaping up:

1. **Do nothing.** Assume that the past mischief was the worst that the bad guys had intended—if in fact there had been bad guys. This

option best fit scenarios in which there had never been intruders, or in which the intruders had been mere tricksters, not really malicious.

2. **Shut down the company, except for operations that could run manually, as soon as possible and rebuild critical production systems from development files.** This was the "playing it as safe as possible" option, but it had an unfortunate side effect: the shutdown of most of the company's operations would last long enough and be noticeable enough from outside IVK that it would need to be explained. And there were risks. The IT team assumed they could rebuild from development files, but the documentation on how to do that had not been kept up to date. They would eventually get it done, but it might take longer than estimated. Also, because data would have to be restored from backups, this option did not address possible data corruption issues; if bad guys had subtly adjusted the data in some way, they might have done it in the past, in which case the problem would be present in backup files too; this would be undetectable. And if customer data had already been stolen and copied to somewhere outside the firewall, this option would, of course, do nothing to address that.

[handwritten margin note: If bkup files are remotely located, then How they can be corrupted?]

3. **Build a mirror site from development files and shut down the original product systems; rebuild original production systems only after the mirror site is up and running.** It would cost money and take time, probably a couple of weeks, to assemble the necessary facilities and equipment. More bad things could happen while all this was coming together. But this option would not require shutting down the business or explaining why IVK was shutting down the business; and it would, if they were lucky, fix some of the problems that might have been left behind by bad guys—if there had been any bad guys.

[handwritten margin note: best option]

Barton's team had a definite preference for playing it safe; they liked option 2. That had been Cho's recommendation as well, before he'd headed home to get some rest.

The disclosure issue was, as expected, more complicated. Some argued for coming totally clean concerning the possibility of an intrusion. Their line of argument went something like this: "We weren't adequately prepared for this attack, so we don't know what happened. Since we don't know what happened, we need to avoid making convenient assumptions about what we *would* know if we had been more adequately prepared. The evidence is strong enough to dictate telling the world that we suspect our customer data has been stolen, or could have been." Barton couldn't quite imagine recommending this to Williams, however.

The most popular position called for contacting customers whose records had been accessed on the day of the attack and perhaps some number of days before—this could be discerned from logs—and warning those customers that their information might have been compromised. There was little agreement on how many days before the attack they should start. It was possible, of course, that the intruders had been inside the firewall for weeks, months, or even years—if, Barton kept reminding himself, there had been intruders at all. Gordon was a broken record on this point: "We have no evidence of an intrusion," she kept saying. "Just suspicious circumstances." The fact that IVK was contacting customers in this way would undoubtedly find its way into the press. But it would not be nearly as dramatic as a big public announcement, and the company might get lucky and the story would end up on the back pages, especially if something distracting was going on in the news. There was even talk about waiting for a distracting event to hit the papers before contacting customers.

A few argued for no disclosure at all. Like the "do nothing to deal with the attack" strategy, this was a "wishing for the best" approach. But it could work out. And if it did, it would be preferable to the other courses of action. If the unknown circumstances were such that this was the best approach, then the other options would all have been foolhardy overreactions. One could imagine a scenario in which there had been no intruders, but IVK, playing it safe, effectively committed corporate suicide by announcing that customer data might have been stolen. Doing that in "no intruder" circumstances would rank high among the all-time dumbest business decisions. But there was no way, of course, to know if these circumstances in fact prevailed.

Barton's direct reports, after much tired and occasionally heated discussion, settled on the immediate rebuild option, explaining it as the sort of maintenance that Barton had warned about at the analyst meeting, and a limited disclosure to customers only, at a time not too far in the future when the news situation was favorable to IVK. Barton thanked them and sent them all home. Fenton and Cho would, Barton knew, be back later, and he suspected Gordon and Ruben had plans to come in on Saturday morning. But the decision on what to recommend was now Barton's. His team had done all they could.

Sometime after 4:30 p.m., Barton called Williams to say that he was ready to discuss options. Williams informed him that the entire senior leadership team of IVK would convene at 8 a.m. on Saturday morning to decide what to do. "We could do it this afternoon," said Williams, "but I think you should sleep on it. So you can be really certain of what you recommend." You didn't have to listen carefully to hear the threat in the CEO's words.

Before he left for home, Barton called Maggie. She was out of town again, which really stunk. He'd managed a call to her from LaGuardia the day before, so she knew roughly what was going on. But he badly needed to talk through the options with her.

"Now wait a minute," she said, when he explained what seemed to be the choice of his IT team. "You've got to be practical here. What's Carl going to be okay hearing?"

"I don't know, Maggie," said Barton. "But there are legal issues that come into play around disclosure."

"Yes, but disclosure *now* puts IVK in deep trouble with *certainty. Not* disclosing might result in big problems, but that's *less* than certain."

"Some of the problems might involve lawsuits, even jail time, for all I know. Do you know, could we get in criminal trouble for anything here?"

"I'm not a lawyer," said Maggie, "but I think it's unlikely you'll end up in jail."

"I could get fired."

"That's certainly imaginable."

Barton groaned. "What do you recommend, Maggs?"

"Moderation. A reasonable middle option. You're very tired right now, Jim. Get some sleep, okay? Don't make an extreme choice when you're out of sorts. You might just survive this."

"I hope so," said Barton.

"I hope so too, sweetie," said Maggie, her voice thick with as much empathy as could be conveyed across a mobile phone link.

Friday, June 29, 8:28 p.m. . . .

Barton was ordering his second beer when the kid appeared. As the bartender cleared away the half-eaten remains of a sandwich, the kid settled in beside Barton and ordered a Coke.

"You don't look so good," said the kid.

"Is it that obvious?" Barton asked.

"What's up?"

Barton couldn't share the details, of course. He got across that there had been a major problem and that the CEO was upset enough to call an 8 a.m. Saturday meeting. Barton managed to imply that there might even be legal concerns involved.

"It's not all my fault," said Barton, "but it's a pretty big screwup."

He fell silent. The kid said nothing; he seemed to be thinking hard.

"So, IVK, right?" asked the kid. Barton nodded. "That's Carl Williams, right?"

"That's right," Barton said, surprised that the kid knew the identity of the IVK CEO. Barton didn't remember mentioning Williams by name before. Maybe he had, though.

"Knowing Williams," said the kid, "I'd say you should recommend nothing that might endanger his turnaround of the company. Keep up appearances. That'll be his inclination."

"What do you—?" Barton stammered.

"What do I know?" the kid interrupted. "Nothing, really. What you've told me."

"You know Williams?"

"No." The kid paused to take a sip. "This is your moment, man. Don't listen to me. Trust your gut."

Barton wasn't sure what else to say. He and the kid talked for a few minutes about baseball, then the kid finished his Coke and stood up. "Got to pick up my date," said the kid, "a nonvirtual one this time." He tossed a few dollars onto the bar. "Be sure to come by next week. I want an update."

"Sure," said Barton. "I won't offer you a job this time. I might not be able to deliver it."

The kid laughed, slapped Barton on the back, and departed. Barton finished his beer, walked home, and fell into bed exhausted, remembering to set his alarm for early the next morning.

Saturday, June 30, 8:56 a.m. . . .

"So, this *is* a recommendation," said Williams.

"This is a recommendation," said Barton.

"You think we should shut the company down—excuse me—major parts of the company, not the whole thing—so that we can be sure we don't have any further problems as a result of this attack. *If* there was an attack."

"There was an attack, we just don't know if the database problem was part of it."

"And we explain the outage as a service upgrade."

"Which it is."

"And then we contact customers whose data records have been accessed in the past week, and let them know that they should be especially vigilant about identify theft, because there is a small chance that we might have lost some of their private identify info, Social Security numbers and the like."

"Social Security numbers, name and address, date of birth," Barton confirmed.

"And you think we should wait a few days to begin contacting customers, try to coordinate these contacts with a busy news day, and maybe spread them out a bit over time so that the number of people we're contacting will be difficult to discern."

"The last part, how we contact customers, is a suggestion, not part of the recommendation."

They were assembled in the boardroom. Williams stood, as usual. Leadership team members sat silently around the table. From Barton's right, it was Eva Dillard, VP Corporate Planning; Ed McLaughlin, VP Financial Management; Maria Navarro, VP HR; Ben Lao, Director of Collections; Momoko Sato, VP Capital Markets; Graham Wells, VP Legal Affairs and General Counsel; Omar Willis, VP Business Development; Ehsan Nisar, VP Customer Service; and Niels Hansen, Barton's successor as head of Loan Operations.

None of the others said anything. Barton was the only one who'd spoken since the meeting began, other than Williams.

"Graham?" Williams turned to the company's chief lawyer.

"I like the idea of playing it safe by shutting down the computer systems to make sure we've done everything we can. And I think we can probably get away with a 'careful' customer contact strategy; we're simply gauging our actions to the urgency of our good-faith assessment of the situation."

"Other thoughts?" Williams looked around the room. The others stirred, nodding and murmuring agreement with Barton and Wells.

"There might be opportunity in this," said Willis. "We could play up how much we care about customer security in some of our marketing, cite the shutdown as an example."

"That sounds a bit like tempting fate," said Hansen. A few others chuckled nervously.

"Depending on the number of customers we're talking about," said Nisar, "perhaps we should call them, not write to them. Maybe those of us in this room should make some phone calls."

Nods of agreement around the table. Williams was listening, but he wasn't nodding, laughing, or speaking. A silence stretched out across the room. Williams dispelled it.

"So you all think," said Williams, "that this sounds like a good way to go?"

Again, there were murmurs of agreement.

"What if," Williams asked, "a reporter or analyst puts two and two together, the maintenance outage and the warnings we're sending to customers, then wants to know about the attack?"

"How would a reporter or analyst know about the attack?' asked Hansen.

"I don't know," said Williams. "Maybe a rumor. Our employees know about it. Think none of them has mentioned it to a friend?" No one answered. Williams continued: "I'm not going to let anyone coast on this decision. Let me see hands—who thinks we should adopt the plan that Jim Barton has recommended?"

Haltingly, exchanging uncertain glances, the executives raised hands into the air, in the end indicating unanimous agreement.

Williams surveyed the room, eyes circumnavigating the table as if counting. Then he turned away, moved to the window. For a long time he stood, looking out. The others lowered their hands. *Such a flair for drama, this guy*, mused Barton. *All the long pauses and stalking around.*

Williams turned back: "I don't agree," He said quietly. He took a deep breath and filled his lungs with air, suddenly inflating, threatening to explode—which he then proceeded to do:

"I WAS HIRED," he said, now shouting, "to turn this company around. That's just what I'm going to do. We will NOT shut the company down. And we will NOT say to anyone that we think, maybe, possibly we might have—perhaps, perchance, conceivably—lost customer data. That would be not knowing what we are doing. It would be unprofessional. It would be incompetent. It does not rise to my standard of performance. Carl Williams doesn't run companies that way."

He paused to inhale again, then focused his attention on Barton. The room grew very still. *This is it*, Barton thought, *I'm history.*

Unexpectedly—miraculously—Graham Wells chose just that moment to speak up: "I can't go along with you on this, Carl. This is a very dangerous course you're proposing. At least I think you are proposing it. In my professional opinion, we need to play it safe here."

"You're not the CEO," Williams said, turning on Wells. "It's my decision."

"That may be," said Wells, "but it's my career that you're putting at stake, and those of all the rest of us. My professional ethics too. In good conscience I cannot go along with this. I feel we must come forward with some sort of disclosure, no matter what the consequences. We must do the right thing here."

Williams settled into the empty chair at the head of the table. He propped both elbows on the table, folded his hands together, then positioned his chin atop his hands. Calmly, he said: "So that's what you think, is it?"

"Yes," said Wells, "it is."

"I agree," said Hansen. "We need to choose a strategy that allows us all to move on to our next job, even if this one doesn't work out."

"Move on to your next job," repeated Williams, again calmly, still staring at Wells. It was unsettling how calm he had become.

"Yes," Hansen said.

Now Williams looked at Hansen, who was nodding, nodding, seemingly forgetting to stop nodding, then at the others who were not nodding, who were carefully not moving at all. Williams said: "Well, I say no. We're not moving on, we're not giving up on this company. I'm going to turn this company around. It's what I came here to do. It's what I will do."

"I can't go along with this," said Wells.

"I've got a real problem with it too," said Hansen.

"Anybody else?" Williams asked. No one said anything. Williams stood, went again to the window, waited. He waited for a long time. Then he turned.

"Very well," he said quietly, "the two of you are fired. Before you tell anyone what you think has happened inside IVK, I suggest you consult your employment and nondisclosure agreements. I think you'll discover that if you, as a former employee, cause damage to this company with remarks that are not provably accurate, then we will have legal recourse. You are, as of about twenty seconds ago, former employees. So I'd recommend that you be careful. Because I will—this is a promise—cause you difficulties if you have the poor judgment to violate any aspect of these agreements. You *will* have trouble 'moving on to your next job.' Let me say this even more clearly: When I finish with you, you'll be lucky if you can afford a doublewide trailer in a two-bit trailer park. Now get out, both of you."

"Carl, maybe we should take a moment, let things settle down a bit . . ." Maria Navarro, the HR chief, began. She stopped when Williams beamed a borderline deranged expression in her direction.

Williams returned to the window. Wells and Hansen looked at each other, then stood and left the room. For nearly five minutes, no one moved or made a sound.

Suddenly, Williams turned, swelled to what seemed like twice his normal height, raised his right arm horizontal, index finger outstretched, and pointed directly at Barton. "And YOU!" He was shouting, but he stopped. His head rolled on his neck: once, twice, three times, as if he were about to cough up something, some obstruction keeping him from breathing. Then air and sound came rushing out:

"YOU!—" he repeated, "Will need to take over Loan Operations again until I figure out who to turn it over to. Do NOT—and I mean DO NOT—let Loan Operations distract you from your duties in IT. And DO NOT let this ever happen again. Do you understand?"

"Yes, Carl," Barton whispered.

"This meeting is adjourned," said Williams.

As the remnants of the leadership team filed from the room, Williams took out a cell phone and punched in a call. Barton heard Williams say, "Hi Charlie, regret bothering you at home, but we've got a situation here. We're going to need you to put together a crack legal team to help us with a little emergency. Wells is out of the picture . . ."

Trudging down the hallway outside the corner office, Barton passed beyond earshot of the conference room, his peers alongside him. He felt compelled to say something: "I'm really sorry about all this."

No one responded. Barton turned and headed to his office.

REFLECTION

Which option for securing IVK in the aftermath of the security incident would you choose?

What would you disclose?

Did CEO Williams make the best decision for IVK? — *decision errors Do not say anything, do not do anything.*

Why didn't Williams fire Barton?

CHAPTER TWELVE

COMMUNICATION

Tuesday, July 3, 10:33 a.m. . . .

Barton had forgotten that Wednesday would be a holiday until Raj Juvvani showed up at his office, apologetic because he had long-scheduled plans, a wedding, that would take him out of town for the rest of the week. The poor guy seemed genuinely fearful as he confessed to having a "problem"—that was the word he used for it. At first this surprised Barton. Juvvani seemed to expect a harsh reaction to his news. But it shouldn't have. Word of the tumultuous meeting on Saturday morning, the dual firing of Wells and Hansen, had spread through the company like a brushfire. Barton had overheard emotional voices in the hallways asking why Hansen, popular with his employees, had been fired while Barton remained. He could see their point. Barton knew Hansen well, had mentored him. Wells had never been much more than a bureaucratic annoyance, but Hansen was a real loss.

Williams would appoint someone to take over for Hansen within the week. The CEO had said so in an unusually long e-mail he'd composed to Barton on Monday. The e-mail had begun by proposing Linda Trilling to take over from Hansen and asking Barton's opinion of the choice. It was a good choice, the one Barton would have recommended, and he told Williams that in an immediate reply.

The rest of the note was a list of references to articles the CEO had read over the weekend, most of them from the Web, but some of them from print magazines. All were about IT management. Collectively, they were a diverse set, in age and subject. Alongside some, Williams had recorded a few cryptic comments: "This guy has some interesting ideas," or "Not so sure about this one; what do you think?" Williams seemed highest on a blog by a guy Barton had never heard of. When he followed the link, he discovered that the author had gained fame from controversy. Barton read, trying to understand why the CEO had been so fond of the guy's writing. After a while, Barton began to get it. But the more he got it, the more disheartened he became.

The writer's formula was the business equivalent of the "shock pundit" strategy so popular on TV news channels: Say something outrageous, something your target constituency wants to hear, then sit back and bask in the howls of protest from people who know better (no publicity is bad publicity). Then do it again.

Throughout the blog, Barton found one controversial statement after another, most just the sort of thing that would play to a general manager's darkest suspicions about those mysterious nerds in the basement doing IT. Barton still had what he considered minimal technical knowledge, but the little bit that he knew told him that this guy didn't have his facts straight. Williams, like most business managers, could not see that, though. Indeed, Barton was still close enough to his past as a business manager and IT skeptic to be occasionally drawn in by the writer's seduction. At one point, reading, Barton caught himself whispering "Oh yeah!"

Usually Williams dictated letters and e-mails, then his assistant added openings, closings, formats—imbuing such documents with a formal tone. But Williams himself had clearly typed the e-mail Barton received on Monday. It lacked the usual niceties and contained typos, punctuation problems, and other evidence of keyboard awkwardness. The whole thing was odd; Barton was unsure what to make of it.

Eventually, as he considered the e-mail yet some more, what it all meant dawned on him: colossal absence of confidence in the CIO and IT function. The CEO had concluded, after the events of the past week, that Barton was in over his head. The fact that Williams had composed the e-mail himself probably indicated how exposed he felt; the only course of action he could think of in his desperate situation was to become a "CIO helper" himself. He didn't trust anyone else to do it. There could be no mistaking it: this e-mail signified a dramatic fall from grace for Jim Barton.

Which created a new set of problems. He could expect to get more "advice" from Williams. From now on he would need to do more than inform Williams of what was happening in IT and recommend plans of action. He'd also have to explain and justify *not* following the CEO's advice, which would continue to be of highly variable quality. Williams was taking an interest in IT—that was a good thing—but the guy didn't know what he was doing—that was a bad thing.

After spending another forty-five minutes following links suggested by Williams, Barton rose and wandered down the hall to Bernie Ruben's office.

"They've lost a lot of confidence in us," said Barton, after telling Ruben about the e-mail, the blog, and what it all meant in his reckoning. Barton knew Ruben heard the subtext of his statement: "Williams has lost confidence in me."

"What do you think we should do about it?" Ruben asked.

"I'm not sure. The meeting on Saturday was really something. I've never seen a CEO get quite so . . . *visceral.*"

"From what I've heard, Wells and Hansen threatened to mutiny. Sounds like that's the one thing this CEO won't tolerate."

"Guess so. Not sure how I emerged unscathed."

"You're not unscathed."

"My sense is that we need to think systematically about this, just as we would any other kind of problem."

"Meaning?"

"We need a step-by-step plan for regaining the confidence of the business managers and CEO."

"Sounds like a long-term project."

"We have to improve things. But we also have to communicate what we're doing to Williams and others in a way that builds confidence."

"The plan Tyra and I have been working on is almost ready for initial discussion. It's not rocket science, but it's very thorough."

"Yes, I've seen it in draft, and I like it." Ruben had sent him a copy the day before. The plan was about firewall upgrades, digital file "fingerprinting," better intrusion detection, purchase of additional processing and disk capacity to allow more logging, additional third-party security audits, procedures to makes sure emergency manuals were up to date, training, rehearsal of emergency procedures on a regular basis, and renewed emphasis on change control. The goal was never again to be in a situation in which they didn't know what to do in an emergency or couldn't tell what should be running on production computers. "Williams will sign pretty much anything security-related, at this point," said Barton, "so let's don't lowball anything. He's expecting a big number."

Ruben nodded. "A big number should help with the confidence issue. Though he probably won't like spending the money."

"As the new guy, he's got some slack to spend money, write some things off. The money is the least of our worries."

"What do you have in mind?" Ruben asked. "Briefings?"

"Frequency of communication is one question," Barton acknowledged. "We could go away and fix a lot of things, then come back to Williams when we can claim a lot of progress. That's one approach. Alternatively, I can request much more frequent and incremental updates. Maybe once a week, a regular agenda item at the leadership team meeting, and an additional meeting every week with Williams. Something like that."

"Think Williams would meet that often on IT? He doesn't seem like that much of an IT guy."

"Oh, he'd hate it," Barton agreed. "But we could, if we think it's the right thing to do, insist. Right now, he wants us to just handle it. He's chosen this 'hope for the best' strategy in reaction to the attack, so he really doesn't want to be reminded of what might still happen."

"Maybe we should just leave him alone for a while, let him settle down."

"Maybe."

"He's agreed to Plan B, right? If we're not going to shut down, we should at least build a mirror site and switch over to that."

Barton nodded. "As long as it doesn't involve a shutdown or any form of public disclosure, he's okay with it."

"What do you think about his approach?"

Barton shrugged. "It's not the one I recommended. If things go south, I'll be dragged down with him. Williams and I are in the same boat. We'll sink or swim together."

"Oddly, that makes you his closest ally, doesn't it?"

"Not one he thinks of very highly." Barton stood. "Tell you what. Why don't you and Tyra think a bit about communication strategy, this question about frequency, anything else you think is important. Also, I'd like recommendations about how we should reach out to the extended business team. Williams is easy in terms of how: I'll brief him personally. But we've also got an issue with the rest of the business. I won't be able to personally brief all of them."

"A newsletter? A regular e-mail?"

Barton shrugged. "Don't know. That's what I'd like you to think about for me."

"Sounds good."

Barton turned to go. Ruben spoke: "Jim?"

Barton turned back: "Yes."

"I think you're going to climb back out of this."

"Thanks for the vote of confidence."

"Deep down, I think Williams knows it too."

"Hope he's right. Hope you both are. Thanks, Bernie."

"Anytime."

Barton departed, moving quickly back down the hallway to see what new problems awaited him. Before he settled in behind his desk, he went to the whiteboard, to record the insight he'd experienced in the conversation with Ruben. He wrote: "Effectively communicating IT-related business issues to business managers requires SYSTEMATIC EFFORT, just like everything else you try to accomplish in business; spend sufficient time on it." He wasn't sure he understood what he meant by "systematic effort." That would come, hopefully.

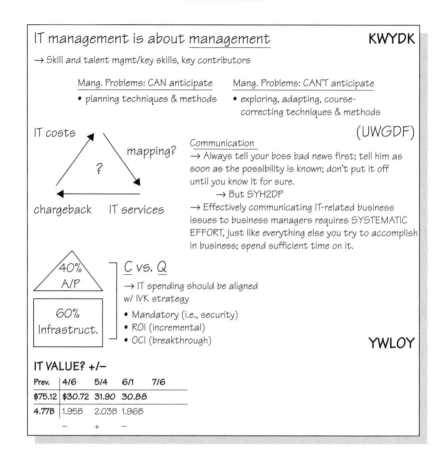

IT management is about <u>management</u>   **KWYDK**

→ Skill and talent mgmt/key skills, key contributors

<u>Mang. Problems: CAN anticipate</u>
- planning techniques & methods

<u>Mang. Problems: CAN'T anticipate</u>
- exploring, adapting, course-
  correcting techniques & methods

IT costs   **(UWGDF)**

mapping?   <u>Communication</u>

?   → Always tell your boss bad news first; tell him as
soon as the possibility is known; don't put it off
until you know it for sure.

→ But SYH2DP

chargeback   IT services   → Effectively communicating IT-related business
issues to business managers requires SYSTEMATIC
EFFORT, just like everything else you try to accomplish
in business; spend sufficient time on it.

40%
A/P

<u>C vs. Q</u>

60%
Infrastruct.

→ IT spending should be aligned
w/ IVK strategy
- Mandatory (i.e., security)
- ROI (incremental)
- OCI (breakthrough)

          YWLOY

IT VALUE? +/−

Prev.	4/6	5/4	6/1	7/6
$75.12	$30.72	31.90	30.88	
4.77B	1.95B	2.03B	1.96B	
	−	+	−	

Saturday, July 7, 6:13 p.m. . . . .

Maggie sipped the drink Barton had prepared for her. She was in town for a change, thanks to the midweek holiday, so Barton was in a good mood, also for a change. There hadn't been much to be happy about lately, so it was nice to have an excuse. The two of them were hanging out, relaxing, doing nothing; they had 8 p.m. dinner reservations at a new restaurant that had recently received a Michelin star, but that was nearby, and it wasn't time to leave yet.

Barton plopped an olive into his own drink and moved across the room to adjust the equalization on his stereo. They were listening to one of Barton's iTunes playlists, a shuffled mix of selections from Broken Social Scene, the Decemberists, DeVotchKa, Hotel Lights, Jack's Mannequin, PJ Harvey, Andrew Bird, Regina Spektor, Zero 7, Yo La Tengo, and others. "Nietzsche" by the Dandy Warhols came on, and Barton found it necessary to crank up the volume. When the vocals kicked in, he turned it back down and settled in on the couch across from Maggie. Despite their rule against talking shop at times like this, the events of the past week had launched that rule out the window.

"Think I should contact Francesco Carraro?"

"Carraro? Who's he?"

"IVK board member. Enthusiast for IT. Remember?"

"Right. And you want to contact him . . . why?"

"He left the door open."

"To what end? For what purpose? Why would you contact him?"

"I thought Williams might want me to go to the board with him to give an update on this attack. The thought crossed my mind that the only reason I have a job still is to absorb fire from the board when we update them about it. But he doesn't seem to be in a hurry to update them. It's consistent with his overall strategy for handling the event: wish for the best, pretend it never happened. But, if he's not planning to update them, this raises an even more disturbing possibility."

"That he's keeping you around to pin the whole thing on you if the ship goes down?"

"Exactly! The old 'I didn't know a thing, and I'm not an IT guy, so how could I?' defense. Variants of it worked for Jeff Skilling at Enron and Bernie Ebbers at WorldCom.[1] Well. Kind of worked. Seemed to work for a while, anyway."

"You sound a little paranoid, Jim," teased Maggie.

"Just because you're paranoid doesn't mean they're not out to get you."

Maggie paused, bit into an olive, then voiced a scenario: "So you bypass Carl and update the board yourself, through Carraro. Carraro goes to the board, the board confronts Carl, Carl confronts you. The two of you end up in a credibility contest. Secret lunches ensue, favors are called in. The board comes to realize that a lot of their own credibility is invested in Williams. Once they do, things end badly—for the both of you, but especially for you. Hmmm . . . No, Jim. I don't think you should contact Carraro. Unless Carl says to."

Barton sank back against the couch. "That won't happen. Not the way things are going."

Maggie slid over next to him. "Maybe you need to be plotting an exit? Your situation is a bit dicey, to say the least."

"Yeah, I'm totally screwed."

"Yes, you are. Totally screwed."

Barton smiled. "That's what I love about you, babe. Brutal honesty."

"That's why clients pay me the big bucks. It's a pretty neat trick. I tell them they're totally messed up, they thank me and pay me $800 an hour."

"That's how *enlightened* executives behave. Some others pretend nothing's wrong and fire people for saying otherwise."

"It's a problem."

"Yes, it is."

"But look at the bright side."

"The bright side?"

"At least he's not threatened by you anymore."

Barton laughed and changed the subject: "Any thoughts on how we ought to rebuild confidence in our IT capabilities?"

"Your communication plan?"

"That."

"Well, it's occurred to me that you might find stakeholder analysis to be of use in formulating your plan. Have you used it before?"

"No. I think I've seen someone give a presentation about it. But it's been awhile. Remind me."

"You were talking about something systematic, this is definitely systematic. You identify stakeholders—the people who can influence the outcomes you care about. You map stakeholders into categories, like "Allies" and "Blockers," then you formulate independent strategies to deal with each category—or even each stakeholder, if the person's influence warrants that. There's a good deal more to it than this, but the basic idea is pretty simple."

"Sounds helpful."

"I can send you something to read on it.* You can take a look, decide for yourself if it's likely to be useful. If you decide yes, I can probably

*See "Stakeholder Analysis" at the end of this chapter.

196

connect you with some consultants who can help you carry out the analysis."

"How often do you think we should communicate with Williams and the rest of the leadership team?"

"He's thinking bad thoughts about you at the moment. When you're not around, his imagination builds those up in absence of evidence to the contrary. I'd say that means getting in front of him soon and as often as he'll put up with. You can't rebuild a relationship without interacting with the person."

"Regular agenda item on the leadership team staff meeting agenda?"

"Absolutely."

"Additional one-on-one meeting with Williams once a week?"

"Or more often, if events warrant. I'm pretty sure you won't make things worse in your personal interactions with him. You're basically pretty competent, Jim. And reasonably pleasant to be with."

"Well, I'm glad you think so, Maggie."

Sunday, July 8, 11:55 p.m. . . .

Barton's breathing slowed and his eyelids settled. He had planned to get to bed early, to start the week fresh. He'd orchestrated his entire afternoon with the goal of sleep in mind: taken a longer than usual run, drawn a steaming-hot bath, popped a sounds of nature CD he'd received as a gag gift into his audio system—even choked down some of Maggie's bitter herbal tea. But a million thoughts had swirled in his mind, placing three fitful hours of torment between bedtime and this moment when, finally, he grew still.

Monday, July 9, 4:12 a.m. . . .

Barton jerked upright in bed, reacting to a burning sensation on his thigh, which faded as he opened his eyes. Moonlight streamed into the room through slatted blinds. Images of a dream came flashing back.

He was in his office, talking with a smartly dressed headhunter about becoming the new SVP and CIO for a large investment bank. In reality, Barton had been contacted frequently by headhunters, but he had never encouraged them, nor had he ever heard from a headhunter recruiting for a CIO position. He remembered spilling hot coffee in his lap when the headhunter mentioned the compensation—it more than doubled his existing IVK package.

If Maggie was right, and he was "totally screwed," maybe this dream was a sign. *Maybe I should start looking for a new job?* Barton fell back into the sheets for two more fitful hours of sleepless torment before his alarm rang to officially start the morning.

Thursday, July 12, 12:16 p.m. . . .

"Starting to get a sense for what it's really like to be the CIO at IVK, I hear."

Bill Davies had a smile on his face that Barton wanted to wipe off. He felt a strong urge to ridicule the guy's tie (brightly colored with a Disney theme). But Davies deserved to gloat a bit. He and Barton were having lunch at a local hotel, neutral ground roughly equidistant between IVK and the site of Bill Davies' new CIO job. Barton had requested the meeting. He'd had a long-term intention to stay in touch with Davies, to try to learn why he had not been effective as the IVK CIO. Barton had not followed through on these intentions. Now, as much as it hurt his pride, he would ask Davies for advice.

Davies had already gotten a pretty thorough account of recent events through his informal network. As they talked through things, Barton was surprised by how much people—his employees in the IT department, ostensibly—had shared with Davies, even though he no longer worked for IVK. The level of information conveyed to Davies violated employment agreements, but there was probably nothing to be done about it. Nothing that wouldn't cause more problems than it would be worth, anyway.

Barton controlled his annoyance and worked on maximizing the value of the interaction with Davies.

"Yes, I know a bit more about what it's like to walk in your shoes now, Bill. And I apologize again for the difficulties we had when you were at IVK."

Davies was not done with vengeance: "Is it true that the attack exploited a hole that would have been plugged if you hadn't killed our upgrade project when you were in Loan Operations?" Davies and Cho had surely laughed long and hard about that, surmised Barton. He decided not to concede full satisfaction to Davies on this point.

"We don't know. We're not sure anyone came in through any holes. We have no evidence of it."

Davies chuckled. "You have to admit, if that's what happened there's a certain amount of irony in it."

"Yes, there is," said Barton, "if that's what happened. And in any case, it was a bad idea, shooting down your project. You were right, I was wrong."

Davies softened. "But you still work there. You must be doing something right."

Barton shrugged. "Not sure about that. But I do still work there, so I was hoping to get your advice on a few things."

Barton thought Davies seemed mildly incredulous. But he became very cooperative: "Sure. If I can help, I'd be happy to."

Very big of you, thought Barton, but he didn't say that.

"Any ideas on how to rebuild confidence in the IT group?"

Davies thought for a moment. "Yeah, sure. Get Cho on it, and Fenton, push that upgrade through fast, do everything else you can think of to upgrade security. When you've got most of it in place, lots to show, present to Carl and the other members of the leadership team. And, most important, make sure nothing else happens in the interim."

"So you would go away, do a lot of work, then come back and tell what you've done."

"What else could you do?"

"Well, I've been thinking about meeting every few days with Carl, to make sure he knows what we're doing and feels that he has input into it, or at least opportunity for input."

"Not the way I'd play it. I doubt he wants to see that much of you right now. My guess is that he's pretty upset. You could do it that way, but I don't really see the difference, content-wise, and the continuous explaining and complaining you'd have to endure would be pretty horrible. Horrible for both of you. I don't think you ought to take problems to the CEO, just solutions. Explain the problems when you know how to solve them."

"Hmmm."

"I'm a fan of the 'Doctrine of Completed Staff Work.' Do you know it? The basic idea is that you take completed solutions to your boss, not questions about what you should do. You only go to the CEO when you understand everything and are confident of your solution. You don't go looking for input. Especially in an area like IT. Hard for you, torture for them."

"The Doctrine of Completed Staff Work."

"I'll send you a copy."*

"Thanks." For a guy who'd had such a hard time at IVK, Davies had a lot of ideas. "Let's order some lunch, Bill. I'm buying."

"You don't have to do that . . ."

"I insist. You're providing the advice, I'm buying the lunch."

"If you insist," Davies said, looking pleased, Barton thought.

Friday, July 13, 8:54 p.m. . . .

Barton settled in at Vinnie's. The kid was already there, finishing a burger and watching a baseball game on the flat-screen TV above the bar.

"I missed you last week," said the kid, taking advantage of a commercial break.

"Sorry about that," said Barton. "The holiday and all, you know? And it was kind of a rough week."

"Meeting on Saturday morning go well?"

"No, I wouldn't say so. Williams kind of lost it. Fired two people."

"But not you."

"No, not me."

"Interesting."

*See "The Doctrine of Completed Staff Work" at the end of this chapter.

"I think he's keeping me around to take the blame if there are more unfavorable developments."

"Or maybe he genuinely needs you."

Barton shrugged. "I don't know. But I think I'm just going to play it straight ahead. Do my job. Do as much as I can to address the weaknesses that our little problem exposed. Do as much as I can to rebuild confidence in my team and my own judgment. It's going to be slow, but we're going to press ahead, be as thorough and systematic as possible."

"Sounds like a good plan."

"Not sure my troubles are over, though. I don't really approve of the course of action Williams chose. He overruled my recommendation."

"That hurt your feelings?"

"Nothing like that. I just don't think the choice he made is wise. And I'm worried that it puts me at risk too."

"Time to depart?"

"I've thought of that, believe me. I just don't want to go that route right now."

"Still got things to do, eh? Feeling the urge to bring things to a better situation?"

"Maybe that's it. Whatever it is, now doesn't feel like time to move on. If I'm going to go, Williams will have to fire me."

"I'm impressed."

"Ha! That's just because I can't tell you the details of how badly I messed up."

"Maybe not, but I think I get the idea."

The kid shifted focus back to the game. The home team was down four runs in the bottom of the seventh inning, but they had loaded the bases with nobody out, a situation that required total fan attention. Barton was happy to put his own situation aside for a while and add his cheers to the home team's cause.

REFLECTION

Conventional wisdom suggests that it's important to "manage your boss." As a CIO, what is the best approach to managing your boss? How should Barton handle the bad "advice" coming from Williams?

How should Barton communicate with people outside the IT department to rebuild his organization's credibility?

In an environment of Internet access and real-time information, how effective is the "Doctrine of Completed Staff Work"?

Stakeholder Analysis

As the structure of the business firm has evolved away from the hierarchical, vertically integrated form associated with the industrial sector of the economy toward more complex forms in which power is decentralized, and integration among organizational entities is less clear-cut than before, the new organizational forms are more political, in an operational sense, than bureaucratic, and are marked by stakeholder groups that form temporary coalitions to influence patterns of behavior.[a] Within such political structures, organizational change is effected by mobilizing key stakeholders to support specific projects and plans. Stakeholders possess the influence or position to promote desired changes. Some stakeholders also provide critical resources—time, money, and staff. Others possess substantive input and expertise.

Stakeholder analysis can be particularly useful to a CIO who is pursuing an initiative to transform a company's IT infrastructure from a bottom-up evolutionary architecture to a secure, stable, scalable IT network architecture. Unless each key stakeholder (individual and group) is identified and its stakes with respect to a new IT architecture mapped out and understood, it will be very difficult for the CIO leader to realize his/her short- and long-range plans and goals.[b] Stakeholder analysis is therefore a useful technique for injecting some degree of certainty and control into what is most often a highly political, even controversial, process. Furthermore, given the numerous choices of direction a CIO leader has in pursuing an architecture program (i.e., systemwide or niche), a CIO is apt to pursue the most suitable course of action—that which leads most efficiently to the desired ends—if he or she first assesses the different stakeholder groups affected by the program to determine where sources of support and/or resistance lie.

From a practical point of view, stakeholder analysis can assist the CIO leader to:

1. **Identify the universe of stakeholders.** This includes stakeholders at the corporate level (president, CEO, COO, so forth), at the line-of-business level (group VPs, technical staff, users), and from outside the organization (consultants, advisers). Analyze these

groups in terms of how critical they are to a project, and then assess their motivation to support or resist the process.

2. **Assess stakeholder importance and influence.** Stakeholders do not have equal impact on the architecture process. Some control critical resources necessary to a project and have potential to be "Allies"; others have the power to facilitate, transform, or block implementation at different stages of the process, and have potential to be "Network Members."

3. **Determine stakeholder interests and motivations.** Stakeholders with mutual interests (whether personal, political, or business) are classified as "Allies" and "Network Members." Stakeholders with conflicting interests are classified as "Blockers" or "Slowers."

The architecture stakeholder map emerges from this analysis:

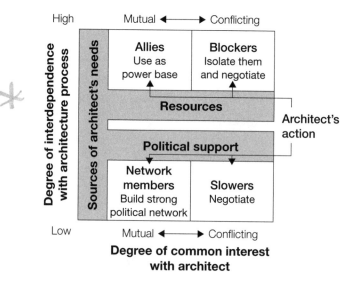

Allies share the architect's interests and vision. They sponsor and/or provide project resources, including funds, manpower, and time. They provide the power base.

Network members share common interests, but are less directly involved in the architecture process on an ongoing basis. They are a political resource for mobilizing otherwise recalcitrant groups.

Blockers are stakeholders who are logically and strategically important to the architecture process, but whose conflicting interests make them less-than-enthusiastic supporters. They require negotiation.

Slowers are stakeholders whose indirect cooperation is needed, but who do not overtly support the process; they may put up indirect or subversive resistance. Slowers also require negotiation.

a. This analysis is adapted from Richard L. Nolan and Deborah M. Kolb, "Architecture Leadership and Stakeholders," *Stage-by-Stage* 7, no. 4, July–August 1987 (Lexington, MA: Nolan, Norton & Co., 1987), 1–9.

b. Architecture serves up blueprints for the technology infrastructure—applications, data, and communications—that are manifestations of the overall business strategy. At the same time, architecture is as much about organizational structure, culture, and practice as it is about technology.

The Doctrine of Completed Staff Work

Completed staff work is the study of a problem, and presentation of a solution, by a staff member in such form that all that remains to be done on the part of the commander is to indicate approval or disapproval of the completed action.[a] The words "completed action" are emphasized because the more difficult the problem is, the more the tendency is to present the problem to the commander in a piecemeal fashion.

It is your duty as a staff member to work out the details. You should not consult your commander in the determination of those details, no matter how perplexing they may be. You may and should consult other staff members. The product, whether it involves the pronouncement of a new policy or affects an established one, when presented to the commander for approval or disapproval, must be worked out in a finished form.

The impulse, which often comes to the inexperienced staff member, to ask the commander what to do, recurs more often when the problem is difficult. It is accompanied by a feeling of mental frustration. It is easy to ask the commander what to do, and it appears too easy for the commander to answer. Resist the impulse. You will succumb to it only if you do not know your job.

It is your job to advise your commander what she or he ought to do, not to ask what you ought to do. The commander needs answers, not questions. Your job is to study, write, restudy, and rewrite until you have evolved a single proposed action—the best one of all you have considered. Your commander merely approves or disapproves.

Do not worry your commander with long explanations and memos. Writing a memo to your commander does not constitute completed staff work. But writing a memo for your commander to send to someone else does. Your views should be placed before the commander in finished form so that the commander can make them his or her views simply by signing the document. In most instances, completed staff work results in a single document prepared for the signature of the commander without accompanying comment. If the proper result is reached, the commander will usually recognize it at once. If the commander wants comment or explanation, she or he will ask for it.

The theory of completed staff work does not preclude a rough draft, but the rough draft must not be a half-baked idea. It must be complete in every respect except that it lacks the requisite number of copies and need not be neat. But a rough draft must not be an excuse for shifting to the commander the burden of formulating the action.

The completed staff work theory may result in more work for the staff member but it results in more freedom for the commander. This is as it should be. Further, it accomplishes two things:

1. The commander is protected from half-baked ideas, voluminous memos, and immature oral presentations.

2. The staff member who has a real idea to sell is enabled more readily to find a market.

When you have finished your completed staff work the final test is this: If you were the commander, would you be willing to sign the paper you have prepared and stake your professional reputation on its being right? If the answer is no, take it back and work it over, because it is not yet completed staff work.

a. This generally applied military doctrine was circulated through U.S. Army General Mac-Arthur's Headquarters during World War II. See, for example, "Standard Operating Procedure" (Memorandum), U.S. Department of Commerce, January 10, 2005, http://www.ita.doc.gov /hrm/sop/documents/000_completed_staff_work_&_c3q_2005_01_10.pdf (accessed August 2008).

207

PART FOUR

THE HERO BREAKS THROUGH

CHAPTER THIRTEEN

EMERGING TECHNOLOGY

Wednesday, August 8, 9:38 a.m. . . .

Jim Barton slammed his office door and slapped a notepad down hard onto the desk.

"Why," he asked of no one in particular, "does every interaction with those guys have to be like a trip to the dentist?"

The leadership team meeting had just broken up. It had been longer than usual; there was a lot to work through. Much of it had to do with IT. Most of that had amounted to listening to people complain.

The meeting hadn't even begun when Williams told Barton that they'd have to reschedule a short meeting on their calendars for Friday morning. The plan was for a fifteen-minute update—just fifteen minutes—but Williams, as it turned out, would be off-site during this time. It would be the third meeting in a row that Williams had canceled. "Is it the fact that we're meeting on Friday? Would a different day be better?" Barton had asked. "No," responded Williams. "Friday's fine, just not this Friday. What's on our agenda this morning?"

Barton had been trying to update his peers and Williams frequently on firewall upgrades and other security measures, as Maggie had recommended. But Barton had to admit that Davies was right about one thing: Williams really didn't like to talk about IT.

The meetings were sheer torture. Barton had trouble explaining things to Williams. Security was a pretty technical area, after all, and Barton was not himself a technical guy. But the alternative—bringing Cho and maybe Fenton to the meetings with him—worked against Barton's other purpose, to rebuild the relationship between himself and the others. Having a hovering sidekick to whom he kept turning would make him seem unprepared and too—something. Too Davies-like, maybe. Williams already had trouble hearing what Barton was telling him; often an explanation of something IT related ended with Williams saying, "No, I don't quite understand, but I'm okay with you deciding. Let's move on." At one particularly horrifying juncture, an exasperated Williams had exclaimed to Barton, "Speak English, man!" Not "Habla inglés?" exactly—that notorious question an exasperated Jim Barton had once used to goad a hapless Davies—but too near it for Barton's comfort. More than once, Barton had taken out the document Davies had sent him, about "completed staff work," to look for something useful, something to make the meetings with Williams less painful.

Barton wanted to think that at some level Williams appreciated what he was doing. But he wasn't sure. Since the security event in June, people seemed less willing to assume that Barton and the IT group were doing things for good reasons. They were more inclined to second-guess, or label ideas "dumb" without taking the time to understand them.

A version of this problem had filled most of the time in today's leadership team meeting. Someone had raised a question about why the start of an IT project had been delayed several months. The answer, Barton thought, was obvious: security upgrades needed to take priority. Surely everyone could agree to do the most urgent things first? In fact, everyone *had* agreed. But the first question provoked a lengthy round of questioning about the way other IT projects had been reprioritized. Barton and his staff *had* reshuffled priorities, but Barton had made a point of communicating the proposed reordering to all his peers, so they could provide feedback or object. If anyone had seen a problem, Barton would have happily addressed it. But no comments had come back, none at all, and the IT department had gone ahead with reprioritization. Since Barton had taken over control of the IT budget in May, it was his decision, officially. But he'd intended to make the decisions in collaboration with the others. Now no one was acting collaborative.

As Maggie had put it back in May, it was Barton's neck alone in the noose, and now the others seemed inclined to yank on the rope. In the aftermath of the June event, no one deferred to Barton because of his former status as a big-shot business manager. Instead, it was yank, yank, yank on the rope.

"Maybe," Barton said aloud, as he settled into his desk chair, "it's time to go back to a committee structure for priority setting. Maybe Davies had it right in the first place." Davies had insisted on a committee with representatives from each of the business areas to decide IT priorities. It operated very slowly and, worse than that, it allowed business units to set aside concerns related to technical risks. The event in June had been directly traceable to this very problem. But Barton could not, of course, point that out because *he* had been the business guy who had railroaded his project through, displacing the security project that would have prevented the intrusion. *If there had been an intrusion—* there was still no evidence of it and nothing more had happened. The "hope for the best" policy that Williams had chosen against so many recommendations seemed to be working out. "Yet another way," Barton muttered, "that I've been wrong lately."

He looked up at his whiteboard, wondering what principle he should add. Something about keeping his neck out of the noose, perhaps. But he didn't want to give up control of the budget. That would just take them back to the bad old days. Somehow, there had to be a reasonable course that was none of the above. He made a mental note to discuss it with his IT managers.

For the moment, though, he needed to turn his attention to the final item that had come up in the meeting. One of his colleagues had asked, out of the blue, "What are we doing in the area of Web 2.0?" Barton might have been unprepared for this question, but Bernie Ruben had forwarded him an e-mail attachment on the subject a couple of days before. Some kid in Ruben's organization was very hot on the business potential of "Web 2.0," whatever that meant. Barton had not actually opened the attachment yet, but he'd been able to respond in the meeting with something like, "Yes, well, I've just received a report from one of my staff on that very subject; there could be important implications for us in some of the emerging technologies in that category. I haven't had time to look at the report carefully though, so let me get back to you on it at our next meeting." No thanks to Barton's own resourcefulness, he had looked reasonably good at this point in the meeting, because he'd seemed semiprepared to respond to this question.

Barton located Ruben's e-mail and clicked on the attachment . . . *Got to get a better handle on Web 2.0 before the Monday staff meeting* . . . The attachment opened . . . Barton picked up the phone to call Ruben . . . Barton began to read about blogs, YouTube, social networking, Facebook, MySpace . . . He wanted to talk to Ruben and the report author before Monday . . . *Social networking, apparently a way to improve collaboration inside the firm* . . . Ruben's phone went to voice mail, so Barton left a message asking him to call . . . *A way to reach out to customers, new and old, through nontraditional channels* . . . Barton considered phoning the report's author directly . . . He noted references in the report to a *MIT Sloan Management Review* article on "Enterprise 2.0" and to a Cutter Special Report on "Harnessing the Power of Social Networks," need to get those . . .[1] He decided not to call the report author at that moment.

"STOP," said Barton, to himself. "Stop. Do one thing at a time." Since the attack, about five weeks now, Barton had been trapped in a cycle of reacting, chasing one thing after another, fighting one fire after another. His attention was fragmented most of the time. This made it impossible for him to get any momentum back, to formulate coherent plans. He knew he had to beat this cycle. He just wasn't sure how.

Let's see, Barton thought, *if I can begin to get things back together. Right now. I will read. I will do one thing at a time. I will act, not react.*

He shut his eyes, then slowly opened them, beginning to read the report, careful not to let his mind jump to anything else. With his frame of mind thus changed, he began to find the subject interesting. Eventually, he found his way to a section at the bottom of the report, which listed some of the people within IVK who were participating in the so-called "Web 2.0 revolution." Some items in the list were active links to blogs. Barton clicked on one and found himself reading about one guy's experiences working in the customer support center at IVK.

Who can access this? Barton wondered. He thought he remembered reading that these blogs were all publicly accessible.

Clicking back over to the report, he confirmed this: all the listed blogs were accessible to anyone, on the Internet. He clicked back to the blog by the Customer Service guy, scrolled down the page and found, to his dismay, a description of a day in June when all the systems at IVK went down for a while. It was the day of his analyst meeting in New York City. The author even speculated, jokingly, about the cause of the outage; his lighthearted list included viruses and hackers.

"You've got to be kidding!" Barton cried out before he stood and went storming down the hall in search of answers.

Tuesday, August 14, 11:35 a.m. . . .

"It seems to me," said Ruben, "that we need two policies here: one for the specific issue of blogs and other similar Web 2.0 technologies. And another for how to identify emerging technologies that may be relevant to us in some way, so they don't blindside us the way this one apparently has."

Barton sat quietly, listening to others discuss.

Tyra Gordon responded to Ruben: "And there's the specific issue of what to do about this particular blog, especially the entry about the June outage."

"It hasn't caused us any difficulties so far," said Raj Juvvani. "Maybe it won't. It doesn't look like very many people read this blog. The blogosphere is an ocean. One guy's blog is a speck of sand."

"They're not all specks," said Gordon. "Some are widely read."

"Not this one," said Juvvani.

"In any case," said Ruben, "it's not obvious that we could take down that blog entry. It's cached on the Internet. Someone's got a copy. If we take it down, that'd be like shouting 'Pay attention to this!'"

"Plus," Juvvani said, "some of my guys know the blog's author. If we tried to get him to take it down, they think he might blog about that. Which would make things infinitely worse."

Eyes turned toward Barton, looking for signs of life. He said nothing.

"Three questions, then," said Ruben. "One: What, if anything, should we do about this blog entry?"

"Nothing," said Juvvani. "We should do nothing."

Ruben nodded and continued: "Two: What should be our general policy about blogging based on inside information from within the company?"

"Tons of implications here: legal, protecting proprietary info, and more," said Gordon.

Ruben, still nodding, continued: "Three: What should be our process for spotting emerging technologies and analyzing them to see how they might be relevant to us, for better or worse?"

Barton spoke: "My first inclination would be to put in place a rather restrictive policy on blogging. That's what Williams would say. We've got to control this."

"Have you discussed it with Williams?" braved Gordon.

Barton shook his head. *I can barely get him to meet with me*, thought Barton. He said: "I don't really know how to bring this up. If he learned that there was a description on the Web, accessible to anyone, of the outage we experienced on June 28, he'd probably fire all of us. It's exactly the kind of disclosure he vowed we would not make."

Fenton spoke up: "Just having a restrictive policy on these things doesn't mean we can ignore the implications of new technologies. I mean, we can prevent people putting unauthorized stuff on their computers. We can tell them they can't talk about work outside of work, certainly not in a blog. But a lot of this Web 2.0 stuff can come to companies whether they like it or not. Ask Nintendo about YouTube. When the wrist strap on the company's gaming remote control turned out to be underengineered, movies of remote controls obliterated by energetic game play, of TVs obliterated by flying remotes, started showing up all over the Web. Before that, Kryptonite locks had a spectacular sales decline that they traced to a video on the Internet showing how to pick one of their locks with a cheap ballpoint pen."

"Can you write up a few of those examples?" said Barton. "I'll use them as a basis for raising this issue with Williams, get some feedback on it. Get him behind putting out a policy on this. For the time being, I'm not a policy to restrict blogging. So, noone can go out of compliance

Emerging Technology

going to tell him about the existing blog entry about June 28. So don't talk it up outside this room. Maybe when we send out the blog policy, our favorite blog author will realize he's out of compliance and take corrective action himself, without us having to single him out."

"That's good," said Ruben, "much better than an effort targeted at the guy. We can design the policy so that it should be obvious he's out of compliance, but in a way that doesn't convey to him that we even know about his blog."

Barton was nodding. "Good. Now, Bernie, you and your team come up with a first draft of the policy. You need to also take the lead in making sure these things don't blindside us again. I want a process, a way of seeing emerging technologies coming and understanding what they mean for us."

"Jim, Bernie, hang on a second," interjected Juvvani. "When you take these issues to Williams, I just want us to be sure that Web 2.0 technologies don't come out looking like the enemy. There's serious business potential in this area, from what I read and hear, and I know our competitors are tapping these technologies, getting ready to offer customers all sorts of new things. I've got a team on my Customer Support staff right now experimenting with a wiki-based discussion forum to get our key partners involved in new service developments; I've got more ideas I'd like to discuss with this group when the dust settles. In the meantime, what we don't want is to end up with a ton of restrictive policies that kill my team's creativity. We're already playing catch-up."

"Raj is right," added Fenton. "There are serious pros as well as cons here. I was just reading in this book, *The Broadband Explosion*, about these two Internet guys, Licklider and Taylor.[2] Back in the 1960s they predicted all sorts of creative communication possibilities on the net—stuff like real-time collaboration, online communities, peer-to-peer APIs. We're well into the twenty-first century, and we're just starting to realize the potential of these technologies."

"Okay," agreed Barton, "We're clearly going to need to discuss this some more, but I'll see what I can include in my conversation with Williams. I'll need to keep it brief. He's not going to want to hear about a lot of hypothetical, futuristic stuff."

[handwritten margin note: importance of an emerging tech.]

"I've got an argument that may work with Williams," added Ruben. "IT is like a high-tech business—high-tech businesses spend about 10 percent of their revenue on keeping up with new technologies, processes, products. IVK needs to keep up too, by scanning new technologies, allocating resources for that purpose."

"Write that down, will you Bernie? Raj, get me a project report on the wiki thing, maybe a few other concrete ideas your team has for adding business value, and back it up with whatever information you have on what our competitors are trying." Barton stood. "Any of the rest of you have something to add, get your ideas to Bernie. Okay?"

Everyone indicated agreement.

"Let's get out of here," said Barton. "I'm ready for lunch."

Thursday, August 16, 4:02 a.m. . . .

Barton sat straight up in bed, startled awake. Through the fog of sudden consciousness, images from his nightmare came forward: he was standing before all of IVK senior leadership and the Board of Directors. A red-faced Williams singled him out with a long finger of ridicule and roared: "YOU! Where did you get that awful tie?" Raucous laughter spilled forth from his colleagues. Barton looked down to see that he was indeed wearing an enormous, holiday-inspired tie . . . and nothing else!

He fell back onto his pillow, emitting a groan of despair: "I'm turning into Davies!"

Friday, August 17, 3:23 p.m. . . .

Despite himself, Barton remained annoyed by the blog leak, and by the idea that now he had Web 2.0 technologies to try to keep up with on top of everything else. He'd have preferred to simply strike it from his list of concerns. But he took a deep breath and reminded himself that this was just another example of having to *know what you don't know*. He could add Web 2.0 to his ever growing "don't know" list. *Were there things he could strike off the list by now? Known things?* he wondered.

He took a fresh look at Ruben and Juvvani's reports. These guys were "in the know," or getting there, and Juvvani in particular was eager to pursue the new technologies. Barton gazed up at his whiteboard, at the priorities scheme. Maybe Web 2.0 was something for the OCI list.[3] One of these breakthrough possibilities, with future value that was hard to perceive up front. He forced himself up to the board and added: "Harness the power of new technologies (don't sweep under the rug): Web 2.0, social networking, what else?"

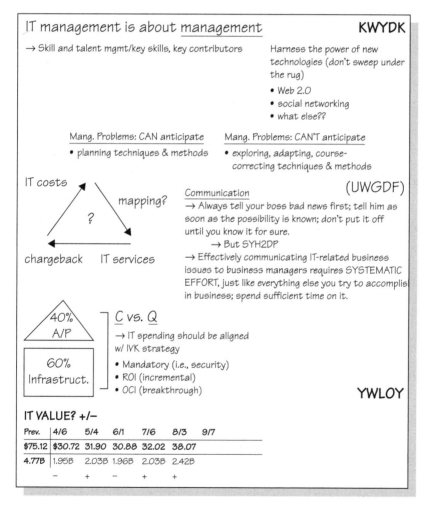

Suddenly, Barton thought of his nephew Jack—maybe he'd know something about this stuff. He was always sending him the wildest links online. The chance Jack would be a source of Web 2.0 information was a good enough excuse for Barton to phone his nephew and ask for some game time this weekend. A few hours of Guitar Hero or Rock Band sounded just about right.

REFLECTION

Given near-universal Web access and the wide use of blogs and social networking, can companies still keep their information "secret"? As a manager, what should you assume people outside the company know?

How would you respond to Bernie Ruben's three questions about blogging and emerging technologies?

What advice would you offer to Barton to help him break the cycle of constant firefighting? Is Barton becoming like Davies? Is this inevitable?

As IT increasingly penetrates into our daily lives, do you think the younger generation (such as Barton's nephew Jack) might do work differently than earlier generations? If so, what kinds of difficulties or opportunities might arise from this difference?

CHAPTER FOURTEEN

VENDOR PARTNERING

Thursday, September 27, 10:55 a.m....

"I tell you, that's simply not going to work!" The speaker pounded his fist on the table. Others in the room let loose a collective sigh. Frustration filled the air like an unpleasant smell.

Barton sat at the back of the conference room, listening. He struggled to control an urge to wade in with his opinion. Two camps had formed, and they disagreed bitterly. Twice before in the span of a week he'd sat through unproductive meetings on this or related topics. The group leading the effort to replace IVK's increasingly decrepit back-office systems, the IR team, had been basically stuck for months now. Someone, or something, needed to break the pattern of dysfunction.

But not Jim Barton. He was the one person in the company who could not do it, who had to stay out of it. He'd dealt a major setback to the effort when he'd canceled the NetiFects contract in May. It had been one of his earliest actions, arguably the most decisive. But, also, Barton knew, the most second-guessed. Barton still believed it had been the right move, but his role in slowing the project down made him both desperate to see the group regain forward momentum and certain that he could not again intervene without creating even greater problems.

When Barton had jettisoned NetiFects, the IVK cross-disciplinary, business-led group that had been working on back-office systems replacement had seemed to take it well. They'd had their own frustrations with NetiFects. Many of them felt satisfaction when Barton summarily dismissed smooth-talking Carlton Leopold. But hard feelings toward Barton lingered among members of the group, borne of the fact that Barton had made the decision to fire NetiFects without consulting them. His unilateral decision to add IT people to the group's membership, justified by an assertion that the group needed more technical experts to ensure adequate evaluation of the merits of solutions proposed by vendors, added insult to injury. Everyone knew that technical evaluation was important. But the group felt that Barton had exerted too much influence.

They had agreed, in response to Barton's urging, that they would avoid the paralysis that had set in last time a result of the sheer size of the project, by starting with a major off-the-shelf package. They would not develop a custom system out of small components, using a systems integrator for new software development, as had been the direction evolving under the previous plan. Instead, they'd start with a big system and use a systems integrator to help install it and, perhaps, customize parts of it. This agreement, however, formed a foundation for three new—and major—disagreements.

The first centered on selection of the off-the-shelf package. The group had narrowed an initial list of more than twenty candidates down to three finalists. Much of this work had been straightforward. Choice of a product also meant choice of the vendor that would become a long-term IVK partner, and many companies that submitted initial proposals were, for one reason or another, unsuitable partners (too small, too close to a major competitor). Others had obviously inferior product offerings. The handful that remained after an early cut had to be evaluated more carefully.

That summer, the group had issued a request for proposal. This RFP asked vendors to self-assess the degree of fit between their product and the specification that IVK had developed when the emphasis had been on working with NetiFects to create a customized system. The IVK team then set out to verify the degree of fit claimed by the top seven vendors. They visited vendor sites, watched demonstrations of software in action, discussed experiences with reference customers, and attended a final presentation by each vendor. Every member of the team had also, in theory, carefully reviewed each of the multivolume proposals submitted by vendors. Upon receiving the proposals, some on the team had joked that the contestants seemed to think they would be chosen based on the weight of proposal binders. The documents made substantial and difficult reading. Gradually, however, the group ruled out candidates from the list of seven. Eventually, three candidates remained, each with significant appeal to a subgroup within the IR team.*

HiOSoft had historically operated primarily as a software company focused on a product line for customers in many more businesses than financial services. Their product fit reasonably with IVK's requirements, but it was arguably the least suitable as installed out of the box. Also, because the company had not been a services firm historically, its proposal relied a great deal on partners; the IVK team agreed that HiOSoft probably ranked third in maturity of service offerings. But HiOSoft's product had one compelling strength: a very open architecture, which would arguably make the customization IVK needed to do in the future much easier. Still, though the product fared well in terms of flexibility, it measured up less well in terms of robustness. The company had been late to the market for industrial-strength, high-reliability products, so there were questions marks in this area that disconcerted some. Other, mostly IT, people believed there was no real reason you shouldn't be able to engineer a very robust system based on the HiOSoft proposal. On the IVK IR team, HiOSoft and its product had support among the smallest minority, much of it from people who had favored the initial NetiFects component-based approach; they also enjoyed disproportionate support from technical members of the IR team.

VerxaWeb had been labeled (by its detractors) "the sentimental favorite." And it was true—people *liked* VerxaWeb. Its products and services specialized in the financial services industry. VerxaWeb spoke IVK's language, and the two organizations fit well together culturally. Their product fit well with IVK's specification. But some on the IVK team felt that the considerably smaller and less financially successful vendor tried *too* hard. They worried about long-term viability of this

*See "Vendor Assessment Matrices" at the end of this chapter.

potential partner. VerxaWeb, some worried, might be a partner that IVK would too soon outgrow.

No one had such worries about ServoLith, by far the largest and most successful company in the group of finalists. Their product focused less on financial services, but fit well with the specification. The concern with ServoLith: whether the vendor's size and success would make IVK, a relatively small company among ServoLith clients, a low-priority customer. Many disliked this vendor based on past dealings. Words used to describe them included "arrogant," "overpriced," and "unresponsive." During the vendor presentations, some had felt vindicated in their harsh assessments when ServoLith failed to produce a technical expert as promised, instead substituting someone more junior. ServoLith representatives said that the promised expert had been detained because of a "personal matter." But an explanation obtained through the grapevine, from someone who knew someone who knew someone within ServoLith contradicted the vendor's assertion. Supposedly, a major company—much bigger than IVK—had summoned the technical expert to *their* site on the day he'd been promised to IVK; the big client's demands had won out when measured against the request from a prospective, smallish client. To some, this was a red flag; it might very well be a behavior destined to be repeated if IVK chose to work with ServoLith. Nevertheless, choice of ServoLith, the industry leader, would be defensible to analysts, shareholders, and executives, no matter how you looked at it. Because this vendor had so many large clients, there were few doubts about the scalability or robustness of their products. Questions centered mostly on whether they would be a sufficiently attentive partner.

To Barton, HiOSoft appeared to be losing out as increasingly strident voices gathered around the other two vendors. Advocates of ServoLith accused proponents of VerxaWeb of ignoring hard facts in favor of mysterious "intangibles." VerxaWeb advocates accused proponents of ServoLith of taking people factors and past experience with that vendor too little into account. Barton thought positions appeared to be hardening, and he saw no indications that the group would break through to consensus anytime soon. If he'd dared enter the debate, Barton would have urged that they focus less on deciding and more on coming up with an agreed method for making a decision they'd all consider reasonable and by which they'd all be willing to abide. But he didn't dare enter, at least not yet.

The second major topic of debate had to do with the proposed contract structure that would define the relationship with whichever vendor might eventually be chosen. In this discussion, the divide had formed around what Barton thought of as "hard-line" and the "soft-cooperation" philosophies.

Hard-liners advocated a service level agreement with, as they put it, "real teeth." If the vendor failed to deliver services as contracted, on the schedule laid out in the SLA, then the vendor would pay significant and painful penalties to IVK. Those who favored this approach believed it would assure maximum effort from the vendor and strong alignment of the interests of the two parties. This group was also more likely to be interested in front-loading the vendor contract in IVK's favor, so that benefits would be realized by the vendor only after the partnership had been in place for a while and the benefits of the partnership to IVK had become obvious. In this sort of scheme, IVK would pay discounted prices to the vendor at first, which would become more lucrative for the vendor as the initiative progressed.

The soft cooperators argued for a more collaborative and less adversarial approach to contracting. They believed the SLA should be in place to eliminate ambiguity in definitions of vendor "performance," but they did not see the point in severe penalties that might, at least in the case of VerxaWeb, actually harm the vendor partner (there was significant overlap between the people of this opinion and those who favored VerxaWeb). This contingent also opposed an adversarial approach to the payment schedule to the vendor, and instead proposed setting up a contract based on fairness and profitability for both parties.

The debate about contract structure interacted with the debate about choice of vendor. In particular, some observed that IVK's ability to dictate contract terms would be considerably diminished if they chose ServoLith. That large company, which could, in the final analysis, easily afford to lose IVK's business, would be less flexible on contract terms and much else. Probably IVK would have to work with them on relatively standard terms that the vendor would disproportionately dictate. The standard ServoLith contract would be designed, no doubt, to avoid any serious teeth that might impact the vendor. In contrast, IVK would have a great deal of contract negotiation leverage with Verxa-Web, whose managers seemed especially hungry for the IVK deal; IVK would be able to put big teeth in the deal, but teeth *too* big might chew hard into VerxaWeb. The coalition of vendors specified in the proposal from HiOSoft offered flexibility in contracting, but also complexity that might be hard to manage. In the HiOSoft proposal, there would not be one SLA but many, each with a different partner vendor.

The third major disagreement centered on what the group had labeled the service delivery model. The three vendors had proposed quite different ways to meet the requirements in the IVK specification, and very different structures of ownership.

ServoLith, for example, had proposed a total solution model, in which the vendor would own the data centers, as well as all the equipment and software in use, and provide services to IVK business personnel and clients over network connections. IVK would pay for these services in a monthly fee, the way they bought power and paid rent. Some members of the group positively loved this idea; they argued that IVK should not be in the business of running data centers or developing basic software systems. They allowed that IVK might want to run its own software in certain areas key to maintaining competitive advantage, but moving nonessential services to a vendor would make it easier, they believed, to focus on the IT services that provided competitive advantage. For most of what ServoLith proposed to do, IVK would never be as expert as the vendor, which had vast experience with many other clients and many more specialized resources than IVK could ever bring to bear.

Those who disliked the "software as a service" model proposed by ServoLith tended to dislike what they saw as the loss of control inherent in the model. The vendor would keep IVK data inside vendor facilities and equipment, and control IVK's access to it. If the vendor proved unresponsive, the result could cripple IVK. In addition, part of the ServoLith strategy of operating this way appeared to be based on their intention to offer solutions developed for one client to their other clients. This could mean, in theory, that IVK-specific functionality would be marketed by

ServoLith to IVK competitors, although the vendor had signaled flexibility in this matter—proposing waiting periods, for example—before remarketing IVK custom features and functionality.

VerxaWeb proposed a solution with very different features. Their representatives went to great pains to reassure IVK managers that they would remain in charge of their own systems and operations. VerxaWeb proposed installing IVK systems on IVK equipment running in IVK data centers (or space IVK had rented from a third party). VerxaWeb's proposal included an option to provide operations staff who would manage IVK systems and equipment inside IVK walls, but it was just an option, and it was as far as their proposal went in that direction. The proposal did not, of course, rule out any future outsourcing, but it represented, on the whole, a more modest service delivery proposal than what had been offered by ServoLith, and one that was also priced more moderately. And VerxaWeb explicitly assured IVK that they would not remarket solutions to IVK competitors. They promised, in fact, not to work for any of IVK's top competitors.

HighOSoft left the question of service architecture completely open. Their proposal had assumed that IVK would be contracting separately with other partners, and the service architecture would be determined by how IVK decided to set up these partnerships. Whatever IVK wanted to do about partnership and contract arrangements would be okay with HiOSoft; they were mainly looking to sell a software package. The only aspect of the solution on which this vendor was inflexible: the broad technical specifications of the service-oriented architecture at the center of their proposal, which set up a standard framework that all the components of the solution would plug into. This approach provided IVK with maximum flexibility, but also maximum relationship overhead. It risked forcing many decisions back onto IVK and causing the same kind of paralysis that had been the norm in the NetiFects era. Unlike the solution proposed by the other two finalists, this one did not explicitly offer "one throat to choke" in its support arrangements. In other words, if something went wrong in the ServoLith model, there'd be only one party to call: ServoLith. The VerxaWeb proposal had a similar feature, and they would likely feel the grip of IVK's metaphorical fingers much more pressingly than would ServoLith. HiOSoft would not object to IVK setting up a single point of contact for service, a single throat to choke, as part of its web of involved partners, but this arrangement wasn't inherent in their proposal.

Barton was not at all confident that he knew the solution to all these problems, but he grew increasingly impatient with the debate. He worried, too, that none of the vendors might be able to do a really good job on such a big infrastructure replacement, at least not on schedule and budget. Barton had read the grim story of FoxMeyer Drug, a $5 billion pharmaceutical distributor that had gone out of business when it switched over to a replacement operating infrastructure and discovered that the new one couldn't handle the required volume of transactions. And that was just the tip of the iceberg. He'd also heard horror stories about candy companies unable to deliver shipments for major holidays and legal battles between companies over whose fault some major failure might be.

As the latest acrimonious meeting ended, Barton thought far too much remained up in the air. It felt to him like a form of torture, following a discussion headed nowhere without being able to intervene. But it was torture of his own making, the result of his own decisions that had seemed right at the time but now cast a long dark shadow. Perhaps he had acted too hastily. Perhaps. But what was done was done. Barton believed he now needed to do something really hard but really essential—trust the team to work through its own difficulties.

Monday, October 1, 11:00 a.m. . . .

As Barton stepped into Maria Navarro's office for their scheduled meeting, he felt himself relax. Maria had that wonderful ability to seem like anyone's confidante. Probably that was a major reason for her success as an HR executive. Certainly it worked with Barton, even though he knew he should be wary. The HR VP was also involved in firings, demotions, and other adverse outcomes. She was, Barton knew, very tough under that warm exterior. But she and Barton had known each other for a long time and had worked together often, so he tended to feel at ease with her.

"How's it going, Jim?" she asked, as she motioned him into a chair. He shut the office door before he complied.

"It's getting better," Barton said.

"Williams has been pretty hard on you, I imagine."

"It's been tough with Carl for a few months, but I'm pressing on. It's getting better," he repeated, not altogether convincingly.

"How about with your peers?"

"You mean do their conversations still stop when I walk up on them? Yes, sometimes. Less often than a month or two ago. I really think we're building back some credibility."

Navarro, in that maddening way of HR managers, was noncommittal. She looked sympathetic, but offered no corroboration that would stake her to a position on how Barton was doing. Then she changed the subject, which was just as well.

"You've got a hiring issue you wanted to talk about, yes?"

"Yes," said Barton. "You remember the NetiFects situation."

"You terminated their contract, as I recall," said Navarro.

"I did. A decision with aftershocks I've been suffering personally. Among the issues we've had to deal with in the aftermath of the divorce: we lost access to some of their very good people. One of them, Ash Srinivasa, is now signaling to us his availability and desire to work for IVK. We'd like to hire him."

"What's the situation with NetiFects? Is that resolved?"

"No. They're still maintaining that we owe them several hundred thousand dollars. I'm arguing that they failed to perform. It won't come to anything. They'll keep billing us, we'll keep refusing to pay. But it won't go any further."

"Unless there's an issue around hiring one of their key people."

"Exactly. Sometimes hiring from a vendor is no big deal. Some vendors expect a certain amount of that. Others make you agree not to do it. NetiFects is the latter kind, although we no longer have a contract with them."

"What kind of contract does—what's his name?"

"Srinivasa."

"What kind of contract does he have?"

"I think there's something in it saying he can't go to work for a client for some period of time without NetiFects' official permission."

"Probably not enforceable. But it could result in a skirmish. How good is this guy?"

"By all accounts, he's very, very good. Worth a skirmish, probably."

"I think we probably go for it, then. They're likely to try to intimidate him into not taking the position. They'll go at him, not us. Or they might just let the whole thing slide. But let me ask you another question," Navarro said. Barton nodded, and she continued: "Why do we need someone this good?"

"You can never have enough people this good," said Barton. "They're very rare."

"But aren't we headed toward more outsourcing in the future?"

"Probably."

"How many very, very good people will we need in that future? Won't we just need smart contract managers?"

"It's a good question," conceded Barton. "I know my guys think we need expertise in-house even when we outsource, so that we can manage effectively. In a way, that's what went wrong with the NetiFects relationship. We didn't have people on it who could supervise their work effectively, and they were taking advantage of that."

"But will we even be able to retain people like this Srinivasa in the long run? How interested will he be in a job that's mostly contract management?"

"Also a good question. My guess is we'll always have some need for really good technical specialists, but I'm not sure how we stay attractive to them if we outsource more of our IT. We need to think about a future when we'll manage more vendor contracts. What does vendor management look like in the long run? What kinds of people will allow us to do it effectively? We'll need to work our way into answers for questions like these, by trying different things, seeing how they work. Minimizing the cost and risk of our experiments. Meanwhile, I think we could use this guy. My people think he'd really be able to help us."

Navarro nodded again. "Let's move forward with it then. Just let me know if you need any more help from me."

Barton stood. "I will."

Vendor mgmt

"Take care of yourself, Jim." She winked at him. Barton felt his defenses falling, then made a deliberate effort to pull them back up. "And use some of that vacation time you're accruing," she called after him, as he started down the hall.

"I'll do that. Thanks, Maria."

Vacation? Geez, it's already October! thought Barton. He hadn't meant to wait so long without going somewhere with Maggie. When he'd cancelled their summer vacation—two weeks in Italy—he was amazed she hadn't dumped him. But he just couldn't see leaving IVK at such a critical time. Who knew what kind of revolt might have arisen in his absence? In a particularly memorable nightmare, Barton had returned from Europe to find Davies reinstated as CIO, sitting in his chair.

In the first few months they'd dated, Barton and Maggie had mastered the romantic getaway: skiing in Aspen, cruising to Cabo; even an impromptu weekend in Paris. They'd always compensated for their awkward schedules, the time apart necessitated by two high-powered careers, by taking really fabulous trips to exotic places when they could get away. Now they were long overdue for one of these. Hadn't Maggie just said something about scuba diving in Bermuda? Belize? Maybe he could make something happen before the month was over. The matter definitely needed tending, Barton thought. Just the possibility of a vacation lightened his step as he headed back to his office to do some research.

REFLECTION

Should acquisition of infrastructure replacement services be an arm's-length transaction or a close partnership transaction?

Which vendor, contract structure, and service delivery model should IVK choose?

How important is "control" to a company like IVK when outsourcing IT? How should control be maintained?

How should IVK hire to support contract management? Will very, very good technical employees be needed in a future characterized by high levels of IT outsourcing?

Vendor Assessment Matrices

Functional criteria	Percentage of fit		
	HiOSoft	VerxaWeb	ServoLith
Electronic application	100	100	96
Credit scoring	82	98	98
Decision processing	75	99	97
Workflow management	78	94	86
Customer service interface	97	100	97
Financial systems interface	100	98	100
Client management functions	87	94	89
Disbursement	100	100	100
Design for robust operation	94	93	99
Scalability	94	91	100
Other	88	89	95

Qualitative criteria	Rating		
	HiOSoft	VerxaWeb	ServoLith
Long-term relationship potential	M	H	M
Research and development capability	M	MH	H
Understanding of IVK culture and challenges	M	H	M
Financial viability	M	M	H
Openness of architecture	H	M	M
Cost	M	ML	H
Technical support capabilities and plan	M	M	M
Dependence on subcontractors in proposed solution	H	M	L
Compatibility with existing IVK infrastructure (DBMS, etc.)	H	MH	M
Compatibility with existing IVK applications	H	M	M
Confidence in project management capability	ML	M	MH
Contract flexibility	H	H	L
Likely attentiveness to IVK concerns	M	H	M
Training capability and plan	M	H	M
Financial service industry experience	M	MH	M
Intangibles, comfort factor	M	H	M
Market position	Second	Third	Leader

CHAPTER FIFTEEN

MANAGING TALENT

Thursday, November 8, 10:13 a.m. . . .

Barton had just begun to check his e-mail when Tyra Gordon knocked gently on the frame of his open door.

"Hi, Tyra," said Barton.

"Got a minute?" she asked.

"More than that, if you need it. Come in."

Gordon entered the office and made a point of shutting the door before settling into a chair.

"What's up?" Barton asked.

"Well . . ." Gordon looked hesitant. "I'd like your advice. I've encountered a situation that I'm not sure how to handle. If you tell me to go figure it out, that's my job, I'd consider it reasonable. But I'd value hearing your thoughts."

"I'll do my best to give them to you straight," said Barton, becoming more curious by the second.

"Okay. Well. You remember Ivan Korsky?"

"Sure, I know Ivan. He's one of your top guys, right?"

"Exactly. He's what you might call a 'uniquely talented member of our staff.' He has a very uncommon combination of skills. He's a top software developer who has at least a ten-times productivity advantage over the next best person we have when he's writing code."

"Ten times?"

"Easily. It's pretty common in this kind of job to see significant disparities in ability. It's not like other kinds of work, where the guy who does it best might be one and a half times faster or better than the next person. In IT, especially in an area like software development, some people work a lot faster and a lot better than others."

"Which surely has implications for how we recruit, supervise, and manage."

"Definitely. But Ivan is not just a brilliant coder; he's also a brilliant architect. He has the ability to envision and design complete solutions that work and scale. Give him a pen and a whiteboard, sit down a bunch of developers in front of him, and you can sit back and just marvel at what comes to pass."

"Sounds incredibly important."

"It's amazing that we've been able to retain him. Microsoft has tried to hire him a couple of times, to make him part of one of their major development groups. Others have too. But he has family in this area and doesn't want to move. There's a constant threat that some start-up might nab him, but we're benefiting from the relative absence of tech companies in our area."

"Do we have a way of formally designating people with this level of talent in our HR management process? We might want to discuss this with Maria Navarro."

"If we lost Ivan, it would definitely set us back months, maybe years. He's not quite irreplaceable; it's been my experience that even when you lose your most important resources, someone eventually steps up to do a pretty good job. But we need to admit that Ivan's replacement would be unlikely to have his unique combination of talents. His replacement would probably surprise us with strong performance, but still wouldn't bring to the table what Ivan does."

"Who else do we have in this category?"

"You'd need to ask the other managers to be sure, but we definitely have others. Raj has one or two, probably not quite like Ivan, but very important to what we've got going on. Bernie has a couple of database specialists who would be very hard to replace, and Paul has Cho, of course, and some others too, networking specialists. We probably have a tendency to overestimate how many such resources we have. It's hard to think of doing without anyone who is currently making a big difference. But things happen and we do manage."

"Maybe," said Barton, "we ought to ask people—managers at your level—to designate a certain number of people in their organizations who are 'Priority 1' resources, or something like that. People we can't stand to lose. Might be useful in our management conversations. Think we ought to work with HR on something like that?"

"Maybe. Depends on how it would work, how useful it would be."

"My half-baked thought," said Barton.

"A good one," said Gordon, "but there might be a lot more thinking to do on how to make such a system most useful. Would we have Priority 2 resources? Priority 3? Should we do some sort of skills inventory, so that we know what each person is capable of? Should it be linked to training? All this sounds good in principle, but it could mislead us into thinking we have the talent thing worked out when we don't. I mean, Ivan has had a lot of training, but what sets him apart is not how many classes he's taken, it's what he's inherently capable of."

"So, back to your original topic, what's up with Ivan? Someone trying to hire him away?"

"I haven't even finished telling you how good he is. In addition to being a terrific coder and architect, he's also a great communicator. Not only can he come up with great designs, he can communicate to others about them. Including managers. This may not sound like a big deal when placed side-by-side with coding and architecture, but it might be the biggest deal of all. It's definitely the least common talent. Especially the 'communicating to managers' part of it. We managers can be a bit thick when it comes to technical stuff, and it's absolutely invaluable to have someone who can make an obscure technical point that entails, say, a cost-risk trade-off, clear to the likes of me or Raj."

"Fenton can go technical with the best of them in his area. But while Raj and I were pretty good technically in our time, that's not our strength, ultimately. And it's been a long time since either of us, or Bernie either, got anywhere close to writing code or configuring a piece of network equipment. The world of technology has changed vastly since we did anything even roughly equivalent to what our people are now doing."

Barton nodded. "It's even worse for me. I never did any of that stuff."

"I can imagine. Though you seem to be holding your own, Jim."

Barton waved a hand dismissively. "If so, it's because I listened well when you explained things to me when I was head of Loan Ops."

"You certainly did."

"So take me back to Ivan."

"Ah, yes. So I spent about half an hour with him this morning. I've got him assigned full-time on the Alpha3 project, which I'm sure you remember."

"I not only remember it, it's high on my list of things to keep tabs on. I was on the phone about it with one of our customers this morning. They are very eager to get the Alpha3 functionality in place. As you know, some of our competitors have also promised similar functionality. It's important enough to customers that they are threatening to move their business if we can't get the project done in a timely fashion. They believe *they're* going to lose customers if they can't offer that functionality once their own competitors have it."

"I know, I know," said Gordon. "It's the most important project we're working on at the moment. The most important anyone in IVK is working on. And from what I understand, and from what you've just been saying, the deadline is not negotiable—we *have* to hit that deadline or there will be very serious consequences for the company."

"Especially," said Barton, "given the company's recent stock and perceived performance woes. Missing the deadline might just confirm the beliefs of those who think we have stumbled after our period of rapid growth. A lot of people out there, analysts especially, are looking for signs that we've *got* our second wind, or, alternatively, that we're *not going to get* a second wind. If we don't, some say we'll be bought by one of our competitors at a discount. It won't be only Alpha3 that determines this. But things like hitting big project deadlines will signal to the markets whether we've proven our ability to move back to the front of the pack. It makes absolute sense that you have Ivan, your best guy, working on it."

"That's just it," said Gordon. "I've assigned him to work on the project full time. But he hasn't been doing it."

Barton's forehead wrinkled. He didn't quite get what Gordon was saying: "You mean he keeps getting pulled off into other things? Fire-fighting?" Barton was imagining his business peers making phone calls to specific developers inside Gordon's and Juvvani's organizations, bullying them into doing things that weren't on the official priority list. As Barton imagined this, his temper rose. "If that's it," he said, "I can make some calls right now."

"We do get some of those problems, but the guys typically bring those right to me, and I handle them," said Gordon. "That's not the problem in this case."

"I don't get it, then."

"Well . . ." Gordon seemed reluctant to say what she was thinking.

"What is it, Tyra? We've worked together for a long time. Whatever it is, you can tell me."

"I feel like a kid telling on my little brother, and that I ought to just handle this without bothering you."

"You said you wanted my advice."

"The truth is, I'm not sure what to do. The truth is, also, that I'm embarrassed. I think this represents a failure of my own management of my own group. I should have known about this."

"If you're trying to whip up my curiosity, you've certainly done it," said Barton. He smiled reassuringly, convinced now that he needed to be involved in this issue that had so disconcerted his trusted manager.

She paused, sighed deeply, then plunged forward. "Ivan's actually been working something entirely unrelated. Unrelated to anything at IVK. His own pet project. As best I can tell, he's been working on it more than half the time."

"What kind of pet project?"

"We put up with a lot of things from some of our best people," said Gordon, now turning protective. "We have to. It's part of how we retain really good people. It's important that we are progressive in the way we treat our people. I don't know if you know this, but John Cho is part of a jazz band. They've made records. Sometimes we give him a few days off to make a new record in a studio. He goes to New York. And we let him come in to work late all the time after he's done late-night gigs in clubs. If we didn't, he'd choose to work elsewhere, and he could. He could walk out any day and have another job an hour later."

"John Cho is in a *jazz* band? Wow. I'd heard that his unconventional work schedule had to do with membership in a band. But I would have guessed punk rock," said Barton.

"He plays saxophone, I think," said Gordon.

"We've gotten off the subject of Ivan." Barton repeated his question: "What kind of pet project?"

"Ivan's been involved in a political movement aimed at getting rid of software patents. He doesn't believe in them. It's sort of a radical open source group. They believe code should be freely available to others, in an ideal world. And they resent efforts by tech companies, and especially opportunistic intellectual property salvage firms, to collect patents that might be the basis for an infringement claim, then sue and settle with companies they accuse of infringement. Ivan has a point, really, a lot of those patents are a problem."

"Yes, but what *kind* of pet project?" Barton was hoping this didn't involve some sort of leakage of IVK proprietary information to someone outside the company. Depending on what it was, that might cost Gordon and Barton their jobs. Williams had a short fuse these days.

"He calls it a 'random patent application generator,'" explained Gordon. "The idea is that it will generate and automatically submit applications to the U.S. Patent Office that look real and take up time and resources, but that are ultimately nonsense. By barraging Patent Office systems with a rapid-fire assault, they hope to totally confound the patent authorities, and bring the whole system to its knees. In a way, it's a version of a denial of service attack, in that it uses up all the resources of the organization on worthless business. But Ivan and his associates would also be delighted, I think, if a randomly generated application resulted in a patent approval. That would have a lot of PR value to them."

"Fascinating, but I still don't see what it has to do with us. Has he pulled IVK into his battle?"

"You mean has he leaked some of our proprietary code, something like that? Oh, no. It's the time. He's spent more than half his time over the past couple of months working on this while we've been under serious deadline pressure on the Alpha3 project. I don't think he's been developing or testing his own private code on our machines, but he's probably been using some IVK resources. E-mail, certainly. And he's remotely accessing his machines at home from our site. None of which has anything to do with IVK business."

"I see. So he has involved us in this, in a way," said Barton. He felt some relief that things had not proved as bad as he'd feared. But he could see why Gordon considered this a problem. "What do you think we should do?"

"That's what I'm not sure of," said Gordon.

"What did you say to him this morning?" asked Barton. "You said you spent time with him."

"Yes," said Gordon, "but I was so startled by it all that I couldn't really fashion a reasonable response on the spot. When we got onto the subject, by accident—I don't even remember how it came up—he was delighted to share it all with me. For half an hour he walked me through the entire project, explained his enthusiasm for it, why he considers it of tremendous importance to humankind—that's exactly how he put it, by the way, said it was of utmost importance to the future of humankind that this issue be dealt with. He didn't say it, but an implication, of course, is that it's more important than the Alpha3 project deadline."

"Think we should fire him?" Barton asked.

"We can't," said Gordon. "Not if we want to have any chance of hitting the Alpha3 project deadlines. We simply can't do it without him."

"Want to wait until we hit the deadline and then fire him?"

"That would seem mercenary of us, don't you think?"

"It would certainly make him an example."

"Might also anger other people. What would John Cho think about it, for example?"

"Maybe there's nothing we can do about it. Maybe he's more valuable to us working on our stuff part time than any replacement would be full time. Of course we need to make sure he doesn't actually launch any of these attacks on the patent office from our computers."

"There's no doubt that he's very, very valuable to us, but I also have a problem with just letting it go. That's not the deal we have with him. We employ him full time. We pay him for full-time work. But he hasn't been giving us full time."

"How do you think he views this apparent violation of his employment contract with us?"

"I think he considers it beyond plausibility that we would not share his concern about the problems in the patent system. I think he honestly expects us to also rank his pet project higher in priority than the Alpha3 project deadline. From what he said this morning, I read between the lines that he likes working for IVK because he thinks we are a good cause."

"I'm guessing that we pay better than his pet project, too," said Barton. "Think you could just sit him down and have a heart-to-heart with him about this? Try to get his priorities a bit more aligned with ours?"

"Yeah, that's probably what I should do. Certainly I need to be clear about what he can and can't do with the company's resources. But it's likely to be a difficult conversation."

"Think I should do it?"

"No, I think that would make it too much like grade school punishment, getting sent to the principal's office."

Barton nodded. "Tyra, I don't have much advice on this, off the top of my head. We can't afford to lose the guy, clearly. Others must know he's not putting all his time into Alpha3."

"Oh, sure. I should have known."

"Oh, yeah, and I should have too," said Barton with a reassuring wink, but without smiling. "How about if you give me some time to think about this, and we reconvene after lunch?"

Gordon nodded her head once, still looking upset. "We'll figure this out, Tyra," said Barton. "We probably ought to bring up this issue in the managers' meeting next week; I want to talk about how we handle these kinds of situations, in case it should happen again. Also, this conversation has got me thinking we should have a much broader conversation about managing talent inside the IT organization."

"Thanks, Jim." Gordon stood. "What time should I come back?"

"Oh, how about 1:30? I've got no meetings until 3. That should give us plenty of time. Think too about whether you need some additional resources to make up for the time lost to Ivan's pet project. We could divert some people from Raj's group, maybe. We've got to hit that deadline."

Gordon shook her head. "I think it's too late to get someone else in there, but we can think about it. We'd lose time getting a new person up to speed, and you can't really substitute anyone else for Ivan. That's why this is such a big deal. We need all of his attention devoted to making this deadline." She paused. "I'm really sorry about this, Jim."

"Sounds to me," said Barton, "like this is more a matter of realizing and adjusting to the changing nature of management in the twenty-first century than anything to feel sorry about."

"Thanks for saying so." She turned and opened the door. Barton knew she'd keep feeling responsible. It was part of what made her a good manager. And they would have to figure out how to make the adjustments necessary to hit that deadline. That was simply not optional.

After Gordon left, Barton's eyes wandered to the whiteboard, where early in his tenure as CIO he'd written "Skill and talent management/key skills, key contributors." He remembered the kid in Vinnie's Bar suggesting an assessment of key skills and contributors as the very first thing Barton should do as a new CIO. But somehow the issue had slipped through the cracks. *Time to resurface it*, thought Barton. *Should have done it already.*

Thursday, November 8, 12:32 p.m. . . .

"That's a tough one," said Bernie Ruben between the last two bites of what had been an enormous BLT. Barton had barely touched his own turkey sandwich. He'd been explaining to Ruben the situation that Gordon had brought to him earlier in the day, and the talking had left Barton with little time for eating. Now he took a bite and listened to Ruben, who wiped his mouth and began to offer his thoughts.

"Tyra undoubtedly feels that this is a failure in her supervisory responsibilities, although I sincerely hope you don't see it that way." Barton shook his head, chewing. "It's a problem. A big one. We depend on them to tell us what is really going on, where the problems really are. And so many of the things we might do to get a better view of what they are doing, an independent view, can potentially backfire, disrupt the communication from them that we really depend on. Developers like

Ivan don't like it when you peek over their shoulders too much, especially when they've been doing their best to explain everything to you. It feels to them like you are checking up on what they're saying. Which is, of course, what you *are* doing. And you can imagine what might happen if someone like Ivan brought the same indignation to his relationship with Tyra Gordon that he brings to his crusade against software patents."

"I don't suppose there's any hope for a technology solution? Monitoring systems, to tell us what people are up to?" Barton asked.

"If you ask me, no. Others might disagree. You can buy software that installs on everyone's computer that tells you what applications people are using all the time. Whether they are accessing sports sites on the Web, or worse. You can get as Big Brother with it as you want. You can use such systems to infer how much time people are spending on the jobs you've assigned to them."

"Whether they're coding, say," Barton tried.

"Yes," continued Ruben, "coding, answering e-mail, surfing the Web, or not working on the computer at all."

"You could probably get sophisticated in how you used that sort of software," observed Barton.

"Yes, but not nearly as sophisticated as guys like Ivan could get. We don't really know what it looks like when guys like Ivan work at their peak. Maybe he's most valuable to us when he sits staring into space 20 percent of the time. Or maybe that's how he's most valuable to us this week and next week it's a different story.

"Imagine a situation like this: We document what everybody does, the time spent performing each kind of work to the nearest minute. Guys like Ivan, operating at a very high level, contribute, let's imagine, twenty-five hours per week in actual coding. Maybe this gets them unfavorably singled out. At the same time, some other employees, who are not performing nearly as well as Ivan, are coding forty or fifty hours a week, in part because it takes them so much longer to do the same jobs. These guys look like heroes using such a measure. Obvious morale problems result.

"The ultimate problem, I think, is that what we want to buy from people is not really their time. We want to buy their smarts, their resourcefulness, their good business judgment, their ideas about new ways of doing things, something like that. Those things don't result from an eight-hour day; those things are hard to measure. But what we can readily measure is their time. The disparity between what we want from people and what we can readily measure makes it really important that we, as managers, interpret what we see well."

Barton stopped in midbite, interrupted by a sudden thought. "You know," he said, "that's what still makes me most uncomfortable in this job. I walk through the IT department, I see people doing all kinds of things. Typing at the computer, standing in the hall with coffee cups, talking. Sitting together in conference rooms, drawing on whiteboards and flip charts. Problem is, I don't know what any of it means."

"Hah!" Ruben laughed. "Like any of us do. But at least we can know what we don't know."

There was that phrase again, Barton reflected.

"Do you think," asked Barton, "that we've got the right IT organization to maximize the value of our talent? I could imagine other ways of organizing. Right now we are effectively organized with two application groups facing the business units they support, and two general services groups. We could go either more toward centralized support models, by pulling all application developers together, say, or more to decentralized models, by distributing technical talent in your group or Fenton's into the applications areas."

"It's a question," conceded Ruben, "that we should revisit periodically. There's been a movement in the industry toward shared services models, which consolidate and centralize services as an alternative to embedding them in specific segments of the business. If we did this, we might put Ivan, the other key people in Tyra's area, and the key people in Raj's area into a central applications group with super capabilities. They would then work on whatever projects were most important to the company, not just the ones most important to the particular business unit to which they happen to face off. Alpha3 would have not just Ivan and whoever else Tyra's got working on that one, but also maybe some of Raj's best talent. Shared service models might also eventually better facilitate outsourcing, if that's where we are heading. In creating a development capability in a shared services group, we are also potentially creating a place to plug in specialized external resources. The processes and procedures we need to create a general shared services capability are similar to the processes and procedures we'd need to deploy vendor capabilities in those areas. This logic probably also applies to areas like security. Maybe a financial services company can't, in the long run, retain enough talent to keep IT solid in an area like security. Maybe ultimately we'll all have to outsource security, or we won't have enough talent in that crucial area. Then the question becomes: what else is that true for?"

"I wonder which would be best for development of our talent," Barton pondered. "Is it better to put a group of superstars together, let them push each other and learn from each other? Or is it better to surround superstars with less-able employees who can learn a lot from the masters?"

"We know only what we have tried," shrugged Ruben. "which is a result of historical tendencies—how the organization grew in response to specific business needs—as much as anything else."

"I'd like to begin a discussion about this in next week's managers' meeting," Barton said. "Have you put together the agenda for that yet?" Barton relied on Ruben to set the agenda for the weekly meeting with Barton's direct reports.

"I have," said Ruben, "but we have room for this. I'll add it."

The two men grew silent as Barton finished his sandwich. When the conversation resumed, Barton changed the subject: "So, any big plans for the weekend?" Ruben began telling about a dog show that he and his wife liked to attend every year. The two of them were amateur dog breeders, specializing in pugs. As he spoke, Ruben's enthusiasm for the topic was apparent. Barton's thoughts drifted, to questions of how he could acquire the expertise to know who his "best-in-show" employees might be: a surprisingly difficult question, he now realized.

Thursday, November 8, 6:18 p.m. . . .

Barton capped the marker, laid it down, and reviewed his whiteboard additions. *What would Ivan Korsky or John Cho think if they read this?*

Barton imagined Cho warming up for a gig, blasting out an elaborate riff on his sax. Something still seemed incongruous to Barton about Cho holding a sax, rather than a guitar. *Maybe I should check out his band some time.*

But not tonight. At the moment, nothing appealed more than his leather couch and some mindless TV. And with that imagery vivid in his mind, he was out the door.

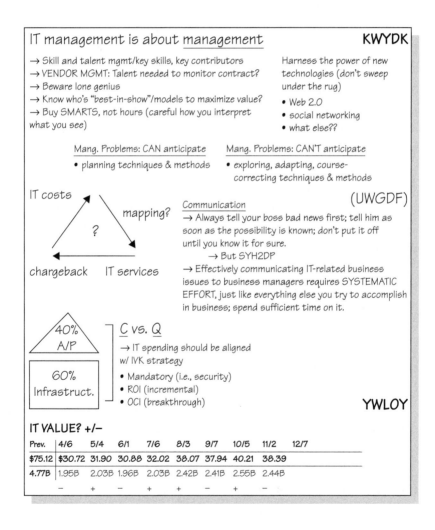

The Hero Breaks Through

These guys are really good, thought Barton. *At least as far as I can tell with my non-expert ears.*[1]

After a stop in Vinnie's Bar for dinner, he'd headed over to a local jazz club to catch the featured act, the John Cho Quartet. Barton settled himself at a back table in a dark corner, then sat back to listen and wish that Maggie could be there. It felt a bit pathetic, being alone, as usual, on another Friday night. But the music soared, lifting his spirits with it.

The quartet included, besides Cho on sax, a drummer, upright bass, and piano. The solos were dazzling—each of these guys was really talented—but the ensemble playing just blew him away. Barton studied the collaboration, what seemed to make it work, and formed some hypotheses.

During a break, Cho, who had noticed Barton partway through a set, stopped by his table to say hello. The two had never had conversations outside official channels—and their work relationship had been, well, rather encumbered—so both interacted awkwardly at first. Barton invited Cho to sit, if he had time; he thought Cho seemed generally pleased to have his boss's boss come check out a gig. Barton hoped he'd become at least a little cooler in Cho's estimation. *Always a good thing*, Barton thought, *as cool is not something I have in natural abundance.*

Barton tried out on Cho some of what he thought he could see in how the ensemble collaborated. "You each have pretty specialized roles," he said. "You, the saxophone, carry the tune a lot . . ."

"The melody, yeah," confirmed Cho, nodding.

"The drum and bass players set the rhythm, help you all keep things together . . ."

"Yeah, they set the groove, keep it going . . ." said Cho.

"The piano seems quite versatile, sometimes a melody instrument, sometimes more like the bass, accompanying, keeping the flow going . . ."

"Yeah, totally. Nice observations," said Cho. "We definitely have specialized roles, and knowing that we each just have to manage our own role is part of the way we can work so well together."

"You seem to take turns with solos," said Barton.

"That's right, pretty much," said Cho, "That's another way we simplify interactions to help us work better together. We decide, pretty much in real time, like with a nod or a hand movement, who is going to solo next. When we're really going good, sometimes we don't literally take turns, in, like, a mechanistic way, but instead we start to have a sort of nonverbal conversation, weaving in and out of solo or 'comping' roles. But having that basic idea of soloing versus comping totally helps."

"And of course you are all technically fabulous players," said Barton.

Cho nodded: "'Technique is the dancer's freedom.' Martha Graham, great dance choreographer, said that. Technique is the jazz musician's freedom too. In our conversation, like within our flow, we have a lot of problems to solve in real time: where to go next, keeping it together, building on each other's ideas. And we see lots of cool opportunities, to try something new, to get rid of an old musical cliché we're prone to, or at least to twist and turn the context so that old clichés sound fresh and new. Our ability to solve the problems and seize the opportunities in real time depends on our technical mastery. But technical mastery is not enough by itself; it's, like, a prerequisite to going beyond it, into true artistry. Plus, the best players combine technique with simplification—with experience you tend to play less, but accomplish more."

"How is it," asked Barton, "that you were able to play that request in the last set so fabulously?"

"You liked that?" said Cho. "Man, that was a tough one. It was not something we'd practiced together. But we all have, like, a similar philosophy as jazz players. We like to take chances, do something that puts us out in new territory. Do that together, but in a way where we might not all take risks all the time. We played it, had a few rough spots; if the soloist goes out on a limb, the other players tend to become more predictable to support the soloist. Probably not audible to most people."

"I heard no rough spots."

"That doesn't surprise me, but we totally had some—places where we made incompatible choices and had to climb back down from those. The bass player had a bit of trouble remembering the piece! He figured it out eventually, but he did it while we were playing."

"No kidding. You would think something that big would be audible, even to my ears."

"I don't know," Cho shrugged. "Sometimes I think that's when jazz is at its best, you know. When you're solving a new problem that drives you into a totally new way of playing. That's when it's really fresh, and that's when it is what it is. That's jazz at its best, man. The rough spots are part of it. You relate to a form, but you try to stretch its boundaries."

"Sounds pretty scary."

Cho shrugged again. "Scary. Exciting. Two nights ago, we started playing one song, and I just spaced. I could not get going. The bass player went into a solo because he could tell I was having trouble, to buy me some time, and when he came out of it, somehow I started off in the wrong key. Now he's a great bass player, but he couldn't close the gap between what I was doing and what he was doing, and I couldn't either, so I just totally stopped playing! The keyboards player went into a different ballad, and we all went with that instead. It was a train wreck, really, and I think some people in the audience could tell, but it wasn't totally terrible. Then later, I started playing a ballad in the middle of something else we were doing and the bass player couldn't figure out what I was doing right away. Eventually he locked in, but it took him a few minutes. It's hard to know how well you are playing when you are in the middle of it. When I was younger I would judge myself more while I was playing. But experience and listening to recordings has taught me that my ability to judge my performance while I am performing is pretty much worthless. It's better just to be in the moment and to trust your own abilities."

"Sounds like you all know certain songs."

"That's part of how we collaborate so well. We have a common language and a lot of shared references. We call them standards. We've all studied a bunch of the same recordings, and memorizing solos is both a way to build your own voice and create a pool of ideas we can later tap into to develop ideas—like Sonny Rollins's sax solo on one of his originals, "St. Thomas," or Miles Davis's solo on "So What" from *Kind of Blue*. We know the chord progressions. We know rhythms, grooves, from different recordings. So, with a thirty-second conversation, we can orient ourselves—even a group that's never played together, if they're good. A certain groove from one recording, a chord progression from another, a Latin version of an old standard, then we improvise around the known parts of it. We lay down certain parameters, and by quickly establishing certain absolute guidelines for the band—tempo, key, groove—we have more mental capacity available to be creative and to focus on the musical context—which, by the way, is different every time we play. It's really like a conversation. The most important element we bring to the table is our ability to listen to each other and make sure our input is relevant to the context. Chops, or technique, if you will, that's really meaningless if not used musically. Make any sense? I'm getting a little out there . . ."

Barton was nodding. "I think I get it. Part of it, anyway. I'm trying to think whether it helps me understand anything about how to manage you brilliant technical guys, in our other lives, at IVK."

"A deep question," said Cho, "But I think there's something there. It's not, like, a perfect analogy, but there's no doubt I bring something from my sax playing to the work I do at IVK."

Just then, the drummer came back out on stage and motioned to Cho. "Gotta go," Cho said. "Thanks a ton for coming."

"Thanks a ton for playing such fabulous music," said Barton. "And for taking the time to explain things to me. This won't be the last time I come to hear you play."

Cho smiled, then headed back up to the stage. Barton took a sip of his drink. He wondered briefly about the size of this quartet. *Does this kind of collaboration scale? If not, what does that mean for how we should organize our top talent?* Important questions, Barton thought, but now was not the time to answer them. Now was the time to listen to excellent jazz.

REFLECTION

What should Barton and Gordon do about the Ivan Korsky problem?

How might IT managers best measure and compare the output of diverse employees? Do you think this measurement should impact the kind of "deal" (contract) that IVK makes with talented employees such as Korsky?

What other kinds of challenges are involved when acquiring, training, and managing IT talent?

What kind of restructuring or "tuning" does an IT organization require over time? How should you decide whether to centralize talent in a shared organization or decentralize it into distributed groups?

What might Barton learn from Cho's explanation of how a jazz ensemble works?

CHAPTER SIXTEEN

STANDARDIZATION AND INNOVATION

Infrastructure standardization policy day at IVK. Barton sat listening to proposals by Bernie Ruben's staff for how the IT department should act against the proliferating complexity of IVK's IT environment, the abundant variety of software and hardware in different versions and brands. Business managers at IVK had grown accustomed to making their own decisions about what business systems and tools to acquire. When they saw something they liked and decided they wanted it, they often bought it if they had budget for it. Sometimes they bought an application without any input from the IT department, then turned around and expected IT to install it and support it. This happened all the time with PDAs, for instance. Some departments liked one variety, others another. All did as they pleased. Consequently, the IT staff found itself supporting e-mail services on four different vendor platforms, and frequently getting blamed for problems that had nothing to do with IVK, problems actually caused by service providers.

But PDAs were the least of the IT department's concerns about infrastructure diversity. PDAs were non-mission-critical devices. When they failed, a lot of wailing and gnashing of teeth ensued, but the company continued to operate. The relics of past battles between different IT department factions were bigger problems.

IVK had historically been a mostly Microsoft shop, but open source and more Unix-based platforms had made inroads. Wherever this had happened, a bridging application had to be developed, which then had to be maintained and modified whenever the application on either side of the bridge changed. And people forgot to include changes to bridging application in project plans, which meant extra work not in the schedule in the best case, malfunctioning systems in the worst case. Often these problems were easy fixes for IT support staff, but the total overhead increased as more of these fixes became necessary. It had happened again and again, whenever enthusiasts for various unfamiliar technologies gained critical mass within IT.

Sometimes a vendor drove the adoption of nonstandard software or equipment. This had been on the verge of happening when Barton fired NetiFects. The vendor had a significant investment in one of the software development paradigms that was a rival to Microsoft's. Most of the know-how NetiFects could bring to bear fit poorly with the IVK legacy infrastructure. The IR group, at the time not very deep in IT talent, had weighted this factor insufficiently in the decision to hire the company in the first place. NetiFects had contributed to the problem by downplaying the extent of their orientation toward this alternative paradigm until after they had a signed contract in hand. Then they had promptly begun lobbying for a major course change in infrastructure standards at IVK. They had argued for this change on the relative merits of the two alternative paradigms, but their true reasons had much less to do with IVK's best interests than their own.

NetiFects did not succeed in changing infrastructure standards at IVK—Barton had fired them before they got the chance. But over the years a number of vendors had successfully executed similar strategies, though not on the scale NetiFects had attempted. Usually these one-off technologies came into IVK when a business unit worked for a while with an external consulting group. The marketing department, for example, had worked with such a consultant for some time and had several systems based on technologies far outside the IVK mainstream to show for it.

More generally, the problem arose whenever the business units decided they just *had* to have systems, whether promoted by consultants or not, that happened to run on different platforms—hardware or software—than those the IT department could comfortably support. Business managers had little sensitivity to this issue. They cared little about the aspects of a system that operated "below the floorboards." They cared only for business functionality, not what DBMS or networking software (for example) an application worked with best. Usually, in such a case, the IT department faithfully purchased the required underlying technology platforms and learned how to install and support it. But costs mounted.

Complexity also. Business units disliked costs associated with non-value-adding components of systems, of course, and so did Barton and the rest of the IT department. But the risks to business operations that arose from ever-increasing infrastructure complexity worried Barton and his IT managers more. The group had discussed some ideas developed by Charles Perrow concerning "normal accidents" or "system accidents" that resulted from the unanticipated interaction of multiple failures in complex systems.[1] These became more likely and more difficult to deal with as the complexity and *coupling* of a system increased. Most IT systems were tightly coupled, because people usually appreciated the benefits of integration—functional coupling—between systems. Real-time operations required tight coupling, for example, and IVK had a standing objective of achieving more real-time transactions. That had been one of the major drivers behind the IR project. But if coupling was essential to the beneficial operation of many IVK systems, complexity was not. IVK could, if its managers had the will, do something about the complexity of its systems, especially those below-the-floorboards aspects that business units cared nothing about. All it took was a willingness to invest in the occasional infrastructure simplification project.

In addition—well, it sounded oxymoronic, but the variety in the company's infrastructure also worked against the IT department's ability to be *flexible*. Dictated infrastructure standards sounded inflexible to business managers, who wanted to maintain their freedom to buy non-standard applications they thought they needed (or applications that required nonstandard infrastructure), but the complexity that arose from lack of standardization meant ever-greater difficulty in making changes to company systems. As complexity increased, IVK systems became more like a large ocean liner, pretty good at carrying its passengers in one direction, but harder and harder to turn to new headings. Gradual reductions in business agility, always step by incremental step, never dramatic enough to become the subject of deliberate business decisions, could eventually leave IVK in a vulnerable competitive position, unable to counter a move by a competitor. One historical case that had been discussed among Barton's managers: A phone company in the 1990s had begun to offer a new "Friends and Family" calling plan that allowed people to call a specified handful of people for free; competitors, because of the evolved complexity of billing systems, had been unable to respond with similar plans for many months, and had lost big chunks of market share during that time.

The current focus on standardization and reducing infrastructure complexity had arisen from a reawakened discussion with the business units, and with Carl Williams, about the reasonable distribution of IT expenditures. Recent calculations suggested that IVK spent nearly two-thirds of its IT budget on just keeping things running, and the rest on new systems, mostly security upgrades that followed the hacker attack on IVK in June and the IR project. The forecast called for a slight improvement in this ratio in the next year or two, as the IR project picked up momentum, but things would be much worse after that. Within four years, on current trends, IVK would spend more than 80 percent of its IT budget on maintaining existing systems. No one, on the business or IT side, could say what the "right" ratio might be between maintaining existing functionality and investing in new functionality, but pretty much everyone agreed that 80-20 was too high. One way to work that ratio down, in the long run, was to simplify infrastructure.

The problem, then, was how to accomplish standardization. Barton listened as Ruben's staff identified three alternative approaches.

The first proposed action was what detractors called the "do nothing" option, although the actual name given this proposal was "voluntary compliance." It called on the business units to voluntarily take into account concerns about the infrastructure required to run a system or tool they wanted to acquire. This approach would have the advantage of requiring business managers to educate themselves about the difficulties that confronted IVK's IT staff. The problem, in the estimation of its critics: the business units would never comply. Nothing would happen. The policy would be ineffectual. Business units wanted this approach because it preserved their right to vary from standards "for a good enough reason."

The second proposal, "strict enforcement," occupied the other end of the spectrum. IT would decide standards and have absolute authority to enforce them. This option also included immediate investments to move off noncompliant platforms. Some business units would have to move to packages and tools that were not their favorites. Proponents of this approach raised good questions: Did it really make sense for IVK to support four different PDA technologies? Did it really matter so much to the business whether they used the "long sleek one" or the "short chunky one?" Business managers tended to see this option as a big step backward, however. IT staff, not surprisingly, were the major advocates; they pointed out that many highly regarded companies, such as Cisco Systems, operated this way, and that it hadn't kept them from being very successful. Listening to the opponents of this option, however, you'd think that the demise of the company was imminent if the plan was adopted. They called it "the tail wagging the dog," and "IT driving business strategy" rather than vice versa. IT staff pointed out that IVK could still vary from standards "for good enough reasons" under this plan. But the IT group would decide what "good enough" meant.

The third option, "gradual migration," was fashioned as a middle option. It involved classifying known technology platforms into three groups: emerging, declining, and standard. "Emerging" technologies would have to be relatively new, and be promising candidates to become future standards (thus compatibility with installed legacy technologies would have to be taken into account). "Declining" technologies would be the opposite, neither particularly promising nor a good fit with existing infrastructure. And "standard" would designate technologies that IVK could best support. Investments in standard platforms would require no justification beyond the usual business case. Investments in emerging platforms would be generally allowed, but their timing (why now?) would need to be explicitly justified. Declining technologies would require CEO approval before being purchased.

This third option abstracted from the discussion of specific systems, though not so far that business units stopped worrying about threats to their favorite nonstandard systems. The idea was that this option would deliver a more standard infrastructure over time. It would provide some flexibility that wasn't present in option 2, and more impetus to change than option 1. But some option 3 skeptics considered it a ridiculous compromise. One put it this way: "Come on guys, this is crazy. If we were a $100 billion company with two hundred thousand employees, that would be different. But we're not. We're supposed to be entrepreneurial. We should bite the bullet, get this done. As designed, I'm not even sure this scheme gets us to standardized infrastructure, and if it does it'll take years. Years of additional cost and risk. Years of more arguing about which platforms should or should not be categorized as Declining. This isn't a solution, it's a way of putting off tough decisions.

Wednesday, December 12, 9:06 a.m. . . .

Barton pondered an e-mail he'd just received from the CEO, asking him to identify specific ways his department could contribute to IVK's top-line growth. The e-mail had gone out to all departments. The topic was not new, but the focus on it was. Barton had been hoping for more attention in this area, as he thought there were many ways that IT might accelerate sales. He'd attempted to bounce the idea around with his direct reports a couple of times, but he found that they were so focused on the cost side of the income statement—cost and headcount reductions, efficiency enhancements—that they literally had trouble thinking about IT's potential to contribute on the revenue side of the income statement. But Barton thought they'd come around. This was a genuine opportunity.

The timing of the issue, its juxtaposition with issues of infrastructure standardization, also represented, Barton believed, an opportunity. He intended to have the two conversations together, to work out with his managers and the rest of the IT staff the relationship between innovation and infrastructure standardization. He knew that some believed that standardization would impede innovation; that was one of the arguments people who resisted standardization were most inclined to make. But Barton was not so sure of that.

Eager to get going on the two issues, he stood and went out to Jenny's desk. He'd ask her to schedule a meeting for the following week, with his direct reports and the next level down managers. It was probably optimistic to think he could assemble that group in a week, but he wanted it to be soon.

Friday, December 14, 9:08 p.m. . . .

As usual on a Friday night, Barton was having a drink with the kid at Vinnie's Bar. *One of these days I'm going to ask him what his name is,* Barton thought. The kid was holding forth as only a mega nerd could, and there would be no interrupting him. Barton had launched the kid on this path with a claim that he (Barton) thought he was starting to know some things. Things he had known he hadn't known at one time. The kid didn't like that kind of talk. "Getting a little cocky, are we?" had been his response.

Then, to Barton's growing amusement, the kid had launched into some sort of fable. Barton listened, but understood little of what the kid was going on about.

"Once there was a great leader in a province of China," the kid began. *Was there something in his Coke?* Barton wondered. The kid continued:

"The leader was retired, and had aged considerably. He'd saved the city at one point in the past, so he was greatly revered, even though he had long since given up being a leader. Now he was known as a wise, kindhearted, and eccentric old dude."

"Ah, *Old Dude,*" repeated Barton. "That's an ancient Chinese honorific, right? As in 'Most Honorable and Revered Old Dude.'"

The kid ignored this hazing and plunged ahead: "Because of his glorious past, the new leaders of the city proposed a festival in the great man's honor. As part of the festival, there would be a sculpture contest. Sculptors would be asked to create likenesses of the great man. Two prizes would be awarded, one based on a popular vote of the city's inhabitants, the other based on the judgments of a panel of sculpture experts. Winning entries would be installed in a place of honor in the center of the city.

"Sculptures were submitted from far and wide. Some were huge full-sized statues, others were short stout busts, still others were small and detailed relief sculptures. The festival came, the contests were held, and two winners were chosen, one the popular choice, another the expert choice. But when it came time to award the prizes, the guest of honor could not be found.

"A quick search of the city determined that the eccentric old gentleman was not there, that he had likely wandered out through the city gates into the countryside, for reasons no one could fathom. He was known to occasionally follow butterflies out through the gates, and most assumed something like that explained his absence. The leaders of the city organized search parties, but very quickly they realized that they had a problem: No one outside the city knew what the great man looked like. If they could not usefully ask country farmers if they had seen the man, the search would be difficult.

"These difficulties perplexed them all until a small child came forward. The little girl pointed out that, thanks to the sculpture contest, the city was filled with likenesses of the great man. Searchers needed only to take a likeness with them to show to people in the countryside and say 'Have you seen this man?' to recover him safely.

"Now the two winning sculptures were everyone's first thought, but on second thought these were much too large. Both were heavy enough to break the back of a horse. Most useful to the search were not the award winners, then, but smaller pieces, especially a series of relief sculptures, each the size of a person's hand, which showed the great man in various poses. Each contained a likeness useful for identification purposes.

"The search parties divided up the small sculptures, set out to find the great man, and returned with him within an hour. The festival could then be finished, the prizes awarded. To celebrate a successful festival, the revelers partied long into the night."

The kid paused, took a drink. Barton waited. Then waited some more.

"And?" said Barton.

"That's it," said the kid. "That's the end of the story."

Barton frowned. "Is it supposed to mean something to me? What's your point?"

The kid looked disappointed. "So which sculpture of the great man was the best?"

Barton shrugged. "The award-winning one?"

"Which award-winning one?"

"I don't know. The popular one."

"But that one was of no use at all in finding the great man."

"You didn't say 'useful.' You said 'best.'"

"I didn't say what I meant by 'best.' You assumed."

"Okay, well if you meant useful, then the small relief sculptures."

"No, you said the award winners were best. Why?"

"Well, they must have been the most realistic. The searchers at first wanted to use them. Would have if they hadn't been so heavy."

"Ah-ha!" the kid said. "Most *realistic*. Now you have fallen into my trap. Are any of these sculptures realistic? Aren't they all just pieces of rock? Surely none of them come close to really being the great man."

"Okay, fine," Barton said. "So of course none of them are real. That's not what I meant by realistic. I guess it depends what you are looking for in a sculpture. Something to use to find the old guy, or something you think is artistically pleasing."

"Right!" said the kid.

"I'm still not following," said Barton. "What does this have to do with anything?"

"I'll spell it out," said the kid. "All these sculptures are representations of the great man, simplifications. By necessity."

"Of course."

"Well, you said you think you know some things. What you *mean* is, you've constructed simplified representations of how those things work. But don't confuse yourself by thinking your simplified mental constructions are *realistic*, or worse yet, *true*. They're no more real than those statues of the great man. You have to judge them by some criteria other than realism. Nothing useful is real. If it's complicated enough to be realistic, it's too complicated to be useful. That's why we build models. Representations. When we say we know things, we just mean we have mental models of those things that we like. Often we like them because they've been useful. But let's not confuse having a useful model with actual knowing."

"What difference does it make?"

"All the difference in the world," said the kid. "A model you like for one thing, a representation that is great by one criterion might turn bad when the criterion or the task at hand changes. The award-winning statues were not very useful when the task changed to finding the old guy. If the searchers had stubbornly persisted in their affection for the award-winning statues, they'd have found the great man much more slowly and probably ruined a few horses in the process. Managers have a problem like this when they fall in love with a particular model of how something works. When they become convinced that a mental model they have of how something works is the *right* one. When they decide that they *know* something. None of us really knows much of anything, when you get right down to it. We like some mental models just because we find them pleasing in some way. We like others because they've been useful in the past. But when we become too wedded to a model, we lose our ability to deal with new situations."

"So what I think I know could be something useful now, but might not be if conditions change."

"Precisely. It's best to get over the feeling that you *know* things. What you have is a toolbox full of personal theories. You keep those favorite theories—models, tools, whatever you want to call them—for a variety of reasons. All I'm really saying is, you need to be aware of why you're keeping them in your kit. And you need to always remind yourself that they are there *not* because they're right, or realistic, or true, or anything like that, but because they've been pleasant or helpful in a defined set of circumstances. Sort them, store them, and label them in accordance with the circumstances in which they are valuable. You wouldn't use a hammer for a job that needs a wrench. The best managers, in my opinion, take this sort of toolkit approach to what they do. Bad ones try to use a hammer, or a wrench, or whatever they regard as the one true tool, for everything."

"Wow," allowed Barton. "You learn all this in Second Life?"

"Of course not. Some of it's from World of Warcraft."

"I play that with my nephew," said Barton. "Guess I should play it more often."

"You should," said the kid. "You definitely should."

Barton grew silent. His remarks had been facetious, but the kid's story did really have him thinking. If he took the idea seriously, he really *knew* nothing about being a CIO. But then, neither did anyone else. Maybe that put him on more equal footing with the others. Or maybe his knowing he didn't know things put him on better footing. Maybe that had been the point of that phrase all along.

REFLECTION

Can the IT trend toward ever more maintenance be stemmed?

What should be the ideal ratio of maintenance to new applications?

Is there a trade-off between standardization and innovation? How are the two related in most companies?

What do you think of the kid's toolkit approach to management? How could you apply his ideas?

PART FIVE

MASTER OF TWO WORLDS

CHAPTER SEVENTEEN

MANAGING RISK

Wednesday, February 20, 11:10 a.m. . . .

Jim Barton sat back in the blue chair at the CEO's office table, taking a momentary break from his meeting with Carl Williams, astounded at the conversation they'd been having. Williams had wandered off to refresh his coffee but promised to come right back. The two men had been talking since 10 a.m. No one-on-one meeting with the CEO in Barton's recent memory had lasted this long, and Williams appeared eager to continue. The relationship between the two had been better since the first of the year, for reasons Barton didn't completely understand.

True, things looked better for IVK than they had for a while. The stock price had risen just past $50, much better than when Williams had taken over, though not yet nearly as good as the historical peak. Improved stock performance had earned them all nice holiday bonuses, and of course the CEO's bonus would have been especially nice. But Barton doubted that a bonus, however good, could account for the renewed interest shown by Williams in discussing IT. Barton almost wondered if it might be the result of a New Year's resolution, or something like it.

Whatever the reason, Barton loved it. He and the CEO were having a real conversation about topics—security and availability—that Barton had expected to be difficult. The time had come to decide exactly what to spend on some major upgrades. The IT managers had decided to put business continuity and high-availability upgrades into the proposal with the security upgrades, network consolidation, and other infrastructure simplification initiatives, since all involved cost-versus-risk trade-offs. Only the CEO could decide how much risk it was reasonable to bear, but Barton had been unsure he'd get the help from Williams that he needed in order to make the decisions.

At the end of Monday's leadership team meeting, as others stood up to depart, Barton expressed to Williams his emphatic belief that the two of them should schedule a lengthy session to talk through options for risk management and reduction. Barton had prepared this "elevator pitch" to maximize delivery of message in the shortest amount of time, in the most accessible possible way. But he'd held out little hope that the strategy would work. The CEO had surprised Barton by clearing Wednesday morning—two days later!—in response to Barton's impassioned plea.

Some things had been done the previous summer, right after the June DoS attack, mostly emergency actions to secure against obvious threats, to fill holes in the company's defenses that had been suddenly recognized. The big problem with proposals to fix additional security and availability problems (those that remained): they ranged very widely in cost. IVK could pay *a little* more for *some* additional security, availability, and business continuity improvements. Or they could pay *a lot* more for *even more* additional "protection." However much they spent, IVK could never be sure of complete protection against all risks. You could prove that risks existed by finding them and pointing them out, but not that none remained—not seeing any being not at all equivalent to there not being any—so 100 percent protection was a pipe dream. The question on which Barton needed guidance then: how much protection should they purchase? They needed a framework to use in thinking about this. Barton had some ideas, but really everything depended on what seemed reasonable to the CEO.

Early on in the conversation, things had taken an unusual and, it now seemed, fortuitous turn. About ten minutes into the meeting, as Barton explained that things could still go wrong no matter how abundantly and skillfully they deployed prevention measures, Williams started talking about poker.

"Sure, I get it," he said. "Even when you've got a strong hand, things can go against you."

He proceeded to tell a story about playing "In-Between," a poker variation in which you needed to draw a card "in between" two that you'd already drawn. Williams was holding a two and an ace (the lowest and highest cards in this game), so he could only lose by drawing another two or another ace. Anything else would be in between and he'd win. He held two of the eight instances of two or ace, so only six remained in the deck. That meant, Williams explained, his probability of drawing a winning card was (52–6)/52 or about 88 percent. In this particular game, there was no better hand than the one he held.

Reasonably enough, he'd bet big, drawing in a couple of others who also put in a lot of money. Patting himself on the back for spectacular execution, already anticipating the feeling of triumph as he leaned across the table to rake in the pot with both hands, Williams had drawn his next card and turned it face up: a two.

A highly improbable outcome, but not impossible. And a loser.

"Craziest thing was," Williams explained enthusiastically, "the same thing happened again later that night. Again I was holding an ace and a two. Again I bet big. Again, people thought I was bluffing. And again I drew a two. It was an important experience for me. The decision I made, to bet big holding a two and an ace, was entirely sound. Both times. But the particular outcome stunk. Happens in business too. Sometimes you make the sound choice, and still lose. Luck has something to do with it, always."

And sometimes, Barton thought but did not say, *you make a bad decision and get a good outcome,* meaning the chance Williams had taken in not disclosing the possible hacker attack in June. Remarkably, at that moment, Williams expressed exactly the same idea:

"The flip side is also true. Sometimes you make a questionable decision and things turn out okay. Like they did for us after the hacker attack in June. Occasionally you win by counting on luck. Shaky decision, good outcome. It happens. Sometimes you have to go for it."

What do you mean "us?" Barton mused. *It was you that made that shaky decision, in conflict with my advice.* Nevertheless, it surprised Barton that Williams was so thoughtful about what he had done back in June. Barton had considered Williams's decision not to disclose what had happened a purely emotional, spur-of-the-moment thing. Now he realized that Williams had been thinking about it with quite a bit more nuance and subtlety. Counting on being lucky, with eyes wide open. A bad decision, even Williams admitted—but the way you had to play it sometimes, he clearly believed.

"But not too often, I guess," Barton said, surprising himself with his candor.

Williams laughed. "Exactly right! Do that too often, you'll lose your shirt, in poker or real life. But now and again, on rare occasions . . ." He grinned at Barton widely, making him a confidant. Barton couldn't help grinning back.

Then, to Barton's great delight, the poker game analogy grew into a much larger frame for the conversation about risk that he'd wanted to have—indeed, needed to have—with the CEO. In fact, it expanded into a much bigger frame than any Barton had in mind, thanks to Williams.

"The first thing you have to do in poker and in business," said Williams, now holding forth eagerly, "is decide what kind of player you are. You can minimize risk, minimize losses by playing a very conservative strategy, only betting big when you have good cards, bluffing occasionally to keep the others off balance. Problem is, you never win big that way. People start to read you, realize when you're betting they ought to fold. But you don't take risks, so you rarely lose big either. It's a pretty good strategy. If I were running one of our big competitors, that's the way I might play it. But IVK is not an incumbent. We can't play it that way."

Barton inserted his own analogy, not poker based but, he thought, appropriate: "Reminds me of the 'risk escalator' analogy." Williams showed no signs of recognition but looked interested. Barton continued: "IVK and its competitors are like people trying to walk up a down escalator. You have to keep moving, just to stay in place. Stop and you move backward. Some competitors are in front of others, but the order can always change. There's a switch that any of you can adjust that controls the speed of not just your own escalator, but all the escalators. If you can get ahead by being a better climber and then speed up the escalators, you make things very hard on your competitors. It's the risks a company takes that speed up the stairs for everyone."[1]

Williams nodded. "I like it. We stumbled a while back and drifted backward. But not being an incumbent, we still have to take risks, have

270   *CEO — Risk taker*

to speed up the escalator. It's why we do all the things we're attempting in client management, the things our competitors have been obliged to follow. Problem is, while taking these risks, we got a little sloppy, got a bit uncoordinated, stumbled, and slid back. That doesn't change the fact that the kind of player we are in the poker game is one that has to take risks, not a leader who can sit back and minimize losses."

Barton could scarcely believe how well these remarks by Williams set up what they needed to talk about. "So, Carl, that is a great context for the decisions we need to make about security and availability upgrades. As you say, we're playing a riskier game. We do more sharing and transfer of data between our own systems and our partners. We invest in new systems—especially Web-based systems that clients see and use—more aggressively. Every time we make such an investment to try to speed up the escalator for our competitors, there's a question about how bullet-proof we ought to make our operations against accidents and people with bad intentions. There are all kinds of gradations. There's also project risk that arises when unexpected complications make it difficult for us to deliver functionality as planned and expected."

"So if we continue with the poker analogy," said Williams, "you have to think about a few factors when you decide whether to bet, whether to take a chance. What is the risk of the downside? Big or small? And if you experience the downside, how costly will it be? Will you lose a lot or a little?"

"That's exactly analogous," said Barton. "Our highest priorities are risks that are likely and can generate big costs."

"We'd need to see big benefits possible before we took on those risks," said Williams.

"That's right," said Barton. "And we might be willing to make additional investments to mitigate some of the risk, with the expectation that the return will be great."

"So that's a reasonably easy case to decide," said Williams.

"I agree," said Barton. "But it's your decision how much to invest in additional risk mitigation. The more you invest, the less dramatic your return, even assuming the probabilistic risk is not realized."

"It's like deciding to take a risk but also buying insurance. How much coverage do you want?"

271

"Exactly," said Barton. "So I have a list of these for you, examples of big risks we're taking in replacing systems, with questions about how much insurance to buy to offset uncertainty. Not an actual insurance policy, but technologies we can implement or steps we can take, at a cost, to reduce the probability or the consequence of an unlucky outcome."

"What about other categories of risk? Low probabilities and high costs, or high probabilities and low costs, or low of both? It's a two-by-two."

Barton stood, moved to a whiteboard and drew a two-by-two table.[2]

		Downside risk	
		Tolerable	Intolerable
Cost of protection	High	Bear the risk	Capitalize costs of risk mitigation
	Low	Lowest priority	Mitigate ASAP

He explained: "Most of the action, as you can see, is on the right. We've already handled everything we can see in the lower right, the intolerable-risk, low-cost-to-mitigate cell. The hard one's in the upper right. For things in this category, we can decide not to do the things that generate those risks—that would mean, typically, reconsidering some element of our business strategy, whether something we've said we want to do is worth the risk—or we can decide it makes good sense to take the risk and invest in mitigating it—buying insurance, in effect."

"What's a 'tolerable risk'?" Williams asked, looking at the left side of the table.

"Good question," said Barton. "Generally, it's one with not much potential cost, but it would be worth reviewing the ones we've put in that category, to make sure that what we think is tolerable and what you think is tolerable are the same thing."

Williams nodded in agreement. "But I see what you mean about the upper right. The dicey area."

"Yes. I've got a list of things I want us to walk through, one by one, to see if they seem like the insurance you want to buy. But before we do that, there are two more things I want to point out."

Barton paused, and Williams responded with a nod.

"First," said Barton, "it's important to realize one of the implications of the left-hand side of this chart, especially the upper left. If we bear some risks, it means we will have some problems. On the availability side, it means sometimes things won't work, not because anyone has done anything wrong, but because we've decided to bear a risk and the cards came out wrong for us. On the security side, it means the number of hacker incidents we can expect every year is greater than zero."

"Hmm," said Williams. "But if we've categorized things correctly, those hacker attacks will do little damage."

"That's right. But it doesn't mean they won't be alarming. Same with the risks we decide to bear from an availability standpoint. The classic example of a place we might choose to bear some risk is by not investing in making sure our PDAs receive e-mail no matter what. It would cost a lot to make PDA e-mail delivery very reliable, and I'm not sure it's worth it. But there's no doubt that people will howl—and loud—when the service breaks down. I want you and other managers to understand that this will happen sometimes because we have not made the investments in bulletproof e-mail delivery to PDAs. It's simply not the best way to invest the money our owners entrust to our decision making. An outage of this kind doesn't necessarily mean IT has gotten something wrong, just that we've decided to live with some risk in that area."

"Sounds right to me," said Williams. "I agree that we don't want to spend too much on bulletproofing PDA systems. People can get their e-mails off their PCs for a while."

"Great," said Barton, sitting back down. "It'd be great if you could say something to that effect in a leadership team meeting the first time we hear a lot of grumbling about a PDA e-mail outage."

Williams nodded. "I get it," he said.

"So here's where the second issue arises. We need to decide whether we want to adopt a general policy concerning levels of security and availability we think are appropriate. Do we want everything to be at least a certain amount safe? And then we can protect especially valuable things even more? Do we want to have levels of safety, call them level 1, level 2, and so on up to level 5, and everything in the same level is equally safe? Or would it be better to decide the security level required for each data item and make things safe at the data item level in differing degrees?"

"I'm not sure I appreciate the difference."

"Doing it at the data level will allow us to decide how much we want to protect each service or data item. There will be more overhead in doing all this deciding, but it will also prevent us from overprotecting some assets and underprotecting others, as we might do in protecting large groups of assets to the same degree. If we categorize, we'll undoubtedly protect some things too much, others too little. But if we protect at the data and service level, we have to understand that we can no longer simply give people access to a category and trust them to behave. For data items that are extremely valuable, we'll track everything that happens to them. This means a lot of monitoring of employee activities. Anyone who deals with our most sensitive data assets or our most critical services we'll essentially spy on, keeping track of everything they do. Some people may not like that. And there'll be some initial investment we need to make in shifting to this philosophy."

"And the alternative is . . ."

"Classic authentication and authorization. What we and most other companies do now. We categorize assets and services, then anyone with sufficient access rights can get to them. If they have the access rights, we don't monitor at the data asset level. Of course we still have some monitoring in place, intrusion detection, that sort of thing. But our protection is more categorical."

"And more trusting."

"Right. So there's a cultural sensitivity here."

"We *are* a financial services firm."

"We are indeed."

Williams sat forward at the table. "Let's go through your list of possible upgrades. By the time I've reviewed that, I'm sure I'll have some more ideas about these general questions of philosophy."

"Very good," said Barton, again marveling at the CEO's continued engagement in this issue. Barton handed Williams a thin binder and they dived into discussion of specific project proposals.

The remainder of the meeting continued in this highly effective mode. Williams exuded enthusiasm throughout. At one point he hit

Barton with a real stunner, a remark made in passing without further elaboration: "You know, Barton, you do good work. It wouldn't surprise me a bit if you turned out to be the next CEO of this company. I won't be here forever, you know. I'm a turnaround CEO. When things are turned, I leave. Someone's got to take over."

Barton had no idea how much stock to place in this remark. Maybe Williams had said similar things to other senior managers. Right after he said it, he continued the risk conversation, as if he'd made a passing comment on the weather. He'd said, "You might be the next CEO," in the roughly same manner than someone might say "Weather's turning a bit warmer, eh?" Barton had no choice but to stick to the philosophy he'd adopted since the June difficulties: "Keep your head down, keep doing your work in the way you think best." There was no sense in getting carried away by the CEO's casual thoughts. A lot could happen, he knew that, had seen that. A lot would. All Barton could do was his job, trying to make the IT department, and IVK, as ready as possible for whatever might happen.

REFLECTION

What might have changed to make Carl Williams suddenly more responsive to and engaged in Barton's IT agenda?

How should a company decide which IT risks are worth taking? How do you decide how much to spend to mitigate the risks you've opted to take?

Why should a CIO pursue senior management participation and oversight when managing IT risk?

Would Barton make a good next CEO for IVK? In what ways might he differ from past leadership?

CHAPTER EIGHTEEN

LOOKING FORWARD

Monday, March 24, 11:16 a.m. . . .

Jim Barton sat motionless in his chair, trying to make sense of the short conversation he'd just had with Robert Goldman, chairman and CEO of the Earlington Financial Group. Barton could scarcely believe he'd been talking with Goldman himself. Leader of a collection of financial companies in a variety of businesses, Goldman had a fabulous reputation. He was known particularly for his integrity; some speculated that he might someday be tapped to head the Treasury Department. He was known for being likeable, a great person to work for and with. His companies were often on "Best Place to Work" lists. He'd been one of Barton's personal heroes for a while.

The day had begun without a clue as to the extraordinary events in store for Barton. At about 9:20 a.m. he had received what seemed to be a typical phone call from a headhunter. Barton got them fairly often, but few of the jobs interested him, and those that did never panned out. This caller started with what sounded like the usual banter; Barton had been about to cut her off so he could get back to work when the woman on the other end of the line cut to the chase.

"I think you're going to want to hear what I've got to say, Jim," she said. "This isn't the usual kind of call. My client is prepared to make a job offer to you today."

That got Barton's attention. She was cagey about who the client was, but described the company in enough detail to allow Barton to narrow it down to three or four firms. From the sound of it, they were somewhat bigger than IVK, in a related industry, and rather more successful, or at any rate less recently troubled. As the conversation continued, Barton realized that the headhunter was trying to arrange a conversation between one of her client's executives and Barton for later that day. Deep down, he was still pretty pessimistic that this was anything worth spending time on, but he agreed to take an 11 a.m. call.

"Great," she said. "The call will be with Robert Goldman, of Earlington Financial."

Barton laughed. "No way," he said.

"Yes, I can assure you it's true."

As soon as he was off the phone, Barton surfed around a bit on various company Web sites, to see if he could discover a connection between Earlington and IVK. After about twenty minutes he found that Francesco Carraro, an IVK board member, was also on the board of directors of a financial software company. Another member of that board was none other than Robert Goldman.

Maybe this is for real, Barton mused.

The phone call at 11:00 had removed all doubts. Goldman himself called, and he hadn't just called to talk. Less than five minutes into the call, Goldman offered Barton the COO position at one of his major companies, one with a superb track record. The company was bigger than IVK. The job would be a step up, a career advancement of real magnitude. And they were offering a surprisingly large amount of money.

"We're going to need to hire a CIO as well," said Goldman, "We'd like to get you in place so that you can hire him or her. It is our understanding that you know a thing or two about that job."

"It's hard-won knowledge," said Barton, "but I'm not sure how good it is."

Goldman chuckled. "I'm sure it's very good, *and* hard-won," he said. "Just think about it. I'll give you a call back in a day or two?"

They're moving fast, thought Barton.

"What's the next step if I say I'm interested?" Barton asked.

"No next step, Jim. If you say 'yes,' the job is yours."

The last time Barton remembered being speechless, it had been roughly a year earlier. *Come to think of it*, Barton thought, *exactly a year. Or, rather, a year and a day.*

"Jim?" said Goldman. "You still there?"

I did it, Barton's thoughts continued. *I lasted a year.* Oddly, it was the first time he'd thought of the anniversary.

"Jim?" repeated Goldman.

"Oh, I'm sorry, Bob. Yes, of course. I will give it a lot of thought." *Had he just called Robert Goldman "Bob"?*

"How about Wednesday, then? By then perhaps you'll have more questions you'd like to ask." Barton had been so dumbfounded by the offer that he'd been unable to think of more than two or three questions. He'd felt unprepared, but Goldman hadn't seemed to mind.

Once off the phone, Barton tried to decide what to do next. He had an 11:30 meeting with his direct reports in the conference room down the hall, but it wasn't quite time for that yet. His eyes came to rest on the whiteboard.

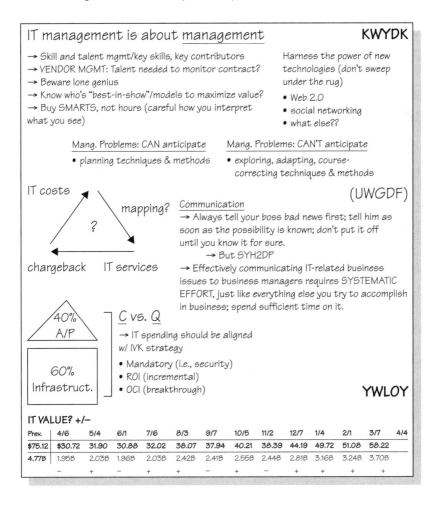

IT management is about management   KWYDK

→ Skill and talent mgmt/key skills, key contributors
→ VENDOR MGMT: Talent needed to monitor contract?
→ Beware lone genius
→ Know who's "best-in-show"/models to maximize value?
→ Buy SMARTS, not hours (careful how you interpret what you see)

Harness the power of new technologies (don't sweep under the rug)
• Web 2.0
• social networking
• what else??

Mang. Problems: CAN anticipate
• planning techniques & methods

Mang. Problems: CAN'T anticipate
• exploring, adapting, course-correcting techniques & methods

IT costs   (UWGDF)

mapping?   Communication
      ?   → Always tell your boss bad news first; tell him as soon as the possibility is known; don't put it off until you know it for sure.
                          → But SYH2DP
chargeback   IT services   → Effectively communicating IT-related business issues to business managers requires SYSTEMATIC EFFORT, just like everything else you try to accomplish in business; spend sufficient time on it.

40%
A/P   <u>C</u> vs. <u>Q</u>
             → IT spending should be aligned
60%   w/ IVK strategy
Infrastruct. • Mandatory (i.e., security)
             • ROI (incremental)
             • OCI (breakthrough)   YWLOY

IT VALUE? +/−

Prev.	4/6	5/4	6/1	7/6	8/3	9/7	10/5	11/2	12/7	1/4	2/1	3/7	4/4
$75.12	$30.72	31.90	30.88	32.02	38.07	37.94	40.21	38.39	44.19	49.72	51.08	58.22	
4.77B	1.95B	2.03B	1.96B	2.03B	2.42B	2.41B	2.55B	2.44B	2.81B	3.16B	3.24B	3.70B	
	−	+	−	+	+	−	+	−	+	+	+	+	

It was a lot more crowded than it had been. The cryptic notations that covered it were, as he'd told Goldman, earned through tough experience. But Barton still wasn't sure they amounted to much. He'd set out a year before to create a management framework he could apply to IT. He felt good about what the whiteboard summarized, but he'd need a lot more distance before he could be sure the board's contents were really worth something. Maybe this new position would provide him with that distance.

He'd have to take the new job, of course. Things at IVK had improved a lot in the past few months. He and the IT department had crawled a long way back from that horrible day at the end of June when he'd had to worry about being fired for the first time in his career. But this offer would install him in a position like the one he'd originally expected and wanted in IVK, under Williams. Only it would be with a bigger company. And not under Williams, but under someone he'd always admired.

The hacker attack, if that's what it had been, had not produced additional consequences. It looked as though Williams had been right to insist that they disclose nothing. The stock price had recovered a good bit of its former value. Things were looking up. But thinking about the whole thing still gave Barton a sick feeling. He would be happy to get beyond worries of becoming a scapegoat. Carl Williams was already getting accolades from many quarters for his "turnaround" of IVK. Barton had come to respect the CEO as well, especially after hearing his explanation of the philosophy behind the risk he'd taken with the possible security breech in June. And, of course, there was that bombshell remark that Williams had unleashed in passing, that Barton might well be the next IVK CEO. Hard to know how seriously to take that. Barton couldn't quite get past the sense that he had seen the real Williams on that fateful Saturday morning in June. And he wasn't sure he really liked the man.

On the other hand, he would hate to leave his team. They had done a lot of good work together. There was so much still to be completed. How would he ever be able to tell them?

Barton was about to call Maggie, to get her reaction, when a glance at his watch reminded him of his 11:30 meeting. He grabbed a notepad and hustled down the hall. He couldn't recall the purpose of the meeting, and it hadn't been entered in his calendar. It wasn't in the room where his team usually met. For some reason, someone had booked the biggest conference room in the building. Perhaps a project team had needed the room they usually used for these meetings.

When Barton turned the corner into the room, he was startled to see that it was packed with people. The room exploded with applause. It looked like, more or less, the entire IT department. There in front were Ruben, Gordon, Juvvani, and Fenton. A bit further back, he saw John Cho in his signature black skull t-shirt, smiling broadly, clapping earnestly. Not far from him were Ellen Ripley and Gary Geisler. On the conference room table, he saw a huge cake. The writing on it said "Congratulations, Jim, on your one-year anniversary!"

The ovation went on and on. Barton had received many accolades and frequent acknowledgements of achievement during his life, beginning with success in sports in school, continuing with academic achievement in college, and carrying on into his career. People had often signaled appreciation for Jim Barton's work. But no acknowledgement, he realized, had ever meant more to him than this one. These people had undoubtedly been skeptical of him as a CIO choice; to a person they had surely experienced deep anxieties about what kind of boss he would be. But somehow he had earned their respect.

And it felt great.

Finally, the applause subsided and the room became still. They were all waiting now, wanting to hear what he would say. He took a deep breath, intending to comply with their wishes.

But for the third time in one year, one day, and thirty minutes, Jim Barton was speechless.

Monday, March 24, 7:55 p.m. . . .

Barton rarely went out to a bar on a weekday, but on this Monday he decided to go have a drink. He'd wanted to celebrate with Maggie, and she was in town, but tied up in a client meeting running late. They'd made plans to meet up at Vinnie's when she finished. He'd gone to the bar early to talk with the kid, if he was there. Barton had gotten the impression that the kid ate at Vinnie's most nights.

Just before 8:00, about halfway through Barton's martini, in wandered the kid.

"Hey, I don't usually see you on a weekday. Don't tell me you got fired?"

"Not exactly," Barton smiled. "I'm meeting Maggie here. We're going out for dinner. Hey, I'll introduce you to her."

"I feel like I know her already." Barton laughed. The kid continued: "So, you're looking . . . something. What's wrong?"

"Nothing's wrong."

"What's happened then? Something has."

"What, we have a few drinks together and you think you can read me?"

"You're right," the kid conceded. "Sorry for presuming. So what happened?"

"You know all those times I've offered you a job?"

"Sure. I began to think you might even be serious after a while."

"You bet I was. But now, well, I'm afraid you've missed your chance."

"What do you mean? Come on, quit toying with me. It's getting on my nerves."

"What I mean is that I might not be with IVK much longer."

"Aaaaah . . ." the kid said in a low voice.

"I got a call today from the chairman of Earlington Financial. They want me as their new COO."

"You mean they want you to come in to talk with some board members and executives."

"No. I mean he offered me the job. Don't tell anybody."

The kid whistled softly. "That Goldman," he said. "I had no idea that he was so shifty."

"You know Goldman?"

The kid ordered a Coke and turned to Barton. He frowned and started to say something, then stopped, as if deciding what he *should* say. Then his face changed, and Barton could tell that he had decided, whatever it was.

"Yes, I know Bob pretty well."

"*You* know Bob Goldman?" The kid looked a little hurt. Barton added quickly, "I mean—I didn't mean to be insulting. But you've never given me any reason to think you might know anyone like Bob Goldman. All your geek jokes, I mean. What, you related to him or something?"

"No," said the kid. He paused for effect before adding: "He and I are on a couple of boards together."

"*You're* on a couple of boards with Bob Goldman?"

"Now, now, you just did it again."

Barton winced. "I'm sorry."

"Yes," continued the kid. "He and I have even talked about you a time or two. That shifty dude, I should have guessed he was up to something. I had a hard time figuring out how he knew you. Probably, now that I think about it, through Carraro. He's on the IVK board, right? Now there's a guy who can't putt to save his life. You play golf?"

Barton shook his head. "Who the heck are you?"

"We never have discussed that, have we?" The kid laughed. "I'm Jonathan Luce."

"*The* Jonathan Luce?"

"The one who founded Dazzle, the computer graphics company."

"The computer graphics company purchased by Microsoft for billions."

"Actually, we were first purchased by MediaSpark in a stock deal, then Microsoft bought MediaSpark."

"Why didn't you tell me?"

Luce shrugged. "You never asked."

"All this time I've been treating you like some kind of kid." Barton buried his face in his hands.

"Hey," said Luce, "don't worry. You were essentially correct. I am a nerd, and I'm twenty-nine. I just happen to do some investing, venture capital, and philanthropic work, and I'm on a lot of boards."

Barton could only sigh. It had been a day of surprises. "Who's been toying with whom?" Barton said.

"Maybe I should have told you," conceded Luce. "Listen," he continued, "I don't want to complicate your life or anything, but you know that job you've been offering me?"

"Huh? Yes. How embarrassing . . . *me* offering *you* a job."

"Well, I've been giving very serious thought to returning the favor. Looks like Goldman's got the jump on me—sneaky bugger—but I've got another proposition for you to consider."

Barton looked at him suspiciously: "What?"

"I'm on the board of directors of a pretty good-sized, international bank. It's got to be ten times the size of IVK, at least. We need a really good CIO. What do you think? Want to be that guy?"

Barton shook his head, to clear it. "I'm not a CIO. You know that. I've told you pretty much everything I've done wrong in the past year."

"I think you *are* a CIO, if you want to be. I'm not coming up with this out of the blue. We've talked about it at board meetings. You had emerged as our number-one candidate. I'm improvising a little here by springing it on you like this, but I'm sure the others won't mind when they hear what Goldman has been up to. It was only a matter of time before we would have contacted you."

"But I don't know anything about IT. Doesn't anybody ever listen to me?"

"Oh, come on. I said you have to know what you don't know, but you can't cling to not knowing."

"I should add that one to my whiteboard."

"Huh?"

"Nothing," said Barton. "I'm just blown away, that's all."

"I'll stop pressing. When does Goldman want an answer?"

"He wants to talk again Wednesday morning."

"Wow, that's soon. Do me a favor—don't give him a firm answer until I can get back to you with an offer. I guarantee you it will be a strong package. This is a much bigger company we're talking about. More staff, more resources, more responsibility. And I guarantee you that being CIO won't take you off the CEO track."

Barton remained silent, thinking.

"Well?" repeated the kid.

"Okay," said Barton, "but it would be good if you could get the offer to me as soon as possible, preferably before the call with Goldman. I don't want to keep Robert Goldman waiting. He's always been a hero to me, ever since I read a case about him in business school. I'd like to stay on good terms with him. There's no way I'll do anything like jerking him around."

"That's why we all want you, Jim. You make doing the right thing a habit. And you make it work. It's been quite a day for you, hasn't it?"

"You could say that."

"How long have you been CIO at IVK now? A year at least, right?"

"A year and a day, actually."

"It's been quite a year."

"It sure has," said Barton. "It surely, most certainly has."

Just then Maggie walked through the door and caught Jim's eye with a wave. She smiled at the kid with recognition. "Jonathan!" she exclaimed, crossing to the bar with her hand outstretched. "It seems I run into you everywhere these days. So, do you know Jim?"

REFLECTION

Why would Goldman and Luce now be competing to hire Barton based on his year's experience as CIO and previous experience as a business manager?

Which job offer should Barton accept?

How important is CIO leadership to the viability and success of twenty-first-century companies?

How should senior managers and the board of directors work together to effectively manage the assets and capabilities of a firm?

EPILOGUE

We wrote the IVK story to be representative, in essence if not in detail, of the experiences of many companies as they struggle to manage IT-based capabilities at the beginning of the twenty-first century. Jim Barton's odyssey represents, albeit in compressed form, the journey of IT managers as they strive to lead their companies' efforts in this area. It is exceedingly important, we believe, that managers, regardless of their degree of technical training, be more introspective about these kinds of issues, stories, experiences, and adventures.

IT—especially with its role so greatly enlarged by the arrival of the Internet—has changed not only how we work and conduct business, but also how we (and our customers) play, how we consume, and how we educate our next generations. And yet the IT phenomenon, so evident in the expenditures of every organization, has not yet achieved management attention equal to other areas, such as finance, marketing, operations, and human resources. In far too many companies, IT remains a black box that business managers rarely try to see inside. When business managers do engage in IT discussions, often they bring little expertise to bear. Few feel apologetic about their IT inadequacies. But the time is coming when "I'm not an IT person" will be no more adequate as a manager's defense in the aftermath of a major corporate problem than Jeff Skilling's now notorious "I'm not an accountant"—that CEOs effort to explain his failure to foresee or prevent Enron's spectacular implosion.

One reason for the startling lack of expertise in IT management: the absence of systematic frameworks that are useful in actual practice. To some extent this is the result of the relative youth of the field. IT traces its roots back fifty or so years. Accounting, to take just one example, can trace a similar time line back many centuries. Furthermore, the technologies that underlie IT management, which continuously evolve the possibilities and constraints with which managers work, change very rapidly. The assumption many often make, implicitly at least, is that the content of IT management is too transient to yield to the treatment that other fields have received. This is, we believe, total nonsense. IT management as a subject to be understood, even mastered, contains fundamental elements independent of the underlying technologies.

That said, we do acknowledge that mastering IT management is hard, that attempts at mastery are hindered by some characteristics of the field that, if not unique to IT, are particularly strongly present. Foremost among these is the fact that it remains difficult to tease apart management and technical issues within IT management. Indeed, the daily tasks of managing in the area of IT consist largely of a series of problems of understanding entangled technical and managerial issues, separating them conceptually, and then communicating them to people who should be involved in particular kinds of management decisions. A big part of the difficulty is the absence of categories, and frameworks built up from those categories, that can serve as lenses to see into the experiences of IT management, and that can function as checklists or guidelines for management action. Where such categories and frameworks do exist, they are often presented and communicated in abstract ways that don't seem useful in practice. This is yet another consequence, we believe, of the intertwined technical and managerial nature of IT management. When you have to work hard to tease apart the technical and managerial, and proceed to categorize the managerial and build the categories into frameworks, the frameworks you arrive at can seem pretty far removed from the situations that instigated them. Ironically, although you need to separate technical from managerial to manage IT effectively, you also need to preserve a strong link between the abstractions and the contexts that motivated their derivation, or else the frameworks won't mean anything to most people. This is the problem with most textbook treatments of IT management: they are mostly composed of abstractions distilled from practice, but too distant from their practical contexts to seem relevant.

Our dual beliefs in both the importance of frameworks and the need to retain the practical contexts of IT management that give the frameworks meaning led us to the unusual approach that is the IVK story. The approach is based on the premise that "knowledge can't be told"—at least not fully. Partly because of the conceptual distance between IT practice and the abstract content of IT frameworks, and partly because of the relative youth of the field, the principles of IT management must be derived from experience (real or simulated). They must be discovered within their contexts, discerned as important, stretched to reveal their limitations, analyzed for their inner structure, and theorized into tools in each manager's personal kit, to the point where they can serve as a guide to practical decision making.

To this end, we have amalgamated our experiences as IT managers, board members, consultants, and researchers into a reality-based narrative designed to allow the reader to "walk in the shoes" of a capable business manager learning to lead the IT function during a one-year crash course. The year necessarily amounts to something of a trial by fire. During this one-year period, Jim Barton—and by extension, the reader—is asked to identify key IT management issues, discover underlying principles, participate in debates, make decisions, and experience the consequences of decisions. As in real life, we do not get to rerun the experiment, to see what would have happened had a different choice been made, or had a different roll of the dice come up. Thus, we do not end the chapters of this story by revealing the "right" answers. There are no *right* answers. But there can be, nevertheless, sound processes, well-considered decisions, carefully constructed justifications for actions, and improved outcomes on average. There may be no right answers, but that does not mean that all answers are equally defensible.

Having acknowledged the immature state of the IT management field and the difficulties of arriving at definitive management formulations—not that definitive formulations are abundant in any field of management, IT or other—we must also acknowledge that our approach in the IVK story entails a certain lack of closure. We acknowledge as well that this lack of closure could be an obstacle to discovery of the frameworks that are the ultimate aim of this exercise in management learning. Which brings us to the purpose of this epilogue: we intend it to provide a baseline summary of the IT management knowledge that can be learned through the experience of the story. We won't provide answers here, but we will suggest categories, specific areas in which a capable IT manager might develop systematic approaches, based on situations facing IVK and, by extension, other companies.

You might choose to translate Barton's experience into a different set of categories than those we propose. You look at the issues facing IVK through your own experiences. If you are an IT manager, you can talk about IVK and its people and issues, and use that as a more comfortable way of talking about the analogous issues in your own company. Often it is easier to have a conversation about another company rather than your own company and colleagues, no matter how transparent the analogy might be. We hope the tale of IVK Corporation will be a trigger for useful discussions relevant to your own situation. But there's no doubt that we're asking you to do some work here, to distill the relevance to your situation for yourself.

Seven Categories for Developing IT Management "Systems"

We list below seven candidate areas for IT management "systems," and show some of the issues that need to be dealt with systematically in each. In keeping with our overall approach, we do not provide the "solutions at the back of the book" that many developing managers long for. You'll need to come up with those from your own experiences, perhaps while reflecting upon the IVK story, as they relate to your own company.

1. Communication system (some would say the most important of all IT management systems):

    - How the IT leader interacts with boss and peers, including frequency and style of interaction, degree of collaboration versus completed work recommendation

- How to achieve joint accountability for issues that cannot be decided by IT alone

- How to achieve adequate transparency, so that non-technical managers cannot defensibly claim not to know or understand something they should jointly be accountable for

- How to talk about "below the floorboards" IT issues with business managers (necessary for cost/risk decisions)

- How to participate with other senior managers in visioning, strategy making, promoting, and understanding of future (technology-enabled) possibilities

- Stakeholder analysis, and other systematic means of persuasion

- Communication with the board of directors to involve them in IT issues to an appropriate degree

- Communication with a community outside the company (other CIOs, for example)

2. People management system (arguably, the other "most important" IT management system):

- Hiring, nurturing, and retaining great talent

- Supervision in the presence of profound disparities in specialized knowledge between managers and their employees

- Keeping the lines of communication open with employees you can't conventionally supervise (because often you can't tell what they are doing)

- Coaching, counseling, and directing the focus of highly talented but variously motivated employees

- Keeping account of talent levels of individuals and their skills and training; knowing what your people can and cannot do

3. Cost and value of IT accounting systems

   – Understanding costs, providing cost transparency; directing costs, and allocating budgets in a way that involves the right people in decisions and gives them the right incentives for making the decision best for the company (not their own department or themselves)

   – How IT creates value (Competes versus Qualifiers) and how value can be attributed to the activities and systems that create it; where to invest to maximize return from IT

   – The reasonable distribution of investments over time between compete and qualify activities, and between infrastructure and new applications

   – Which projects to invest in, and how to prioritize projects in a portfolio for highest overall return

4. Project management/implementation system

   – How to manage problems you can anticipate

   – How to manage problems you can't anticipate

   – Managing project scope (when it should be allowed to expand and when it should not)

   – The appropriate "shape" of projects (iterative prototypes or step-by-step) in different circumstances

   – How to budget when allowing for the presence of uncertainty in project timing and cost

   – How to budget when allowing for the need to learn during the course of a project

5. Vendor management system

   – Achieving accountability and synchronicity of motivation between a vendor and your company

   – Selecting vendors (RFP, selection process)

- Contractual arrangements with vendors, especially vendors with which you have long-term relationships (SLAs)

- Relative merits of service delivery model alternatives (traditional, software as a service, etc.)

- Level of expertise that must remain inside your company to manage vendors effectively (do you need rocket scientists or just capable contract managers?)

6. Infrastructure management system

- How much to invest in maintaining versus new capabilities

- How to achieve standardization and complexity reduction, especially when these do not provide direct and obvious business benefits

- Protection of information assets from malicious attackers (cost/risk trade-offs)

- Level of investment in redundancy; availability (cost/risk trade-offs)

- Crisis management

7. Scanning for and analyzing emerging technologies

- Identification of emerging threats and opportunities

- Integrating emerging technological factors into strategies and plans

As we've said, you might categorize differently. You might think we've left things out. You're probably right, for your company at least.

The IT Manager as a Business Leader

Every day influential managers in business make seemingly "good" business decisions, acting as if they know something about IT, even though they don't. The cumulative results undermine the capabilities of entire companies and place remaining IT capabilities at risk of attack or failure. In the past few years, hackers (many no longer amateurs) have had a surprisingly easy time preying on IT networks, stealing hundreds of millions of records containing customers' personal information, creating a rapidly growing illicit industry in identity theft and other forms of fraud. Known intrusions have been increasing at a multiplicative rate, and the trend is expected to continue. IT projects continue to fail spectacularly in large numbers, and in disconcerting manners, moving from "on course" to catastrophe seemingly overnight. Mistakes and accidents shut down transportation, logistics, and factories. These events should set off a loud alarm in the mind of every CEO, board member, and senior manager. Someday, maybe soon, there will be an Enron-like IT disaster. People will be called to account.

The threat from undermanaged IT is more difficult to head off than the accounting-based Enron disaster. The IT threat involves complex and poorly understood technology and its management. IT in most companies has largely been left to the technologists. Only IT network or major transaction system outages, or possibly e-mail failures, have commanded the attention of the CEO and the senior management team. In most companies, senior managers have responded in a typical industrial economy manner: "Fix it, and don't let this happen again." Root causes are rarely identified, debated, or effectively acted on. The time bomb begins ticking: the beginnings of an even more severe IT outage form amid the wreckage and well-intentioned recovery actions from the one before.

Too often, as in IVK, the senior management team talks itself into believing that the problem will just go away. And, with the scrambling of a good IT department, the problem might be avoided during a particular CEO's watch. But the problem does *not* just go away.

At one level, the IVK story seems rather mundane. IT management issues such as the inner workings of an IT chargeout system, the prioritization of projects, the choice of an IT vendor partner, and turnover of IT resources appear as the background noise, the unglamorous blocking-and-tackling in a "gee-whiz" high-tech business. The technology may seem more interesting than the day-to-day challenges of IT management. We'd agree with this assessment. The heart of IT management effectiveness, although essential to the ongoing success of any enterprise, is just not all that sexy. Nevertheless, it has been conclusively demonstrated that the lack of effective IT management decision making on the mundane issues will eventually lead to spectacular and seriously negative consequences. Sound management that leads to effective IT decision making, on the other hand, will have seriously positive consequences. We wish you more of the latter than the former. But that will be largely up to you.

Good luck.

NOTES

CHAPTER ONE

1. This picture is the work of entrepreneur and business consultant Michael Enright. See Hamilton Technology Advisors Web site, http://www.htadvisors.com (accessed January 2008).

2. Tom Field, "Executive Relationships," *CIO*, March 1, 2002, 58.

3. See Richard L. Nolan, *Dot Vertigo: Doing Business in a Permeable World* (New York: John Wiley & Sons, 2001).

4. Enterprise resource planning systems are generally intended to replace poorly architected legacy transaction processing systems. These systems generally integrate data base technology and real-time processing. For more detail on enterprise systems, see Robert D. Austin, Cedric X. Escalle, and Mark Cotteleer, "Enterprise Resource Planning, Technology Note," Harvard Business School Case No. 699-020 (Boston: Harvard Business School Publishing, 1999).

5. See, for example, Roland Meinzer, "Yes, It's Critical That an Executive with a Broad Overview of the Business Oversee the Technology Budgets," *Optimize*, July 2003, 21.

6. Stephanie Overby, "The Incredible Shrinking CIO," *CIO*, October 15, 2003, 1.

7. Ibid.

8. See Richard Nolan and F. Warren McFarlan, "Information Technology and the Board of Directors," *Harvard Business Review*, October 2005, 96–106.

CHAPTER THREE

1. See F. Warren McFarlan and Robert D. Austin, "CareGroup," Harvard Business School Case no. 303-097 (Boston: Harvard Business School Publishing, 2003).

CHAPTER FIVE

1. See Andrew McAfee, Anders Sjoman, and Vincent Dessain, "Zara: IT for Fast Fashion," Harvard Business School Case no. 604-081 (Boston: Harvard Business School Publishing, 2004); or Kasra Ferdows, Michael A. Lewis, and José A. D Machuca, "Rapid Fire Fulfillment," *Harvard Business Review*, November 2004, 104–110.

Notes

2. Nicholas G. Carr, "IT Doesn't Matter," *Harvard Business Review*, May 2003, 41–49.

3. See articles by Erik Brynjolfsson, http://ebusiness.mit.edu/erik/ITandBusinessvalue.html.

4. See Andrew McAfee and Erik Brynjolfsson, "Dog Eat Dog," *Sloan Management Review*, http://sloanreview.mit.edu/wsj/insight/technology/2007/04/27/.

5. This framework has been used for years within the Technology and Operations Management area at the Harvard Business School, in discussion and in teaching. Its exact origins are uncertain.

6. Richard Nolan and F. Warren McFarlan, "Information Technology and the Board of Directors," *Harvard Business Review*, October 2005, 96–106. For a description of the strategic grid, see Lynda M. Applegate, Robert D. Austin, and Deborah Soule, *Corporate Information Strategy and Management: Text and Cases*, 8th edition (Boston: McGraw Hill, 2009).

CHAPTER SIX

1. The Information Security Glossary Web site, http://www.yourwindow.to/information-security/gl_scopecreep.htm.

2. Jim Highsmith, Arlington, MA: Cutter Consortium, March 9, 2004, www.cutter.com. Reprinted by permission; see also Highsmith's book on this subject: *Agile Project Management: Creating Innovative Products* (Boston: Addison-Wesley, 2004).

3. Cyril Northcote Parkinson, *Parkinson's Law, or The Pursuit of Progress* (London: John Murray, 1958); for discussion of this issue in software development, see T. Abdel-Hamid and S. Madnick, "The Impact of Schedule Estimation on Software Project Behavior," *IEEE Software* 3, no. 4 (1986): 70–75; and R. Austin, "The Effects of Time Pressure on Quality in Software Development: An Agency Model," *Information Systems Research* 12, no. 2 (June 2001): 195–207.

4. On this kind of estimation, see, Barry W. Boehm, *Software Engineering Economics* (Upper Saddle River, NJ: Prentice Hall, 1981); on function points, see A. J. Albrecht, and J. E. Gaffney Jr, "Software Function, Source Lines of Code, and Development Effort Prediction: A Software Science Validation," *IEEE Transactions on Software Engineering* 9, no. 6 (1983).

5. Ed Yourdon, *Death March: The Complete Software Developer's Guide to Surviving "Mission Impossible" Projects* (Upper Saddle River, NJ: Prentice Hall PTR, 1999).

CHAPTER EIGHT

1. Robert D. Austin, Warren Ritchie, and Greggory Garrett, "Volkswagen of America: Managing IT Priorities," Harvard Business School Case no. 606-003 (Boston: Harvard Business School Publishing, 2007).

CHAPTER NINE

1. For additional reading on board IT governance, see Richard L. Nolan and F. Warren McFarlan, "Information Technology and the Board of Directors," *Harvard Business Review*, October 2005, 96–106.

Notes

CHAPTER TEN

1. For a fictionalized account of the weapons hackers use to break in, see Carolyn Meinel, "How Hackers Break In . . . and How They Are Caught," *Scientific American*, October 1998, 98–105.

CHAPTER ELEVEN

1. For more information on managing risk and the processes a general manager should spearhead to lessen the likelihood that assets will be compromised, see Robert D. Austin and Christopher A. R. Darby, "The Myth of Secure Computing," *Harvard Business Review*, June 2003, 120–126.

CHAPTER TWELVE

1. See, for example, Shaheen Pasha, "Skilling Gets 24 Years," *Money*, October 24, 2006, http://money.cnn.com/2006/10/23/news/newsmakers/skilling_sentence/index.htm ?postversion=2006102409; and Dan Ackman, "Bernie Ebbers Guilty," *Forbes*, March 15, 2005, http://www.forbes.com/2005/03/15/cx_da_0315ebbersguilty.html.

CHAPTER THIRTEEN

1. Andrew McAfee, "Enterprise 2.0: The Dawn of Emergent Collaboration," *MIT Sloan Management Review* 47, no. 3 (Spring 2006): 21–28; and Eric K Clemens, "Harnessing the Power of Social Networks: Can User-Generated On Line Content Sell Your Products?" with responses by Robert D. Austin, Tom DeMarco, Ron Blitstein, Lou Mazzucchelli, Lynne Ellyn, Tim Lister, Christine Davis, and Ken Orr; *Cutter Special Report*, Vol. 8, No. 7, Assertion 163 (Boston: Cutter Consortium, 2007).

2. Robert D. Austin and Stephen P. Bradley, "The Broadband Explosion," and Jeremy Allaire and Robert D. Austin, "Broadband and Collaboration," in *The Broadband Explosion: Leading Thinkers on the Promise of a Truly Interactive World*, eds. Robert D. Austin and Stephen P. Bradley (Boston: Harvard Business School Press, 2005); see, for example, J. C. R Licklider and Robert W. Taylor, "The Computer as a Communication Device," *Science and Technology*, April 1968, 21–31.

3. Option-creating investment, discussed in chapter 8.

CHAPTER FIFTEEN

1. Some of the ideas in this section come from interactions with Carl Størmer, who conceptualized the JazzCode (see "JazzCode with Carl Størmer", http://www.jazzcode .com); and from our research interview with the legendary jazz bass player, Cameron Brown.

CHAPTER SIXTEEN

1. For an introduction to these ideas, see William Langewiesche, "The Lessons of Valu-Jet 592," *Atlantic Monthly*, March 1998, 81–97; see also Charles Perrow, *Normal Accidents: Living with High-Risk Technologies* (Princeton, NJ: Princeton University Press, 1999).

Notes

CHAPTER SEVENTEEN

1. This analogy is from Bob Charette, a risk management expert at the Cutter Consortium. For a more detailed description, see Tom Demarco and Timothy Lister, *Waltzing with Bears: Managing Risk on Software Projects* (New York: Dorset House, 2003), 12; or access Charette's extensive writings on the subject of risk management on the Cutter website at www.cutter.com.

2. This matrix is reproduced with permission of the author, Dan Geer, from his presentation at the Harvard Business School on July 25, 2007; a similar matrix is discussed in Dan Geer, "The Evolution of Security," *ACM Queue*, April 2007, 30–35.

WAYS OF USING THIS BOOK

The Adventures of an IT Leader is written for IT managers, potential IT managers, those working closely with IT managers, those who want to understand how to use their IT department to greater effect, and those who are simply curious. While the book is useful and (we hope) interesting to an individual reader, we've also designed it to be the focus of discussion. We suggest reading and discussing the book with a peer, or convening a group of readers at a "brown-bag lunch" or other similar session to discuss the chapters one by one. Questions for reflection or discussion are offered at the end of each chapter. There is no particular problem with reading ahead, although reading ahead will not reveal right answers. At IVK, as in life, there are no *right* answers, but rather a set of decisions, made at a certain time, by a set of actors, with the information available, which results in specific consequences from which to profit or learn or recover.

Jim Barton's story unfolds in eighteen chapters. Experienced cumulatively, the story gains dramatic momentum, and later chapters provide opportunities to revisit key issues in more depth as readers gain deeper understanding and familiarity with the characters, the company and IVK's management situation. However, chapters can also be read independently or in smaller batches as suits the needs of particular readers. Here are some options:

- **Option A:** Chapters 1–18 can be read and discussed in eighteen sessions, or fewer if certain chapters are paired together. Suggested pairings:

- Chapter 2: CIO Challenges, and chapter 3: CIO Leadership

- Chapter 4: The Cost of IT, and chapter 5: The Value of IT

- Chapter 11: Damage, and chapter 12: Communication

- Chapter 14: Vendor Partnering, and chapter 15: Managing Talent; or chapter 15: Managing Talent, and chapter 16: Standardization and Innovation

- Chapter 17: Managing Risk, and chapter 18: Looking Forward

If all of these pairings are used, the eighteen chapters can be discussed in thirteen sessions.

- **Option B:** A sixteen-chapter series could be discussed, in which case we recommend skipping chapters 14 and 16. Other chapters could be omitted, depending on your particular interests. Again, using the pairings suggested above could result in twelve sessions with this option.

- **Option C:** A fourteen-chapter series could be discussed, in which case we recommend skipping chapters 13–16 or 14–17. Pairing would bring this option to a less densely arranged twelve sessions.

- **Option D:** Specific issues could be explored in shorter sequences. For example:

  - An introduction to the CIO function could be achieved using chapters 1–3, adding chapters 4–5 to explore the cost and value of IT.

  - The issue of security, risk management, and crisis management could be discussed using chapters 10–12 and chapter 17.

  - Topics such as project management (chapters 6–8), priority management (chapter 8), vendor partnering (chapters 7 and 14), IT and the board of directors (chapter 9), emerging technology (chapter 13), and managing talent (chapter 15) could be discussed independently.

To help with whatever reading program you choose, we've provided a list of acronyms and terms (see "Glossary of Acronyms and Terms").

This material has been used successfully in classrooms at the Harvard Business School "Delivering Information Services" Executive Program, the University of Washington Foster School of Business (executive and undergraduate level), and the Copenhagen Business School (graduate level). If you are interested in using this book in a classroom setting, teaching notes and guides are available. Please contact Harvard Business Publishing for more information.

GLOSSARY OF ACRONYMS AND TERMS

Apache	A public-domain, open source Web server
A/P	Applications portfolio
APM	Agile project management; also applications portfolio management
APP	Aggregate project planning
BGP	Border gateway control
CEO	Chief executive officer
CFO	Chief financial officer
CIO	Chief information officer
CMM	Capability maturity model
CORBA	Common Object Request Broker Architecture
CPM	Critical path method
CRM	Customer relationship management
COO	Chief operating officer
CQ	Competes [versus] Qualifiers
DBA	Database administration
DBMS	Database management system
DoS	Denial of service
DP Era	Data processing era

Glossary of Acronyms and Terms

EAI	Enterprise application integration
ERP	Enterprise resource planning
IDS	Intrusion detection system
IPO	Initial public offering
IR or IRP	Infrastructure replacement project (as used in this book)
IT	Information technology
ITIL	Information technology infrastructure library
Java	A high-level programming language developed by Sun Microsystems
KWYDK	"Know what you don't know" (as used in this book)
Linux	An open source operating system
OCI	Option creating investment (as used in this book)
Oracle	Large software company, focused on database products
OSI	Open systems interconnection
PC	Personal computer
PDA	Personal digital assistant
PERL	Practical Extraction and Report Language
PERT	Project Evaluation and Review Technique
PGP	Pretty Good Privacy
PLM	Product lifecycle management
RFP	Request for proposal
ROI	Return on investment
SaaS	Software as a service
Sabre	Semi-automated business research environment
SLA	Service level agreement
SOA	Service-oriented architecture

SQL	Structured query language (originally SEQUEL: structured English query language)
SSL	Secure sockets layer
SYH2DP	"Sometimes you have to duck a punch" (as used in this book)
TCP/IP	Transmission Control Protocol/Internet Protocol
TPM	Traditional project management
Unix	A multi-user, multitasking operating system
UWGDF	"Understand what got Davies fired" (as used in this book)
VPN	Virtual private network
YWLOY	"You won't last one year" (as used in this book)

ACKNOWLEDGMENTS

We owe thanks to a great many people who helped us conceive and execute this project. Dean Jay Light and the Division of Research at the Harvard Business School (HBS), President Finn Junge-Jensen of Copenhagen Business School (CBS), Dean Jim Jimbalvo of the Foster School of Business at the University of Washington (UW), and the Philip M. Condit endowed chair at UW all provided financial support for this project, and we are certainly grateful for that.

A number of people provided valuable written feedback on earlier drafts. Ryan Nelson and his colleagues Peter Gray, Glenn Browne, and Stefano Grazioli on the IT faculty at the McIntire School of Commerce at the University of Virginia, and Janis Gogan, who coordinates the course on strategic information management at Bentley College, went far beyond the call of any duty and conducted a careful review and provided very detailed comments, which resulted in rather substantive changes. Thoughts provided by F. Warren McFarlan, our colleague at HBS; Bruce Rogow, who runs the IT Odyssey and Private Executive Counsel; Dan Hill, the CIO of Exelon; Jonathan Wareham and Xavier Busquets, both of ESADE in Barcelona; Lee Devin, our frequent coauthor at Swarthmore College; and Cynthia Beath, at the University of Texas at Austin, were also very helpful. Carl Størmer, a man of many talents and interests—entrepreneur, consultant, jazz musician, and author of the JazzCode—helped us immeasurably with the jazz scene in chapter 15, as did Alan Murray, a Novell vice president and computer security expert, with the chapters in which IVK appears to be under attack by hackers; and Francisco de Asis Martinez-Jerez, an HBS colleague in the accounting area, helped us with the financial statements for IVK. We are grateful as well to several anonymous reviewers whose written comments we encountered along the way.

Many more people provided us with guidance in a variety of settings. Dick Nolan's students at the University of Washington in the fall of 2007 experienced the earliest version of the manuscript and responded with great enthusiasm and many helpful reactions. Rob Austin's students at Copenhagen Business School in the spring of 2008 were equally enthusiastic and also prompted many adjustments, as did participants at the Seattle Innovation Symposium in June of 2008 (Mike Eisenberg, Bob Mason, and Gianmario Motta deserve particular recognition), executives at a major corporation who attended an executive education program at UW in April of 2008, and the sixty-five or so senior IT managers who attended Delivering Information Services, an executive education program at HBS in July of 2008.

Numerous others deserve mention. Fellow pedagogues who offered suggestions and thoughts about teaching IT management: Eric Clemons, Wharton; Mark Cotteleer, Marquette; David Croson, SMU; Eph McLean, University of Georgia; and Ed Pritchard, Portland State. Dan Geer, also known as the "dean of computer security deep thinkers," allowed us to reproduce some of his materials from a presentation, and Michael Enright, an entrepreneur and chief technology officer at World-Winner, allowed us to use one of his terrific diagrams.

Still others provided support of many kinds while we were working on this: Gary Pisano, Technology and Operations Management area head at HBS; Eva Zeuthen Bentsen, head of the department of Management, Politics, and Philosophy at CBS; Daniel Hjorth, research director and colleague at CBS; Ole Fogh Kirkeby and Mette Mønsted, both colleagues at CBS; and Henrik Hermansen, colleague and master problem solver at CBS. Subodha Kumar, from the Foster School of Business Information Systems and Operations Management department, assisted in teaching early versions of the manuscript. Niels Bjørn-Andersen and Jacob Nørberg provided invaluable advice and assistance that helped us offer the course at CBS. We are also grateful for the support of Pam McCoy, Ed Kromer, L. A. Smith, and Jocelyn Milici from the Marketing & Communications Department at the Foster School of Business.

Acknowledgments

Several people are notable because of their multifaceted and unflagging support: Karen Coburn, CEO of the Cutter Consortium, allowed us to reproduce her copyrighted material and has been supportive in more ways than we can count. Abbie Lundberg, editor-in-chief of *CIO* magazine, and Brian Watson, editor of *CIO Insight*, have been enthusiastic supporters and have provided valuable important thoughts at key moments.

At HBS, the talented Evgenia Eliseeva deserves mention. At Harvard Business Publishing, we are thankful for the exceptional work of associate editor Kathleen Carr, and a whole slate of people: Heide Abelli, Liz Baldwin, Marcy Barnes-Henrie, Todd Berman, Erin Brown, Mike De-Rocco, Julie Devoll, Stephani Finks, Sarah Green, Jeff Kehoe, Audra Longert, Carolyn Monaco, Jacque Murphy, Christine Turnier-Vallecillo, Leslie Zheutlin, and our excellent copyeditor, Monica Jainschigg. Special thanks to artist Asaf Hanuka and composer Christopher Colucci for adding their skills to the project.

Of course we must also thank our families, who endure the consequences of our scurrying to make deadlines and our long video calls across many time zones on sometimes awkward schedules, but who nevertheless provide their unqualified support.

—Robert D. Austin
Copenhagen, Denmark

—Richard L. Nolan
Boston, Massachusetts

—Shannon O'Donnell
Puget Sound area, Washington

ABOUT THE AUTHORS

ROBERT D. AUSTIN is a professor of managing creativity and innovation at Copenhagen Business School and an associate professor of technology and operations management at Harvard Business School (HBS). He chairs the HBS executive program for chief information officers and is coauthor (with Lynda Applegate and Deborah Soule) of the leading MBA textbook on IT management. Before becoming a professor, he was an IT manager at a major international corporation. He has written more than one hundred published papers, articles, and cases, as well as several books, some of which have received international awards. He is active on editorial and advisory boards for numerous academic organizations and companies.

RICHARD L. NOLAN is a professor at the Foster School of Business at the University of Washington in Seattle and a professor emeritus at the Harvard Business School; he teaches and researches strategic and execution issues on IT leadership. He is active in helping CIOs, senior managers, and boards of directors more effectively apply information resources in their businesses. During a fourteen-year interim period in his career at the Harvard Business School, he cofounded and chaired Nolan, Norton, & Co., a pioneering strategic IT consulting firm, which was later merged with KPMG. He has been a part of the IT industry for over forty years as a professor, a consultant, and a practicing manager.

SHANNON O'DONNELL is a PhD fellow at Copenhagen Business School, where she was previously a visiting researcher at the CBS Centre for Art and Leadership. Her research focuses on innovation in creative industries and the role of technology in collaboration and innovation. She is also a consultant with Cutter Consortium's Innovation and Enterprise Agility practice. Previously, she was a research associate at the University of Washington Foster School of Business, and at the Harvard Business School, where she coauthored several Harvard Business School cases. She was formerly Resident Director and Dramaturg at People's Light and Theatre, an internationally regarded regional theater company outside Philadelphia.